LUTHER
in Context

Robert B. Ives
November 19, 2002
Dillsburg, PA
4861

LUTHER
in Context

Second Edition

David C. Steinmetz

4861

Baker Academic
A Division of Baker Book House Co
Grand Rapids, Michigan 49516

Published by Baker Academic
a division of Baker Book House Company
P.O. Box 6287, Grand Rapids, MI 49516-6287

Printed in the United States of America

Library of Congress Cataloging-in-Publication Data

Steinmetz, David Curtis.
    Luther in context / David C. Steinmetz.—2nd ed.
       p.   cm.
    Includes bibliographical references and index.
    ISBN 0-8010-2609-1
    1. Luther, Martin, 1483–1546. I. Title.
  BR333.3 .S74 2002
  230′.41′092—dc21   2002021567

For information about Baker Academic, visit our web site:
www.bakeracademic.com

Praeceptori et amico suo
Heiko Augustinus Oberman
auctor hoc opusculum dedicavit

CONTENTS

Preface to the Second Edition   ix
Preface to the First Edition   xi
Acknowledgments   xiii

   I. Luther against Luther   1
  II. Luther and Augustine on Romans 9   12
 III. Luther and the Hidden God   23
 IV. Abraham and the Reformation   32
  V. Luther among the Anti-Thomists   47
 VI. Luther and Hubmaier on the Freedom of the Human
      Will   59
 VII. Scripture and the Lord's Supper in Luther's Theology   72
VIII. Luther and Calvin on Church and Tradition   85
 IX. Luther and the Drunkenness of Noah   98
  X. Luther and the Two Kingdoms   112
 XI. Luther and Formation in Faith   126
 XII. Luther and the Ascent of Jacob's Ladder   142
XIII. Luther and Calvin on the Banks of the Jabbok   156

Notes   169
Index   189

PREFACE TO THE SECOND EDITION

The first edition of *Luther in Context* contained ten essays, all of which are reprinted in this new and expanded edition. I have added three new essays not previously published in book form. Two are contributions to the history of biblical interpretation. The first of these essays explores Luther's exposition of Jacob's famous dream of a ladder extending from heaven to earth. The second investigates his account of the puzzling story of Jacob's encounter by night with an unnamed and mysterious stranger, who attacks him without provocation as he camps on the banks of the Jabbok. The third essay examines Luther's understanding of the catechetical mission of the Reformation as a project for the reeducation and re-formation of adults who needed to be transformed as quickly as possible from old Catholics into new Evangelicals.

The Luther you may encounter in these pages is both a man of strong convictions and a figure who seems at times like an unfinished work in progress. On the one hand, Luther could heap scorn on Erasmus, who thought theologians should have a vivid sense of their own limitations and be more tentative in their claims. Luther labeled the more tentative Erasmus a skeptic and assured him that the Holy Spirit was no such thing. "Take away assertions," roared Luther, "and you take away Christianity." On the other hand, Luther never confused settled convictions with intellectual inertia. He was a man of whom it could be said, as G. K. Chesterton once said of H. G. Wells, "you could hear him growing in the night." Although Luther held fundamental views that shifted very little over time, he never found a stopping point in his theology beyond which he could not advance. Fresh ideas rose to greet him from the pages of the Bible. The result was an incredible energy in Luther's theology that did not diminish with his advancing age. This book attempts to reflect both the lively energy and the challenging substance of Luther's thought.

The new essays were first given as lectures at the universities of Bonn, Heidelberg, Erlangen, Northwestern, Wisconsin, and Notre Dame, at the Herzog August Bibliothek in Wolfenbüttel, Germany, and at meetings of the American Society of Church History in New York and Nashville. I want to thank the editors at Baker Books who first suggested including them in an expanded edition of *Luther in Context*. I was delighted to accept their invitation to revise this work and enlarge its scope. I did it gladly in the hope that the revised book will prove useful in new ways to a fresh generation of readers.

PREFACE TO THE FIRST EDITION

This book began as a series of lectures marking the five hundredth anniversary of the birth of Martin Luther. For the most part, the topics for those lectures were assigned, at least in broad outline, by the host institutions. While the sponsoring committees made every effort to base their requests on research I had already done, I found myself nevertheless reading a number of new sources as well as reacquainting myself with familiar issues in the interpretation of Luther's thought. I would like to be able to complain that the preparation of so many lectures on Luther was a tedious chore and to suggest that my hosts had laid an unreasonable burden on me, but in point of fact I enjoyed myself immensely and was only sorry to see the project come to an end.

While most historians would readily concede that the history of Christian theology is an important strand in the larger framework of Western intellectual history, the historical profession has been preoccupied in recent years with questions of social rather than intellectual history. That has been particularly the case in the study of the Reformation. Social historians are painting an increasingly sophisticated picture of the institutionalization of the Reformation in the cities of western Europe and among the various social groupings in the smaller villages. As a result, students of the Reformation have learned that they cannot simply assume that the ideals expressed in books and treatises, or even in pamphlets, sermons, and catechisms, reflect what actually happened in the daily lives of ordinary people.

On the other hand, ideas do have consequences, and in the sixteenth century the ideas that preoccupied Europeans were in large measure religious ideas. Understanding the history of an idea is a complicated art and requires a different kind of training from the training which equips a social historian. Yet the work of the intellectual historian is no less important for understanding and interpreting the Reformation than the currently more fashionable work of the social historian. Luther's world was not simply the social world of a German territorial city; it was not even a world restricted to his European contemporaries. Isaiah, Paul, Seneca, Cicero, Aristotle, Augustine, William Ockham, and Gabriel Biel with all their subsequent commentators and camp followers were as much a part of his daily life as the congregation at the City Church or the guests at his table. Luther was born to theology as Bach was born to music or Dürer to color and light. Theological talk, disputation, and writing were meat and drink for him. It is therefore not possible to capture his full human reality without giving serious attention to his consuming theological vocation.

These essays are exercises in intellectual history. They try to cast light on Luther's thought by placing it in the context of his theological antecedents and contemporaries. A thing is frequently shown in sharper relief if it is compared with something else similar to it, but from which it differs in certain important respects. Circles never seem so circular as when they are set beside an oval or a rectangle. Luther's thought, therefore, is examined, not in isolation, but in comparison with the thought of other Christian theologians ranging from such seminal thinkers as Augustine of Hippo and John Calvin to such relatively obscure figures as Dietrich Kolde and John Pupper of Goch. The one essay which deviates from this norm, "Luther and the Hidden God," is included in this collection because it provides an additional context for matters discussed in other essays.

There is a danger, of course, that a collection of essays on the thought of a particular figure in the past will be episodic and may give a lopsided and unbalanced view of the structure of that figure's intellectual contribution. These studies are certainly not intended to be a well-rounded presentation of Luther's thought on all subjects or to displace the standard introductory handbooks by Althaus and Ebeling. Nevertheless, the essays do examine a wide range of themes and problems in Luther's theology, so that the reader who encounters Luther for the first time in these pages will find a broad sampling of the themes that were important to him.

It remains only to thank my hosts at Cornell, Michigan, North Carolina, Marquette, South Carolina, Bonn, Calvin College, the Kirchliche Hochschule (Wuppertal), and the Luther Jubilee in Washington, D.C., whose kind invitations in 1983 made these essays, and hence this book, possible.

ACKNOWLEDGMENTS

The essay "Abraham and the Reformation" first appeared in *Medieval and Renaissance Studies* 10, edited by G. Mallary Masters (Chapel Hill and London: The University of North Carolina Press, 1984), pp. 94–114.

"Luther among the Anti-Thomists" uses a few paragraphs from "*Libertas Christiana:* Studies in the Theology of John Pupper of Goch (d.1475)," *The Harvard Theological Review* 65 (1972): 191–230.

"Luther and Hubmaier on the Freedom of the Human Will" has appeared previously in German as "Luther und Hubmaier im Streit um die Freiheit des menschlichen Willens," *Evangelische Theologie* 43 (November/December 1983): 512–26.

"Scripture and the Lord's Supper in Luther's Theology" was first published in *Interpretation* 37 (July 1983):253–65.

"Luther and Calvin on Church and Tradition" has appeared in *Michigan Germanic Studies* 10 (Spring/Fall 1984):98–111, and the *Martin Luther Quincentennial 1983* (Detroit: Wayne State University Press, 1984).

Parts of "Luther and the Two Kingdoms" were published in a somewhat different format in "The Nature of Luther's Reform," *The Duke Divinity School Review* 44 (1979):3–13.

"Luther and the Ascent of Jacob's Ladder" was first published in *Church History* 55 (June 1986): 179–92.

"Luther and Calvin on the Banks of the Jabbok" has appeared previously in German as "Luther und Calvin am Jabbokufer," *Evangelische Theologie* 57 (June 1997): 522–36.

The essays are reprinted here with the permission of the respective journals and publishers.

Luther in Context

I

LUTHER AGAINST LUTHER

Throughout his life Luther suffered from periods of depression and acute anxiety. He referred to these episodes as *Anfechtungen,* or "spiritual trials." The terror which Luther felt during such attacks was not a generalized or non-specific anxiety on which he could not put his finger. His terror was all too specific. It was an unnerving and enervating fear that God had turned his back on him once and for all, had repudiated his repentance and prayers, and had abandoned him to suffer the pains of hell. Luther felt alone in the universe, battered by the demands of God's law and beyond the reach of the gospel. He doubted his own faith, his own mission, and the goodness of God— doubts which, because they verged on blasphemy, drove him deeper and deeper into the Slough of Despond. Election ceased to be a doctrine of comfort and became a sentence of death. No prayer he uttered could penetrate the wall of indifferent silence with which God had surrounded himself. Condemned by his own conscience, Luther despised himself and murmured against God.

Philip Melanchthon, Luther's co-worker and friend for more than twenty five years, offers his own eyewitness account of Luther's *Anfechtungen:*

> On those frequent occasions when he was thinking especially about the wrath of God or about extraordinary instances of retribution, such violent terrors afflicted him that he almost died. I have seen him, distressed by his concentration upon some dispute over doctrine, lie down on a bed in a nearby room and mingle with his prayer this oft-repeated sentence: "He has concluded all under sin so that he may have mercy upon all."[1]

As Melanchthon's testimony makes plain, Luther's conversion to a Reformation understanding of the gospel did not put an end to his *Anfechtungen.* Even after the great shift in his theological outlook, Luther continued to suffer periods of severe spiritual anxiety. Probably the doubt which haunted the older Luther most tenaciously was the

1

fear that he was, after all, in error (just as his enemies alleged), and that he had misled thousands of innocent Christians who ought to have been left undisturbed in their traditional piety. "Nowadays," Luther ruefully observes, "I must suffer other thoughts from the devil. For he often casts in my teeth: 'Oh, what a huge crowd of people you have led astray with your teaching!' "[2]

The spiritual trials of the young Luther, however, focused on other matters, on temptations "not about women [this is said in opposition to the medieval preoccupation with sexual sins], but about the really knotty problems,"[3] on "spiritual temptations, temptations about faith and hope, temptations of worthiness and temptations about predestination."[4] Luther's early anxieties were thoroughly medieval, and it was to medieval remedies that Luther first turned to alleviate them. It was only after Luther had tested those remedies and found them wanting that he developed his own alternative theology. In order, therefore, to understand Luther's earliest *Anfechtungen* and their meaning for him, it is necessary to place Luther in context, to recreate, however briefly, the spiritual environment of the late medieval world in which Luther was raised and against which he rebelled.

I

If the older Luther was particularly tormented with doubts about his vocation, the younger Luther's anxieties centered on the confessional.

> I tried to live according to the Rule with all diligence, and I used to be contrite, to confess and number off my sins, and often repeated my confession, and sedulously performed my allotted penance. And yet my conscience could never give me certainty, but I always doubted and said, "You did not perform that correctly. You were not contrite enough. You left that out of your confession." The more I tried to remedy an uncertain, weak and afflicted conscience with the traditions of men, the more each day found it more uncertain, weaker, more troubled.[5]

Roughly speaking, there were two penitential traditions which lived side by side in the later middle ages, sometimes in harmony, more often in a fragile and uneasy truce.[6] The first tradition stressed the importance of the disposition of the penitent in the confessional, the sincerity and completeness of the penitent's confession, and the necessity for finding a competent and sensitive spiritual advisor. The other tradition stressed the authority of the Church and its sacraments, the power of priestly absolution, and the consolation which the faithful can find when they turn their attention away from themselves and focus on the efficacious rites and ceremonies of the Church. It was not impossible to want to stress both the necessity of a proper disposition and the power of priestly absolution, but almost all theologies of penance tended to tilt in one direction or the other.

We can get a layman's eye view of the penitential tradition that stressed the proper disposition for the reception of grace if we read the best-selling German catechism by Dietrich Kolde of Münster, the *Mirror for Christians*, first published in 1480 and issued in forty-six more editions thereafter (an impressive printing history, even by modern standards).[7] Kolde had been an Augustinian friar but transferred to the Observant Franciscans in the 1470s.[8] Since Luther spent four years in Eisenach as a boarder in the house of Heinrich Schalbe, a pious host who was a devoted follower of the Observant Franciscans, there is good reason to believe that Luther heard the Observant friars preach with some regularity during his impressionable adolescent years.[9]

Christians cannot confess their sins properly unless they know how to identify them. Accordingly, Kolde helps the layperson to identify his or her own sins by providing several overlapping paradigms: the ten commandments (which are briefly summarized and then explained at greater length), five commandments of the Church, seven deadly sins, nine alien sins (that is, sins which other people commit but which we assist or in which we take delight), three openly discussed sins and several mute sins (mainly sexual) against nature, six sins against the Holy Spirit, and a gaggle of great sins of the tongue. Kolde is not as systematic or detailed as the manuals for confessors which the clergy read, but he provides much of the same information and conveys many of the same attitudes. For example, in his explanation of the seventh commandment, Kolde not only condemns fornication, adultery, incest, sodomy, rape, and masturbation, but also makes a veiled reference to sexual activity "at unacceptable times and in unacceptable ways" by people who, "like beasts, seek nothing other than the pleasures of the flesh."[10] What Kolde seems to have in mind are married couples who have sexual intercourse during menstruation (which is popularly believed to produce "ugly, misshapen, leprous children")[11] or who adopt positions during intercourse which may increase sexual pleasure but inhibit conception.[12]

Kolde outlines the conditions penitents must fulfil if God is to forgive their sins. The first condition, "that a person not doubt the mercy of God,"[13] corresponds to the first sin against the Holy Spirit, the "skepticism or despair with which divine aid is disdained."[14] In addition, penitents should fear God, believe the creed (summarized at the beginning of the catechism), and love their neighbors. Kolde warns against the foolish strategy of delaying conversion until just before death or of consciously retaining a mortal sin (perhaps because one is too embarrassed to confess it to a priest).[15] Every mortal sin must be listed and confessed insofar as that is possible. To cover lapses of memory one ought to pray:

> O dear Lord, forgive me all my great and serious sins, and preserve me from future sins, and redeem me from all forgotten sins, and give me the favor and grace to serve you cordially, fervently and willingly all my days. Amen.[16]

It is clear from what Kolde says, though he does not use technical theological language, that he is primarily interested in a disposition of contrition on the part of the penitent rather than a disposition of attrition. Contrition is sorrow for sin motivated by love of God. Attrition is imperfect contrition or sorrow for sin in which love of God and fear of punishment are mixed together. Kolde's penitent is contrite; he is "deeply sorrowful because he has greatly angered God his creator and dear Father with great sins for so long."[17] Furthermore, since true contrition is always marked by a desire to confess to a priest, it is not surprising that Kolde's penitent wants "to confess all the sins he has committed, and to purposely leave nothing unconfessed, and to seek a good wise, educated father confessor."[18]

Kolde repeats his advice to seek a "good spiritual father confessor."[19] There are at least two reasons why Kolde is so concerned with the quality of pastoral care offered to a penitent. First of all, some sins, such as arson against church property, are reserved and can only be absolved by a bishop or higher prelate.[20] An ignorant priest might leave the stain of mortal sin on the penitent's soul simply because he does not know the limits of his own authority. Furthermore, if a disposition of contrition is essential for the reception of the forgiveness of sins, laypeople need the expert advice of a wise counselor who can tell true contrition from false and who can ask the kind of probing questions which will assist the sinner to make a full confession. Attrition and contrition are easier to define than to distinguish in practice, since their outward signs are similar.[21] There are certain tests, of course, which the penitent can apply to himself. He can ask himself whether he has "every intention of never committing a mortal sin as long as he lives, even if he could gain everything in the world by so doing."[21] But the safest course is to have an experienced guide who can lead one through the dimly lit passages of the human soul.

Sinners can assist the priest if they remember not only the kinds of sins they have committed since their last confession and the frequency with which they have committed them, but also the circumstances surrounding the commission of those sinful acts: what, with whom, when, why.[23] Knowing the circumstances makes it easier for the priest to determine the proper satisfaction, though Kolde is keen to remind his readers that the most rigorous works of satisfaction established by the priest are insufficient to atone for the least mortal sin committed by the penitent.[24] True Christians must devote themselves to additional works of satisfaction "by groaning, crying out, begging help, giving alms, private mortification of the flesh, sharp clothes or belts around the body, or by disciplines, or vigils, or humbly going on pilgrimages."[25] Kolde establishes a discipline of prayer for penitents which covers the various periods of the day and seems more suited to the cloister than to the life of a farmer or merchant or housewife. The book concludes with prayers that one should recite on one's deathbed.

The historian who reads Kolde hoping for a technical discussion of grace and free will or the merits of congruity and condignity is sure to be disappointed. Kolde offers practical advice to simple laypeople and does not make the theological foundations of his thought explicit. Nevertheless, a certain picture of the shape of Kolde's religious vision does emerge from the pages of his catechism. Although God is merciful and Christ has died for the sins of the world, the emphasis throughout the catechism is on the responsibility of the sinner to act on behalf of his own soul by rigorous self-examination, by good works and self-denial, by prayer and pious exercises. God is willing to forgive the sinner, but there are conditions which must be met and which lie within the power of the sinner to perform. Above all, the sinner must be truly contrite and must make a sincere and complete confession.

II

At the opposite end of the spectrum from Dietrich Kolde stands John of Paltz (d.1511), the Augustinian Observant, whose *Coelifodina*[26] (1502) and *Supplementum Coelifodinae*[27] (1504) were important and influential manuals of pastoral care. While Kolde wrote for the laity, Paltz wrote for simple priests, applying the results of scholastic theology to the pastoral problems which parish priests encountered daily.[28] Paltz belonged to the Observant Augustinian house in Erfurt, in which Luther took his vows, and was even in residence in 1505 when Luther applied for admission to the order.

Paltz found the contritionism of Kolde and of their common great contemporary, the German nominalist theologian Gabriel Biel (d.1495), to be thoroughly unrealistic. The great mass of laypeople are incapable of the level of self-analysis and contrition which writers like

Kolde demand and are certainly unwilling to undertake the rigorous program of prayer and worldly asceticism which Kolde assumes as a matter of course. Paltz wants, therefore, to ground religious security and certitude of salvation in the sacraments and structures of the institutional Church. He locates the heart of the sacrament of penance in priestly absolution rather than in the disposition of the penitent.[29]

We can see best what Paltz is up to if we contrast his view of contrition with the views of Biel. According to Biel, God has established a covenant, the terms of which are proclaimed by the Church in the gospel. God has promised to give saving grace to everyone who meets the conditions of the covenant. What is demanded of the sinner, quite simply, is that the sinner love God above all else and thus make an act of perfect contrition. Sinners can do this because, while sin has damaged their natural capacity for loving God, it has not obliterated it. Grace is given, therefore, to sinners outside the sacrament of the penance and before confession to a priest. Biel loosely ties the forgiveness of sins to the hierarchical priesthood by insisting that the mark of true contrition is the desire to confess to a priest, that a priest is an expert in distinguishing true contrition from false, and that God has an additional gift of grace to give to penitents who submit to the discipline of the confessional.[30]

Like Biel, Paltz stresses the free will of the sinner and the necessity for penitents to assume responsibility for their own sins by turning to God and doing what is in them, though, unlike Biel, he is interested in the penance of Christians who have fallen into mortal sin rather than in the conversion of unbelievers.[31] Furthermore, while Biel downplays the role of the Church in motivating sinners to repent, Paltz explicitly emphasizes the churchly call to repentance through preachers and father confessors. But the principal difference between them is that Paltz stresses attrition as a sufficient disposition for the forgiveness of sins and attempts to support a minimal program of human piety with a maximal program of ecclesiastical guarantees.

Some people, Paltz concedes, are able to exercise their natural capacities to the fullest and can produce a very strong disposition of attrition. God will reward their efforts with saving grace apart from the sacrament of penance by transforming their attrition into contrition. Most Christians will follow a less strenuous path to forgiveness by expressing a somewhat more moderate sorrow for sin, a kind of attrition *ordinaire*. This attrition will be supplemented and filled out by participation in the sacraments of penance, confirmation, eucharist, and extreme unction. Paltz even allows for minimal attrition in the crisis situation of the deathbed. Minimal attrition can be changed by extreme unction into genuine contrition provided that the penitent interposes no obstacle to the working of grace. At the very least, dying sinners should feel pain that they feel no pain at the recollection of their sins.[32]

For those penitents who want the highest degree of assurance that their sins have been forgiven, Paltz recommends the monastic life.[33] God has bound himself in Matthew 19:29 to give grace and final salvation to every monk who lives in fidelity and obedience to his religious vow. Paltz does not romanticize the monastic life, and he is under no illusion that monastic houses are filled with spiritual giants. Quite ordinary Christians are drawn to the monastic life, and the monastic orders must provide at least a minimal program for the strengthening and comfort of the weaker brothers and sisters. In many ways, the cloistered life is simpler and easier than life in the world. What Paltz wants to stress is obedience to one's vows and to the rule of the order one has entered. God gives grace not just to a spiritual elite who live in an intensity of devotion but also to the quite ordinary men and women who see no visions and who experience no ecstasy, but who do their duty in simple fidelity to their vows.

III

It is clear from Luther's autobiographical statements that he had little sympathy with Paltz's minimal program of attrition and obedience. Luther took his cue from spiritual advisors like Kolde, who stressed the importance of rendering satisfaction for sins over and beyond the penances assigned by the confessor, and who attempted to make a sincere and complete confession out of a disposition of contrition.

> I was a good monk, and kept my order so strictly that I could say that if ever a monk could get to heaven through monastic discipline, I should have entered in. All my companions in the monastery who knew me would bear me out in this. For if it had gone on much longer, I would have martyred myself to death, what with vigils, prayers, reading and other works.[34] . . . [M]y conscience would never give me certainty. But I always doubted and said, "You did not perform that correctly. You were not contrite enough. You left that out of your confession."[35]

The brothers in the Augustinian cloister at Erfurt were baffled by Brother Martin's spiritual anxieties and tried to talk him out of them by adopting an argument along the lines suggested by John of Paltz:

> Ah! (they say) what are you worrying about? It isn't necessary: you have only to be humble and patient. Do you think that God requires

such strict conduct from you? He knows all your imaginings and he is good. One groan will please him. Do you think that nobody can be saved unless he behaves so strictly? Where would all the others be, then, in whom you see no such violence? Perish the thought that they should all be lost! It really is necessary to observe "discretion," etc. And so gradually the unhappy soul forgets the fear of the Lord, and that the Kingdom of heaven suffers violence.[36]

Luther drew no comfort from such advice and only found that his conscience had grown "more uncertain, weaker, more troubled."[37] "For I used to ask myself," he admitted, "who knows whether such consolations are to be believed?"[38] While Luther was troubled by scruples and later recalled that he "would not dare to possess a pen without first consulting the prior," he never attributed his anxieties to scrupulosity.[39] The terror Luther felt in the presence of a righteous God could not in his judgment be equated with the fussy anxiety of the scrupulous.

> I knew a man [Luther wrote in 1518] who said that he had often suffered these pains in the shortest possible compass of time, so great and infernal that "nor tongue nor pen can show" nor can those believe who have not experienced, so that if they were completed, or lasted half an hour, or even the tenth part of an hour, he would utterly perish, and his bones be reduced to ashes. Then God appears horrifyingly angry and with him, the whole creation. There can be no flight, no consolation, neither within nor without, but all is accusation.[40]

That is not to say that all the advice Luther received in the cloister proved useless to him. He later remembered with gratitude the words of the anonymous brother who told him in exasperation: "My son, God is not angry with you, but you are angry with God."[41] Of even more help to Luther was the advice of Dr. John Staupitz, Vicar-General of the Augustinian Observants and professor of Bible in the newly founded University of Wittenberg.[42] "If I didn't praise Staupitz," Luther later told his students, "I should be a damned, ungrateful, papistical ass, for he was my very first father in this teaching, and he bore me in Christ."[43] "If Dr. Staupitz had not helped me out . . . I should have been swallowed up and left in hell."[44]

Staupitz was an Augustinian in his theology as well as in his allegiance to the Augustinian Order. He did not ground the certitude of the forgiveness of sins either in the human act of contrition (Kolde) or in the authority of the Church (Paltz). Behind the authority of the Church and the contrition of the penitent is the prior grace of an electing God. God has already shown his mercy to a fallen race in the wounds of Christ. The problem, as Staupitz sees it, is not how to make sinners dear to God (the electing grace of God has already solved that problem), but how to make God dear to sinners. Vigils, fasting, prayers, self-examination, or heroic devotion to good works will not do it. Only God can make God dear to sinners. The love of God is a gift which cannot be earned or anticipated or prepared for. It is not a gift given to the astonishingly virtuous, but to the morally threadbare and tattered.

Most of the advice Staupitz gave to Luther is unremarkable and could equally well have been given by Kolde or Paltz. Staupitz told Luther that temptations were good for him since the devil never disturbed the tranquility of people who were safely in his camp.[45] When Luther trembled before the wrath of a hidden God, Staupitz pointed to the wounds of Christ, which were visible signs (indeed, visible over every altar) of God's steadfast mercy.[46] Even when in a fit of depression Luther moaned about his sins, Staupitz brought him up short by dismissing his transgressions as so many nursery peccadilloes. Luther should keep a list of what real sins are—sins such as blasphemy, murder, and theft—and not assume that every social indiscretion is a mortal sin.[47] All these incidents are recounted by Luther many years later when he is a man in his fifties. While there is no corroborating evidence from Staupitz, since all these conversations were protected by the seal of the confessional, the stories do have the ring of truth.

The only evidence we have from Luther about Staupitz's pastoral advice which is almost contemporaneous with the events just described is a dedicatory letter to Staupitz, which Luther wrote in 1518 and appended to his *Resolutiones disputationum de indulgentiarum virtute.*

> I remember, Reverend Father, amongst your most delightful and salutary stories with which the Lord Jesus used to console me wonderfully, mention was sometimes made of the word "penitence." Then we who had grieved for many consciences, and for their tormentors who give endless and intolerable instructions in what they call a method of confession, received you as a voice from heaven when you said that there is no true penitence except that which begins from the love of justice and of God, and that what they regard as the goal and consummation of penitence is really its beginning. This statement of yours pierced me like the sharp arrows of the Almighty. And then I began to collate it with passages of Scripture which teach about penitence—behold, what an utterly joyful pastime! Words on every side were joining me in the game and laughing and jumping in plain agreement with your outlook, to the extent that, whereas previously there had been scarcely a word in the whole of Scripture more bitter to me than "penitence" (even though I sedulously pretended even to God and tried to squeeze out a contrived and coerced love), now nothing sounds sweeter or more agreeable to me than "penitence." For the commands of God become sweet

when we understand that they are to be read not only in books, but in
the wounds of the sweetest Saviour.[48]

With these words Luther rejected categorically the contritionist understanding of preparation for grace. Morally good acts do not have a
claim on the favor of God. Real preparation for grace is not the
preparation sinners make through their contrition and confession but
the preparation God has made by his election, calling, and gifts. Contrition is the fruit of grace not its presupposition.

Staupitz had taught that God gives his grace to "real" sinners.[49] Real
sinners are people who are not merely sinners in fact (everyone, after
all, is a sinner in that sense), but who confess that they are sinners.
Luther found this notion liberating. Real sinners conform their judgments of themselves to the judgment of God over them and by doing
so justify God. That is, they acknowledge that God is in the right when
he condemns them as sinners and offers them a pardon which they
cannot merit.[50] The problem with human righteousness is not merely
that it is flawed or insufficient (thought it is both). The problem with
human righteousness is that it is irrelevant. God does not ask for
human virtue as a precondition for justification, not even in the sense
of a perfect act of contrition. He asks for human sin.

IV

As any historian knows, the struggle of the young Luther to understand the meaning of true contrition is not the only strand in the story
of his battle with *Anfechtungen*. New ideas about sin, faith, justification, preaching, and prayer came tumbling from his pen in 1513–1518.
It was not a single insight but a score of insights which gave Luther the
courage to face what he feared and to grasp the promises of the gospel
by faith. Nor did he ever outgrow all the advice Staupitz had given him
in the cloister. To the end of his life, he repeated the words of Staupitz
that temptations and trials were meat and drink for him. The faith
which believes the promises of God is a faith which is tested over and
over again. Only through repeated testing by the devil does the bruised
conscience find consolation. That is why Luther calls the devil by a
title generally reserved for Jean Gerson: The devil is a *doctor
consolatorius*.[51]

Nevertheless, when we focus on the sacrament of penance, we are
focusing on an issue central to Luther's new Reformation understanding of the gospel. Luther rejects both attrition and contrition, the
minimalism of Paltz and the maximalism of Kolde, in order to stress

(in a reference to Augustine) that it is not the sacrament but the faith of the sacrament that justifies. Under the tutelage of Staupitz, Luther sees that contrition cannot be the proper disposition for grace, since only the already justified can experience sorrow for their sins. Moreover, the justifying grace which is the proper disposition for the experience of contrition can only be given to sinners who have nothing to offer to God but their sins. The good news of the gospel (at least as Luther understands it) is that that is all that God asks sinners to offer.

II

LUTHER AND AUGUSTINE ON ROMANS 9

The relationship of Luther to St. Augustine is a far more complicated question to resolve than one might anticipate. No one doubts for a moment that Luther was profoundly influenced by Augustine (even if historians like Nygren[1] and Saarnivaara[2] prefer to stress topics like charity and imputation on which they differed) or that Luther regarded Augustine as the one Father really worth intense study. His own knowledge of Augustine, as Adolf Hamel has shown,[3] grew almost geometrically in the period from 1513 to 1518, the period in which Luther struggled to interpret the Psalter and the writings of St. Paul. The difficulty with labeling Luther an Augustinian is that every theologian in the West is to some extent an Augustinian, even though their common commitment to St. Augustine does not prevent them from differing profoundly with one another. How does Luther's Augustinianism differ from the various Augustinian theologies of the middle ages? In what sense is it appropriate to call Luther an Augustinian theologian?

There are three ways to approach this question. One way is simply to compare the teaching of Augustine on a given topic with the teaching of Luther. When we compare them this way we find, for example, that Luther is not interested in Augustine's theory of knowledge (few theologians of Luther's generation would have been!) but is fascinated with Augustine's theory of grace. That does not mean that Luther sees sin and grace altogether from Augustine's point of view. Augustine regards love rather than faith as the central principle of justification and even accepts a role for human merit in the process of salvation. Augustine would not have known quite what to make of Luther's doctrine of justification by faith alone with its stress on the imputation of the righteousness of Christ to the believing sinner. Still, they do agree about the doctrine of predestination and the absolute priority of grace in redemption.

The difficulty with this approach to the relationship between Luther and Augustine is that it compares *our* knowledge of Luther with *our* knowledge of Augustine without raising the prior historical question of Luther's knowledge of Augustine. There is always the possibility that Luther may not agree with Augustine on some point, not because he rejected Augustine's position but because he was unacquainted with it. Furthermore, what seems an eccentric interpretation of Augustine by Luther may in fact reflect a common misreading of Augustine by Luther's contemporaries and thus give us no insight into the peculiar workings of Luther's mind.

A second approach focuses on the theological environment in which Luther read Augustine and the angle of vision or tradition of interpretation characteristic of the religious community to which Luther belonged. H.A. Oberman has suggested that the Augustinian Order is a crucial ingredient for understanding Luther's relationship to Augustine.[4] The Augustinian Order claimed to have been founded by St. Augustine as the Franciscan Order had been founded by St. Francis, a claim which had no foundation in fact but which nevertheless had important historical consequences for the character and vision of the order. The Augustinians became the textual critics of the later middle ages, concerned with better editions of St. Augustine and more accurate citation of authorities. The order was also home for one of the more remarkable theologians of the fourteenth century, Gregory of Rimini, known for his fidelity to some of the more unpopular ideas of Augustine on sin and grace. According to Oberman's reconstruction, there is an Augustinian theological tradition within the Augustinian Order, formed especially by Gregory of Rimini and mediated to Luther by John Staupitz, a tradition which is re-formed by Luther into the new theology of the Protestant movement.

What this theory implies and what its weaknesses are, I have discussed elsewhere in detail.[5] Suffice it to say here that in my judgment Gregory is not a theologian whom Luther reads at the earliest stages of his development, that Staupitz is no disciple of Gregory, that the most important books young Luther reads are not by Augustinian friars, and that Luther shows from the very beginning an astonishing independence of all his teachers, even the most Augustinian. Even Staupitz seems to be less a mediator of theological ideas to Luther than a skilled counselor who enabled Luther to face what he feared and resolve for himself his acute theological anxieties.

A third approach attempts to skirt the problems inherent in the first two by concentrating on Luther's own use of Augustine, particularly in his early biblical commentaries. This is the approach recommended by Leif Grane,[6] who applied it to Luther's lectures on Romans 1–8, and it is the approach I want to follow in this essay. By focusing on Luther's actual use of Augustine we are able to accompany Luther into his theological workshop and gain insight into his exegetical method. I have chosen Romans 9:10–29, a passage on which Augustine comments several times during his life and on which he changes his mind substantially. The issues discussed here are important to Luther as well, who must select among the varying interpretations given by Augustine as he attempts to understand the Pauline text.

I

The earliest exegesis of Romans 9 which we have from Augustine is the *Expositio quarundam propositionum ex epistola ad Romanos,*[7] written in 394, while Augustine was still a presbyter in Hippo Regius. It was written, therefore, about the same time as Augustine's great work against the Manichaeans, the *De libero arbitrio*. The Manichaeans explained the existence of evil by pointing to a cosmic clash between Light and Darkness. Bits of Light had been trapped by Darkness and could now be found in the souls of the elect. The process of redemption was the process of extracting Light from Darkness and reestablishing the proper boundaries between each. This dualistic scheme identified evil with the material world and offered redemption to a small group of the elect who, completely by accident, had become receptacles for particles of Light. Augustine attacked this deterministic worldview and argued that evil had its origins in the free will of the rational creation. Augustine in 394 is keen, therefore, to stress human free will and to avoid any suggestion that human beings are helpless pawns in the hands of a blind destiny. His first exegesis of Romans 9 reflects these concerns.

The problem for Augustine is that Romans 9:10–29 seems to suggest that human beings are in the hands of a destiny over which they have no control and which does not operate according to the ordinary rules of fair play. The problem which troubles St. Paul is the unbelief of Israel, its rejection of Jesus of Nazareth as the Messiah. Does the unbelief of Israel invalidate the promises and covenants of God to Abraham and his descendants? The answer, of course, is no, because the boundaries of the true Israel are not determined by physical descent alone. God is sovereign and free and may constitute his chosen people any way he pleases. If he chooses to set aside Jews and make Gentiles children of Abraham by faith, that is his sovereign prerogative. It is the will of God and only the will of God and nothing beyond or beside the will of God which defines the true Israel. Indeed, this electing purpose is already evident in the Old Testament when God chooses Isaac over Ishmael and Jacob over Esau. Moreover, the God of Isaac and Jacob not only shows mercy to whomever he wills, he even confirms the reprobate like Pharaoh in their stubbornness and disobedience. Paul supports his argument with a string of texts, including the unsettling words from Malachi (1:1–2): "Jacob have I loved, but Esau have I hated."

Augustine moves swiftly in his exegesis to dampen any suggestion that Paul intended to undercut the freedom of the will when he appealed to the example of Jacob and Esau. The election of Jacob over Esau is based on foreknowledge, not foreknowledge of their good and bad deeds but foreknowledge of their faith.[8] The process of the justification of the sinner begins with divine calling or *vocatio,* an initiative which lies wholly with God and which cannot be merited by any human activity.[9] However, the response to this calling—namely, faith—lies wholly within the power of the free will of the sinner.[10] God elects believers to justification because of the merit of their faith.[11] This justification consists primarily in the reception of the Holy Spirit.[12] The justified sinner now performs works of love because of the activity of the Holy Spirit and the cooperation of the human free will.[13] Without the presence of the Spirit and its gifts, particularly the gift of love, there would be no impulse to do good; without human free will, there would be no morally good works or perseverance in the new life of love.[14] Through perseverance in good works, human beings merit eternal life.[15] "God never predestined anyone unless he foreknew that he would believe and follow his calling."[16]

Augustine has some reason to feel satisfied with himself. In his *Expositio,* he has preserved the initiative of God, absolutely with respect to calling and relatively in the gift of the Holy Spirit, while maintaining the freedom of the human will. What looks like an arbitrary exercise of sovereign power—namely, the choice of Jacob over Esau or the destruction of Pharaoh—is capable of a rational and morally satisfying explanation. God preferred Jacob because he foreknew Jacob's positive response to the divine call which would be offered to him. By the same token, the hardening of Pharaoh's heart was a just penalty for his obstinate unbelief. In both cases, it is the faith which lies in the power of human free will which is determinative.

In the *Retractationes* or revisions written years later, Augustine indicates that he has three problems with his early exegesis of Romans 9: (1) he did not make clear that election is a grace which cannot be merited by any human activity, even the act of faith; (2) he did not indicate that faith is a gift of God given by the same Spirit which empowers believers to do good works; and (3) he did not distinguish sufficiently between the call of God which is directed toward the whole human race and the special call, the *vocatio secundum propositum dei,* which is extended only to the elect.[17] If faith is not purely a human act, but a human act which is also a divine gift, then the explanation that God preferred Jacob because of his foreknowledge of the merit of Jacob's entirely free act of faith becomes untenable. Election cannot be a passive response to human activity if the faith with which Jacob believes is itself a gift.

Augustine's decisive break with his early exegesis of Romans 9 comes in his *De diversis quaestionibus ad Simplicianum,* written around 397 and directed to Simplician, who succeeded Ambrose as the bishop of Milan.[18] The shift follows the lines suggested in the later *Retractationes.* Augustine can no longer regard the faith which responds to the call of God as simply an act of human free will. God must attract and empower the will to believe, even though the human will is not set aside or bypassed in the act of believing. After a prolonged consideration of the case of Jacob and Esau, Augustine now comes to the conclusion that election by foreknowledge is election by works, even if one calls the work faith.[19] It is inconceivable that St. Paul, who wrote the epistle to the Romans to undercut human confidence in good works, could ever have intended to teach election based upon them.[20]

The problem, therefore, as Augustine sees it, is not that faith is a gift of God but that this gift is not given equally to all human beings. Does the reason for the unequal distribution of the gift of faith lie in the human free will? Are some people more willing to hear and believe the gospel than others?[21] As attractive as this solution seems, it will not do. What human beings share equally is an unresponsiveness to the gospel. The human family participates equally in an inheritance of sin and disobedience. The predicament is universal and absolute and admits of no exception. Both Jacob and Esau deserve divine judgment and condemnation. Both belong to the *massa peccati.*[22]

One must distinguish, therefore, not between degrees of receptivity on the part of human beings but between kinds of calling on the part of God. While the gospel is directed toward the salvation of the whole human race, one must distinguish between effectual and ineffectual calling.[23] Recipients of the effectual call hear and obey it; recipients of the ineffectual call either remain indifferent to it (Esau) or are confirmed in their obstinate rebellion against God (Pharaoh). If anyone protests that this distinction in calling is inherently unfair, Augustine appeals to a higher hidden justice which transcends human notions of right and wrong but which bears some analogy to them.[24] At any rate, if God did not elect Jacob to justification apart from all consideration of merit, whether of faith or of works, then both Jacob and Esau would be lost, and no one would be saved.[25] Without election, the predicament of Esau is not improved; the situation of Jacob is merely worsened.

There are brief discussions of Romans 9 in many of Augustine's anti-Pelagian writings, particularly *De spiritu et littera, Epistula 186 ad Paulinum, Epistula 194 ad Sixtum, Contra duas epistulas Pelagianorum, De gratia et libero arbitrio, De correptione et gratia, De praedestinatione sanctorum, De dono perseverantiae* and the *Opus imperfectum contra Iulianum.*[26] While these writings add some points, particularly on the question of perseverance, the main themes of Augustine's mature exegesis have already been set in the letter to Simplician. In the *Enchiridion*, written around 421, Augustine returns to the question of God's justice and argues that while Jacob is the recipient of a wholly gratuitous mercy, Esau has meted out to him the punishment which is justly his.[27] Both belonged to the *massa perditionis*, and it was only the call of God which separated Jacob from it. All of this is familiar from the letter to Simplician, including the pastoral observation that election teaches the faithful to praise God rather than to glory in their own works.

II

Of the fourteen works by Augustine which discuss Romans 9, Luther cites seven in the course of his exposition of the whole epistle. He does not cite, however, *De diversis quaestionibus ad Simplicianum* at all and only begins to use the *Expositio* in his gloss on Romans 5:5. The sole writing by Augustine which Luther cites in his exposition of Romans 9:10–29 is the *Enchiridion* 98–99. Indeed, in the interpretation of this section Luther turns to Erasmus and Faber Stapulensis more often than to Augustine.

Nevertheless, important elements of Augustine's mature exegesis of Paul are repeated by Luther in his treatment of the text. Luther agrees with Augustine that the election of Jacob over Esau is based neither on inheritance nor on merit of any kind. Both Jacob and Esau are evil because of original sin, and both belong by birth to the mass of perdition.[28] Goodness is the result of God's election, not its precondition. Predestination teaches believers humility; it teaches them that they are not able to justify themselves by the exercise of their free will.[29] Grace raises believers up "before and beyond" the exercise of human volition.[30]

While Luther presupposes the Pauline exegesis of the older Augustine, his exegesis introduces a number of themes not found in Augustine's interpretation of Paul. For example, the idea that human virtue is a product of divine election and reckoning is used to attack Aristotle's notion that the habit of virtue is attained through the repetition of morally good deeds.[31] Paul interpreted with the assistance of Augustine stands as a warning against the fascination of scholastic theologians with Aristotelian philosophy.[32]

Similarly, while Augustine appeals to the hidden higher justice of God (as exemplified by the parable of the workers in the vineyard), Luther is satisfied to make the bald declaration that "there is no other reason for his justice and there can be no other than his will."[33] Since God's will is by definition the highest good, men and women ought to stretch every nerve to see it done and not worry whether it conforms to customary notions of right and wrong. Even reprobation cannot be evil if it is willed by God. Human beings regard the will of God as evil only because they cannot manage it.[34] In short, Luther interprets the theme of divine sovereignty in what appears to be a rather Occamistic fashion: good is good because God wills it. The meaning of that goodness cannot be discovered in advance by human reason, but only experienced by the faithful who resign themselves to it. "If one wills what God wills, even if this means to be damned and rejected, one has no evil. Then one wills what God wills and patience enables one to bear it."[35]

Luther's pastoral concerns color his exegesis and are not exactly the same as Augustine's. Augustine had worried, both before and after his letter to Simplician, about the role of the human free will and about the psychological impetus which moves the will to faith or morally good deeds. Luther, on the other hand, seems willing to state Augustine's conclusions without embracing Augustine's psychology: "A man owes his ability to will and to run, not to his own power, but to the mercy of God who gave him this power to will and to run."[36] He can even refer to human beings as "instruments of God" and compare them to an ax in the hand of a cutter (an analogy which he draws from Isaiah 10).[37] An ax in the hand of a cutter is not an image which does justice to Augustine's rather more subtle description of the activity of grace on human volition. Luther does, however, want to make the pastoral point that human willing and running are not in vain when they are God's work in a man or woman.[38]

The pastoral problem which seems uppermost in Luther's mind is the problem of certitude of salvation. He touches on it several times. In the scholium on 9:15, remarking on the underlying Hebrew text (Exodus 33:19), "I will have mercy on whom I will have mercy," Luther notes that the Hebrew is "indefinitely put. It speaks of mercy more in terms of a chance without specific reference to predestination."[39] The mode of expression seems to Luther to imply that God wants to discourage people from speculating about predestination, their own or their neighbor's.[40]

At the end of the scholium on 9:16, he returns to this problem. He indicates that predestination is a question which should be reserved for the "strong and perfect," since the discussion of this mystery is "theology in the best sense of the term."[41] He claims that he would not have brought the subject up at all, except the order of his lectures on Paul compelled him to do so.[42] While predestination is "very strong wine" and "solid food" for the spiritually advanced, Luther confesses that he is a babe in Christ who needs milk. "Let him who is as I am do likewise. The wounds of Christ, 'the clefts in the rock,' are safe enough for us."[43]

Luther's reference to the wounds of Christ is a reference to pastoral advice, which Luther elsewhere claims he first received from John Staupitz. To look to the wounds of Christ is to contemplate the Savior who was crucified for the sins of the world; more particularly, for the sins of Martin Luther and the other "babes in Christ" who are distressed by the merest thought of the mystery of election and reprobation. It is the redemptive love of God directed toward sinners and revealed in history through the crucified Savior on which the weak should fix their attention.

In the scholium on 9:19–20, Luther tries to console anxious Christians who find the question about the justice and fairness of God naturally springing to their lips, and who are terrified that they have committed blasphemy by entertaining such doubts. God is not "impatient or cruel," particularly to those timid souls who are "under the overwhelming power of an assault" upon their faith.[44] The point for Luther is that the very anxiety which the believer suffers is itself the strongest evidence that no blasphemy has occurred.

> If a man is filled with fear and trembling because he has uttered a blasphemy, this is a sign that he did not really want to do it and that he did it innocently. This dread of evil is an evident sign that one has a good heart. Hence, the best cure for such thoughts is not to be concerned about them.[45]

In the scholium on 9:17, Luther returns to the Augustinian theme which links the doctrine of predestination with humility. After a lengthy discussion of Latin, Greek, Hebrew, and German words for power, Luther offers two interpretations of what Paul means by referring to the demonstration of the power of God in the career of Pharaoh.[46] The first interpretation is tropological. God demonstrated his power in Pharaoh in order to show the elect their weakness.[47] By reducing their power to nothing through the far greater power of Pharaoh, God taught the elect not to glory in their own strength. Liberation from bondage in Egypt was due to the power of God alone. In this interpretation, power is linked to salvation through the humiliation of the elect.

A second interpretation, however, which seems more probable to Luther, links the power of God to the destruction of the reprobate.[48] Jacob is made good not because of his ancestry or merit but because God is merciful to him. Similarly, Pharaoh is not made good because God is not merciful to him. This interpretation links 9:17 ("That I might demonstrate in you my power") to 9:18 ("He has mercy on whom he will, and whom he wills he hardens") and demonstrates more clearly that the will of God lies behind both election and reprobation. While Luther may prefer not to talk about predestination at all, he is also unwilling to soften the doctrine by equating election with foreknowledge, even if one means by "foreknowledge" the foreknowledge of faith. Luther is not drawn to the position of Augustine in the *Expositio,* though he knows it, but stays with the position of Augustine in the *Enchiridion,*[49] however much he may fear that Augustine's mature position is too strong a drink for the immature theological palate.

III

If we compare the exegesis of Romans 9:10–29 by Luther with the various interpretations of that passage by Augustine, as we have done in this essay, we will find that certain conclusions rather naturally suggest themselves to us:

1. Neither Augustine nor Luther is particularly concerned about the problem which is uppermost in Paul's mind. Paul wants to know whether the unbelief of Israel has invalidated the covenant which God concluded with her. What place in the history of salvation remains for Israel, especially in view of the new and astonishingly successful mission to the Gentiles? Has Israel been permanently set aside in favor of a New Israel, composed of Gentiles and a remnant of the Old Israel? Paul's reflections about Jacob and Esau are set in that context rather than in the context of the salvation of the elect from the mass of perdition which is fallen humanity. That is not to say that the question is altogether neglected in the commentaries we have read. Luther, for example, spends a great deal of time in chapter 11 discussing the place of the Jews in the economy of salvation and even castigates the anti-Semitic theologians of Cologne who attacked Reuchlin in the Pfeffer-

korn affair.[50] But the immediate context for his exegesis of Romans 9 is the universal context of the predicament of the human race before God rather than the more particular context of the relationship of Israel and the Church. In that approach to the text he is following lines already suggested by Augustine.

2. While Luther knows both the young anti-Manichaean Augustine and the old anti-Pelagian Augustine and makes use of exegetical writings from all periods of Augustine's life, he clearly prefers the old Augustine to the young in his exegesis of Romans 9. Luther does not talk about effectual and ineffectual calling (the so-called *vocatio congrua et incongrua*) or worry about some role for free will in the psychology of faith. He embraces the most severe statement of Augustine's position on predestination (a position from which Augustine himself at times attempted to retreat) and states it as a conclusion which is indisputable. The will of God is the cause of both election and reprobation. All human beings belong to the mass of perdition because of original sin. Jacob cannot merit his election but is an object of inexplicable mercy from God. All of these Augustinian ideas are so firmly embedded in Luther's mind that Luther does not seem to notice that St. Paul never mentions a *massa perditionis* or *massa peccati*. Augustine has encapsulated for Luther the substance, if not the exact language, of Pauline teaching. One cannot regard Luther as merely a conventional Augustinian on these points, since the vast majority of medieval theologians tend to stress more than Luther does the justice of God in reprobation and to bring that doctrine into greater harmony with human notions of fair play. Where Luther is dependent on Augustine, he is dependent on the old anti-Pelagian Augustine, who knows that the will must be healed before it can ever come to faith or serve God.

3. Having said all that, it is astonishing how little of the rest of Luther's exegesis of Romans 9 comes from the comments on that text by Augustine. St. Paul as read through the lenses provided by Augustine creates certain acute theological and pastoral problems for Luther, but Augustine himself plays very little role in the resolution of those problems. One can detect in Luther's exegesis the explicit help of Erasmus and Faber and the implicit help of Biel and Staupitz. But the mixture of ideas is Luther's and reflects his own personal relationship to the text and his own experience of the anxieties which the text creates. While Augustine worries about free will and the justice of God, Luther devotes his attention to certitude of salvation and the understandable fears of the spiritually weak. At the same time, very few of the young Luther's most characteristic theological themes—the strange and proper work of God, the hiddenness of God underneath a

contrary appearance, or the contrast of a theology of the cross with a theology of glory—find expression in this section of his exegesis. When confronted with the doctrine of election, one stands in "fear and trembling" before an "abyss of horror and despair."[51] Only when the eyes of the heart are purged by meditating on the wounds of Christ can one confront this mystery without terror. It is this immediate pastoral response to the text which marks Luther's exegesis off from Augustine's and gives it its peculiar character.

III

LUTHER AND THE
HIDDEN GOD

The center of Luther's understanding of Christianity is the proclamation of a God who is both hidden and revealed. The notion of a hidden God is certainly no new idea in Christianity. According to the book of Acts, Paul announced to a bemused Athenian audience that the altar dedicated to the unknown God was in reality an altar dedicated to the God and Father of Jesus Christ. The heretic Marcion, himself a devout admirer of Paul, pressed Paul's point further by suggesting that the Christian God was hidden not only from the ancient Greeks but also from the ancient Jews. Neither Plato nor Moses knew anything about the merciful God of the New Testament until he was revealed by Christ. Though Marcion's exaggerated doctrine of the hiddenness of God was rejected by the Orthodox community, Christian theologians continued to argue that the Christian Gospel is a message about a transcendent God who at one time had been hidden but who is now revealed.

Usually, however, the revelation of God was not thought of as something altogether exclusive to the Christian Church. God had revealed himself in the natural order as well as in the oracles of the prophets and apostles. Men and women, made in the image of God, were able by the exercise of their natural reasoning powers to discern the hand of God in the biological and physical processes of nature and in the providentially guided events of history. This natural theology needed, of course, to be supplemented by revealed theology, since sinful men and women must learn about God the Redeemer as well as about God the Creator. Natural theology is no substitute for instruction concerning the mysteries of redemption, but it forms a foundation and a starting-point for such instruction. The God who was hidden is revealed not only from faith to faith in the Gospel but also to ordinary human reason in the world of nature.

I

There are two senses in which Luther can speak of the hiddenness of God. He can speak of a God who is hidden outside of revelation, unknown and as unrevealed unknowable, and of a God who hides himself within his revelation, undisclosed in the very act of disclosure. Of the two senses, the first is by far the easier to grasp. Just as two people cannot begin to understand each other until they speak and by the act of speaking disclose something of their character, their hopes, their fears, their prejudices, their aspirations, so, too, God cannot be understood until he discloses himself through word and deed. Although Luther believes in natural law and that human reason is able to discern principles of morality which conform to the will of God, however imperfectly, he is not interested in attempting to construct a natural theology. What can be known of God through creation is perverted by a fallen human race into idolatry. Though sinners know that there is a God, they refuse to take God as he is but insist on subsuming the Godhead under their own narrow self-interests. Rather than modifying their notions of what God is like to conform to God's self-disclosure, they construct for themselves a tame and gracious God who conforms to their hopes and expectations.

Luther's lack of interest in natural theology has, I think, at least two roots. The first has been suggested already. Nature would have been an important source for the knowledge of God were it not for the fact of human sin. Luther regards all created things as *larvae* or "masks" of God. The doctrine of divine transcendence does not mean that God is removed from creation. Indeed, Luther stresses the immanence of God in the world in such strong and unguarded language that he sounds at times almost pantheistic. God is not merely present in eucharistic bread; he is present in all common bread and in the wheat from which bread is made. The transcendence of God is not equivalent to his absence. On the contrary, transcendence means that, while God is present in every creature that surrounds me, his presence is inaccessible to me apart from his Word. In one of the most striking passages in the *Tabletalk,* a passage echoed by John Calvin in the first book of his *Institutes,* Luther argues that in a fallen world the

> article concerning the Creation from nothing is more difficult to believe than the article concerning the Incarnation of Christ. . . . For sin has so blinded human nature that it no longer knows the Creator, although it catches a hint of His works, especially in the order of the world! Man does not even know his own sin, and thinks his blindness is the highest wisdom. If only Adam had not sinned, men would have recognized God

in all creatures, would have loved and praised Him so that even in the smallest blossom they would have seen and pondered His power, grace and wisdom. But who can fathom how from the barren earth God creates so many kinds of flowers of such lovely colors and such sweet scent, as no painter or alchemist could make? Yet God can bring forth from the earth green, yellow, red, blue, brown, and every kind of color. All these things would have turned the mind of Adam and his kin to honor God and laud and praise Him and to enjoy his creatures with gratitude.[1]

Furthermore, natural theology, with its inferential methods and its proofs for the existence of God, seems rather pointless to Luther. The universal phenomenon of religion is already sufficient proof for Luther of the ineradicable human perception that there is a God. The very fact that human beings find it worthwhile to construct idols and pray to them is evidence that the existence of God is a datum indelibly written on the human heart. All human beings know without being told that there is a God and that they are responsible to this God. What they do not know is what this God is like.

Because God is hidden outside his revelation, Luther is adamantly opposed to any attempt to uncover the naked being of God through speculative reason or religious ecstasy. The dazzling glory of the being of the hidden God would blind and terrify us if we could uncover it. God must hide his glory in his revelation; he must accommodate himself to our finitude and sin. The gospel is the good news that we are not required to ascend to God through prayer, self-denial, and the discipline of reason and desire. God has descended to us as a child on its mother's lap. He has met us at the bottom rung of the ladder, on our level rather than on his. Holiness may alarm and terrify us, but no one is frightened of a child.

O, what a ridiculous thing, that the one true God, the high Majesty, should be made man; that here they should be joined, man and his Maker, in one Person. Reason opposes this with all its might. Here, then, those wise thoughts with which our reason soars up towards heaven to seek out God in His own majesty, and to probe out how he reigns there on high, are taken from us. The goal is fixed elsewhere, so that I should run from all the corners of the world to Bethlehem, to that stable and that manger where the babe lies, or to the Virgin's lap. Yes, that subdues the reason. Do not search what is too high for thee. But here it comes down before my eyes, so that I can see the babe there in its mother's lap. There lies a human being who was born like any other child, and lives like any other child, and shows no other nature, manner and work than any other human being, so that no heart could guess that the creature is the Creator. Where, then, are all the wise men? Reason must bow, and must confess her blindness in that she wants to climb to heaven to fathom the Divine, while she cannot see what lies before her eyes.[2]

The fact that the hidden God has disclosed himself in Christ does not mean, however, that this self-revelation of God is exhaustive. In his self-revelation, God tells sinners all that they need to know, not all that they would like to know. Theology for Luther is neither a science of God in the sense of propositional comment on the being of God nor a study of religious phenomena in the sense of critical reflection on human religious experience. Luther regards theology as an ellipse with two foci. Authentic theology is concerned with God in his relationship of judgment and grace to the self and the self in its relationship of disobedience and faith to God. It is concerned with nothing which stands outside that relationship and reconceives all traditional theological topics from the perspective of that ellipse.

When Luther observes that a theologian is made by *meditatio, tentatio,* and *oratio* (meditation, temptation, and prayer), he wants to emphasize that theology is not a neutral discipline like geometry, which can be studied dispassionately in abstraction from the self and its concerns. Theology deals with a God who stands in a relationship to me and who lays claim to my life, whether I acknowledge that relationship or not. Where I am not included in my reflections about God, there is no Christian theology but only philosophical speculation. Only as God reveals himself to me through his Word, only insofar as I am confronted by this God and my faith is awakened, can theology be engaged in at all. Everything which stands outside the circle of light cast by revelation is impenetrable darkness.

To the hiddenness of God belongs the mystery of predestination. Luther urges believers to turn their eyes away from the *deus absconditus,* the hidden God who elects and damns, and focus them on the *deus revelatus,* the revealed God who has shown a merciful face in Jesus Christ. The hidden God hardens the heart of Pharaoh, rejects Esau before he is born, and wills the death of sinners. The will of this hidden God is inscrutable. It is not merely undisclosed; it is concealed.

> To the extent, therefore that God hides himself and wills to be unknown to us, it is no business of ours. For here the saying truly applies, "Things above us are no business of ours."[3]

Luther does not mean to suggest that the hidden God is no concern of ours. There is only one God, even though that God is both hidden and revealed and even though there is a dangerous side to the hidden

God which revelation does not dissipate. What Luther is arguing is that the hiddenness of God outside of revelation is not a subject for critical investigation. Christian theology must begin with the God revealed in the humanity of Jesus Christ. It must resist all temptation to speculate about the nature and being of God apart from Christ and must focus on the self-disclosure of God in this man.

> Begin your search with Christ and stay with Him and cleave to Him, and if your own thoughts and reason, or another man's, would lead you elsewhere, shut your eyes and say: I should and will know of no other God than Christ, my Lord. . . . But if you abandon this clear prospect, and climb up into God's Majesty on high, you must stumble, fear and fall because you have withdrawn yourself from God's grace, and have dared to stare at the Majesty unveiled, which is too high and overpowering for you. For apart from Christ, Nature can neither perceive nor attain the grace and love of God, and apart from Him is nothing but wrath and condemnation.[4]

II

It is precisely at this point that Luther encounters a difficulty. Faith has as its object hidden things, the so-called *res non apparentes,* "things that do not appear," of Hebrews 11. Hiddenness belongs to the very nature of revelation. One cannot juxtapose the hidden and the revealed God as though they were antithetical to each other. The revealed God remains hidden, not only outside his revelation but also in it. Indeed, hiddenness, particularly hiddenness under the form of a contrary appearance, is the form of God's self-revelation.

Luther provides a lucid example of this theme in his sermon for the first Sunday in Advent, 1533. The sermon comments on the triumphal entry of Jesus into Jerusalem on Palm Sunday (Matthew 21:1–9) and focuses on the word of the prophet Zechariah which is cited by Matthew as an explanation of the event (Zechariah 9:9): "Rejoice greatly, O daughter of Zion; shout, O daughter of Jerusalem: behold, they King cometh unto thee: he is just, and having salvation; lowly, and riding upon an ass, and upon a colt the foal of an ass."

> Yea, of a truth, He will be a king, but a poor and wretched king who has in no way the appearance of a king if He is judged and esteemed by outward might and splendor, in which worldly kings and princes like to array themselves. He leaves to other kings such things as pomp, castles, palaces, gold, and wealth; and He lets them eat and drink, dress and build more daintily than other folks; but the craft which Christ the poor beggar-king knows, they do not know. He helps against not one sin

only, but against all my sin; and not against my sin only, but against the whole world's sin. He comes to take away not sickness only, but death; and not my death only, but the whole world's death. This, saith the Prophet, tell the daughter of Zion, that she be not offended at his mean advent; but shut thine eyes and open thine ears, and perceive not how He rides there so beggarly, but hearken to what is said and preached about this poor king. His wretchedness and poverty are manifest, for He comes riding on an ass like a beggar having neither saddle nor spurs. But that He will take from us sin, strangle death, endow us with eternal holiness, eternal bliss, and eternal life, this cannot be seen. Wherefore thou must hear and believe.[5]

Luther contrasts the entry of Christ, "the poor beggar-king," into Jerusalem with the customary entry of "other kings" into their capital cities. Christ has "in no way the appearance of a king." Kings wear fine clothes; they ride purebred stallions and are accompanied by an entourage of important and influential people. They are met by the chief citizens of the city, lodged in comfortable rooms at public expense, and offered delicacies to eat and drink. Christ, on the other hand, enters the city alone, on a donkey, without saddle and spurs, and is greeted by children and old men. Nevertheless, even though the royal power of Christ is hidden under his beggarly appearance, Christ is in fact a king, a king whose power over life and death puts the merely political power of kings to shame. The danger, of course, is that onlookers will judge the event by what they can see and not by what the prophet Zechariah says. The word of the prophet is the clue to the meaning of the event. Against what the eye can see, against what reason, prudence, and common sense dictate, the onlooker must deny the evidence of his senses and grasp the word of the prophet by faith. He must close his eyes and open his ears. The revelation of God is hidden under a contrary appearance; in his self-disclosure, God remains concealed.

Luther's view of the hiddenness of God is intimately connected with his view of faith. The fundamental human predicament is unbelief. Men and women will not put their ultimate trust in God, will not receive their lives as a gift from God, but place their ultimate trust in themselves, in their world, in created reality. Human nature is proud, and human beings must be tackled in the depths of their pride. Human pride is broken down by the hidden revelation of God which always contradicts human expectation.

In his early lectures on Romans, Luther gives an illustration of what he has in mind. A patient in a hospital has an immediate perception of his illness. He knows without waiting for a diagnosis from his physician that he is running a fever, that he is suffering from nausea and headaches, that his joints are stiff, and that certain sudden motions give him sharp pains in his arms. What he cannot tell from experiencing the symptoms of his illness is whether he is getting worse or is on the mend. The physician, however, is in a position to make a dispassionate judgment about the real condition of the patient.

Suppose, said Luther, the doctor tells you that you are on the mend. You can, of course, put your faith in your symptoms and assume that the doctor is trying to keep from you the cruel truth that your illness is terminal. Assessing the empirical evidence with your own reason and common sense, no other conclusion is possible. Or you can, against the evidence of your senses and the pessimistic conclusions of your intellect, trust the word of your physician and assess your situation from his perspective. The fact of your beginning recovery is hidden under the contrary appearance of your virulent fever. You can grasp it now by closing your eyes to your symptoms and opening your ears to the word of your physician, who contradicts by his prognosis your immediate experience of pain.

While no analogy is perfect and while Luther does not mean to suggest that God as a physician of souls merely announces a natural recovery of spiritual health of which he is not the cause, the illustration does make certain important points. Empirical evidence cannot be trusted, particularly when it is assessed by fallen human reason. I am brought in touch with my real situation by listening to the Word of God, which contradicts my own assessment, and by trusting it. Faith means letting God be God, accepting the scandal of his hiddenness and trusting him in spite of reason, experience, and common sense.

At this point, however, a further difficulty surfaces for Luther. Just as it is inadequate to contrast the hidden and revealed God as though the revealed God were not also hidden, so, too, it is inadequate to contrast the empirical evidence which the eye sees with the audible Word which interprets the self-disclosure of God hidden beneath it. The Word which the revealed God speaks is both Law and Gospel, both wrath and mercy, both no and yes. The Law no less than the Gospel is the Word of God. This Law condemns me as a sinner in such a way that my conscience agrees with that judgment. Unless I can overcome God's "no" spoken in the Law with God's "yes" spoken in the Gospel, the last enemy to keep me from God will be God himself.

Luther unforgettably describes the predicament of the believer in sermons preached in 1525. In the first sermon, Luther ruefully admits that the Law condemns him as a sinner. If he agrees with the Law, he is lost; if he says no to the Law, he must have a firm basis for that no. While sinners cannot say no to the Law, Christ can. The Law has no

basis on which to condemn him. Therefore, Christ gives to believers
the no to the Law which he has merited for them.[6]

In the second sermon, Luther comments on the story of the Syrophoenician woman (Matthew 25). The woman asks Jesus to come to
her home and heal her daughter, who is ill. Jesus replies harshly that
he has come solely to the house of Israel and has no mission to the
Gentiles. He cannot, he says, give the children's bread to dogs. The
woman replies: "Truth, Lord: yet the dogs eat of the crumbs which fall
from their masters' table." Jesus approves of her reply and says to her,
"O woman, great is thy faith: be it unto thee even as thou wilt."

> Is not this masterly? She catches Christ by means of his own words. He
> compares her to a dog, which she admits and she asks no more than
> that he let her be like a dog as He Himself judges: Whither could he
> turn? He was caught. No dog is denied the breadcrumbs under the
> table. They are its rightful share. Therefore He takes heed of her and
> submits to her will, so that she is no longer a dog but is become a child
> of Israel. And this was written in order that we might be comforted and
> that it may be made manifest to us all how deeply God hides his grace
> from us, and that we should not judge Him according to our feeling and
> thinking about Him but in accordance with His Word. For here you see
> that Christ, although he showed himself hard, pronounced no final
> judgment by saying "No" to her; but all His answers, though they
> sound like "No", are yet not "No" but are indefinite. Therewith is
> shown how our heart should stand firm in the midst of temptations, for
> as hard as we feel Him, so Christ feigns to be. Our heart hears and
> understands nothing but "No" and yet it is not "No". Therefore sweep
> your heart clean of such feelings and trust firmly in God's Word and
> grasp from above or underneath the "No" the deeply hidden "Yes" and
> hold on to it as this woman did and keep a firm belief in God's justice.
> Then you have won and caught him with His own words.[7]

Just as the revealed God is hidden in his revelation under the form
of a contrary appearance, so the "yes" of this revealed God in the
Gospel is hidden under the "no" spoken to guilty sinners in the Law.
If I say "yes" to God's "no," if I embrace God's "no" as the final
reality, then God himself keeps me from God. Against God's opposition to me in the Law, I must break through to God's mercy in the
Gospel. I must grasp underneath God's "no" the deeply hidden "yes."
I must borrow from Christ a "no" to the Law which is not rightfully
mine. I must with the promises of God in the Gospel outwit the denun-
ciations hurled at me by the Law. Behind the strange work of God's
wrath, I must believe in the proper work of his mercy. Not only is God
hidden under the form of a contrary appearance; so, too, in a certain
sense, is the Gospel.

III

Recent scholarship has shown a new curiosity about Luther's preoccupation with the devil. It is true, of course, that Luther has a great deal to say about the devil as the chief adversary of God. At times, Luther can sound almost dualistic, so graphically does he portray satanic opposition to God. Yet, as terrible as the devil is and as ferociously as he rages against the little flock of true believers, the fact remains that the devil is God's creature and cannot act beyond the limits set for him by God. His "no" to the Church and the individual believer is a penultimate "no". His wrath is a terrible thing, but it is a creature's wrath and not the wrath of God. The devil is not the final arbiter of human destiny, though he would like to be. The last word in this as in all things belongs to God.

For that reason, the central theological problem for Luther remains the problem of God. The mercy and compassion of God are always set against the background of God's hiddenness. There is a God who wills and does not will the death of a sinner, whose life-giving promises in the Gospel are hidden under the death-dealing prohibitions of the Law. The thought which terrifies Luther is not that the devil is his enemy but that God might be. Therefore, Luther clings with both hands to the revealed God against the hidden God, to the Gospel against the Law, to what is heard against what is seen.

Faith has to do with a revelation which in certain important respects must remain hidden. If God did not remain hidden in his revelation, he would become accessible to sight, and faith would be superseded. Because God is hidden and revealed, never one or the other but always both at once, faith is never superseded as the appropriate human response to the self-revelation of God. The doctrine of the hiddenness of God thus leads in Luther's thought inexorably back to the doctrine of justification by faith alone.

IV

ABRAHAM AND THE
REFORMATION

The story of the Old Testament patriarch Abraham plays a central role in two of the major religious disputes of the sixteenth century.[1] One dispute, curiously enough, concerns the relation of Abraham to the rite of circumcision and is mainly confined to certain Protestants of a generally Calvinist orientation who support infant baptism and to other more radical Protestants, primarily Anabaptists, who vigorously oppose it.[2] Abraham becomes for the German and Swiss Reformed a symbol of the continuity of the people of God in history and of the gradual transition rather than abrupt disjuncture which separates the Old Testament from the New. It is a fascinating debate and one whose importance for the history of Protestantism in the sixteenth century cannot be sufficiently stressed. Nevertheless, it is a dispute which we shall for the moment ignore.

The second debate, and the one with which we shall concern ourselves, actually antedates the Protestant Reformation and is stimulated by a quotation from the Pentateuch (Genesis 15:6): "Abraham believed God and it was reckoned to him for righteousness." St. Paul was fascinated with this quotation and used it to undercut the arguments of Jewish Christians who wished to bar from membership in the Church all Gentiles who had not first embraced a kind of minimal Judaism.[3] Against these Jewish Christians, Paul argued that Abraham was accounted righteous by God not because he had submitted to the rite of circumcision or because he kept the moral and ceremonial precepts of the Torah (Abraham, after all, was dust long before Moses was born), but because he trusted a promise given to him by God.

What made Abraham's faith so remarkable in Paul's estimation was that the promise defied ordinary human expectation. Abraham was promised a son whose offspring would become, in the language of the anonymous author of Genesis, as numberless as the sands of the seashore or the stars in the heavens. Abraham was an old man when he received this promise and a much older man before he saw its realization. To compound his difficulties still further, Abraham was married to an aging and chronically infertile woman. When Sarah, his wife, first heard of the promise to Abraham, she laughed. That seems, on the face of it, not a totally inappropriate response.

But Abraham, to use the happy phrase of Erasmus, united two contraries; that is to say, he "hoped in things despaired of."[4] He had utter confidence in a God who creates fresh possibilities for the faithful where all ordinary human possibilities have been exhausted. This unconditional trust in the promise of God, a trust which flew in the teeth of the accumulated contrary evidence, became the basis on which God acknowledged Abraham as a righteous man.

The conclusion which Paul drew from this story was enormously significant for the self-understanding of the early Church. If Abraham had been justified by faith rather than by the rite of circumcision or the observance of the Torah, then a relationship to God based on faith is more fundamental than a relationship based on adherence to a code of moral and ceremonial precepts. There is a sense, then, in which Christianity with its stress on faith in God's promises antedates Judaism with its emphasis on obedience to the Law. Gentiles who stand in a relationship of faith to God are in a certain sense children of Abraham and are permitted immediate access to baptism and membership in the covenant people of God. They are not obliged to undergo a prior and preparatory conversion to Judaism. That is not all that St. Paul has to say about Abraham, but it is enough to give the flavor of his argument.

With the decline of Jewish Christianity, and with a corresponding decline in a largely Gentile Church of interest in the relationship between Christianity and post-biblical Judaism, the argument of Paul was put to other uses. The problem for Christian theology after the death of Paul was no longer the relationship between Israel and the Church but rather what constituted the proper relationship between faith and works. After all, while Paul insisted that Abraham was justified by his faith, James argued just as doggedly that Abraham was justified by works. How were these apparently contradictory assertions to be reconciled?

The thesis that Abraham was justified by his faith became increasingly problematic in a Church which distinguished between *fides informis* (faith that can coexist with mortal sin) and *fides formata* (faith active in love), *fides implicita* (a habitual belief in what the Church teaches) and *fides explicita* (the conscious and explicit assent of the mind to Catholic truth), *fides quae* (the content of faith) and *fides qua* (the act of faith), *fides acquisita* (faith acquired through natural means) and *fides infusa* (faith supernaturally infused), *credulitas* (intellectual assent to true doctrine) and *fiducia* (trust in the promises of God).

When Genesis 15:6 spoke of the faith of Abraham, did it have in mind *credere Deum* (belief that God exists), *credere Deo* (belief that God's words are true), or *credere in Deum* (a loving confidence in God)? What was the relationship between Abraham's faith, however understood, and the Old Testament sacrament of circumcision? Did circumcision have a causative role *ex opere operantis* (on the basis of the interior disposition of the administrator or recipient) or *ex opere operato* (on the basis of the performance of the rite), *ex natura rei* (on the grounds of intrinsic value) or *ex pacto Dei* (on the grounds of a divine covenant)? Or was circumcision merely a sign and not, properly speaking, a sacrament at all? Questions such as these, which would have perplexed St. Paul, came gradually to replace the older issues generated by the separation of Christianity from its Jewish environment.

In spite of the importance of Pauline interpretation for the history of the Church, relatively little attention has been paid to it by historians.[5] This neglect poses an especially acute problem for students of the Reformation, since theologians in the sixteenth century devoted themselves to a study of the letters of Paul with an intensity unprecedented in the history of the Christian Church.[6] Protestants are frequently credited with this revival of interest in Pauline literature, and it is true that Protestants contributed a disproportionate share of the commentaries on Paul; but the renaissance in Pauline studies was well under way before the Reformation began, as the writings of Ficino, Erasmus, Colet, and Faber Stapulensis amply testify. While Catholic commentators on Paul are not so numerous as Protestant exegetes, significant commentaries on Paul were written by such important and influential cardinals as Cajetan,[7] Sadoleto,[8] and Seripando.[9]

It would not be possible in a single chapter to sketch the whole sweep of Pauline studies or even to summarize the weight of sixteenth-century scholarly opinion on each of the themes developed by Paul in the course of his epistles, but it would be possible and, I hope, profitable to take one theme—namely the crucial problem of Abraham's justification by faith—and show three important moments in the history of the interpretation of that single theme.

I have chosen three commentators, two Germans and an Italian, who did not know each other personally but had common ties nonetheless, and who embodied theological tendencies in the interpretation of Paul consciously opposed by the other two. The first commentator is Wendelin Steinbach (1454–1519),[10] professor of theology at the University of Tübingen, who lectured on Paul's letter to the Galatians in 1513.[11] Steinbach was the foremost disciple of the German nominalist theologian Gabriel Biel and the editor of his published works. Indeed,

Steinbach so subordinated his career to the career of his master that his own lectures on the Bible were never published during his lifetime. Steinbach represents an approach to Paul which reflects the theological presuppositions of German nominalism.

The second commentator, not surprisingly, is Martin Luther (1483–1546), professor of biblical studies at the University of Wittenberg. Luther was thoroughly trained at Erfurt in the theology of Gabriel Biel and reacted violently against it. He lectured on Romans in 1515–16, Galatians in 1516 and 1531, and on the Abraham stories in Genesis in 1538–39. In his lectures on Paul, Luther rejected point by point the main assertions about Abraham advanced by Steinbach. Even though Luther did not read Steinbach's lectures, he correctly anticipated the exegetical points which Steinbach had made. While later Protestant commentators did not slavishly repeat Luther's exegesis of Romans 4 and Galatians 3, they did accept—as the commentaries of Zwingli,[12] Bullinger,[13] Brenz,[14] Melanchthon,[15] and Calvin[16] demonstrate—the thrust of Luther's argument.

The last commentator is Girolamo Cardinal Seripando (1493–1563), general of the Augustinian Order, archbishop of Salerno, and papal legate to the Council of Trent.[17] Seripando had been commissioned by Pope Paul III to make a special study of the writings of the Protestants so that the theological points raised by them could be intelligently addressed. He was sympathetic to the Augustinianism of the Protestants, though it was in his opinion an Augustinianism which had lost its Catholic bearings and had therefore seriously misrepresented the original sources to which it appealed. He was one of the most influential figures at the Council of Trent and, even though some of his opinions on original sin and justification were not finally accepted, he nevertheless shaped the outcome of the important conciliar decisions on those topics. In his posthumously published commentaries on Romans and Galatians, Seripando rejected the exegesis of such Catholic interpreters as Steinbach and such Protestant interpreters as Luther. He tried to find a Catholic middle way between a reading of Paul which conceded too much to Pelagius and one which broke too sharply with antecedent tradition.

The clash of these three competing interpretations of Paul, particularly of Paul's teaching concerning the faith of Abraham, is a fundamental dispute and is regarded by the commentators themselves as ultimately irreconcilable. The dispute is intense because each interpretation of Paul presupposes, contains, and implies a competing vision of the nature of the religious life. In this argument, the figure of Abraham, who was a symbol for Paul of what united Jews and Gentiles in a common faith, becomes for sixteenth-century interpreters of Paul a symbol of what separates Protestant from Catholic, heretic from orthodox, the truly devout from the ungodly.

I

During the last years of his life, Wendelin Steinbach, who represented Occamist theology at Tübingen from 1486 to 1517, found his theological assumptions challenged to the hilt by his study of the epistles of Paul and by his wide reading in the Amerbach edition of the writings of Augustine.[18] Steinbach had been taught by his mentor, Gabriel Biel, that sinners could, by the proper use of their natural moral endowments, earn the first grace of justification by a merit of congruity.[19] Such a view came perilously close to the Pelagian views which Augustine had so roundly condemned. Not that Biel thought for one moment that his views were Pelagian! On the contrary, he was convinced that he had added all the proper Augustinian safeguards to his doctrine of grace to preserve it from any such charge.

Still, the concentrated reading of massive doses of Augustine and Paul provide unsettling for Biel's erstwhile disciple, Steinbach, who was more accustomed to dealing with their writings as a series of vetted quotations in a manual of theology. Paul and Augustine, taken in context and at face value, held positions which directly conflicted with the fundamental principles of Occamist thought. It was all very unnerving for Steinbach, who would have preferred to discover that all his favorite authors sweetly harmonized with each other. Instead, Steinbach found that his most important ancient authorities clashed dreadfully with his most esteemed modern ones.

The problem, however, was largely a hermeneutical one.[20] Steinbach was willing to concede (who, after all, could deny it?) that certain opinions of Paul and Augustine, if taken at face value, could not be harmonized with certain opinions of Biel, but then, too, not everything uttered by Paul pleased Augustine in its stark and unqualified form. Even the old Augustine found it necessary to go through his writings with a blue pencil, adding footnotes and marginal notations. In short, theological language is historically conditioned. It is affected by the pastoral or polemical situation in which the theologian finds himself when he writes.[21] Ways of talking about God which are appropriate and useful in one historical epoch may prove misleading, even dangerous, in another.[22]

It is possible to take any number of examples of the historical character of theological language from the writings of Augustine.[23] For example, Augustine appears to deny that human moral activity can be virtuous or good from its very nature (*bonum de genere*) without the gift of infused love.[24] While Steinbach admits that infused charity belongs to the substance of the act of loving God and that good works should have a habitual relationship to God as their final end, he is not willing to deny free will or virtue to sinners who are still outside a state of grace.[25] If the literal sense of Augustine's proposition is true—no virtue without charity—then it is impossible for a sinner to earn justifying grace by a merit of congruity, a position Steinbach wants desperately to maintain. If one distinguishes, however, between Augustine's way of speaking and the real content of his theology, this tension is dissipated, and Augustine can be shown to harmonize with the best Occamist theology.[26]

What is true of Augustine is also true of Paul.[27] When Paul asserts that Abraham was justified by his faith and implies that Abraham was justified by faith alone, he is putting forward a claim which any competent theologian knows is not true. James 2[28] as well as I Corinthians 3 and 13[29] demonstrate that the faith which justifies is a faith formed by love (*fides caritate formata*).[30] Steinbach is enough of an Occamist to believe that there is no inherent power in charity which by its own nature merits eternal beatitude. The law that a sinner must have a habit of grace is a regulation established freely by the ordained power of God. Love, therefore, has no necessary causality but only a conditional causality or causality *sine qua non*.[31] Still, it is infused love and not faith which is the real principle of justification.[32] What on earth could Paul have meant when he claimed that Abraham was reckoned as righteous by God on no other ground than his faith?

What we have here, in Steinbach's opinion, is a particularly outrageous example of Paul's peculiar *modus loquendi* or manner of speaking. When Paul says that Abraham is justified by faith and implies by this that Abraham is justified by faith alone, he is using a way of talking appropriate for catechumens who are not yet fully aware that faith alone (in the sense of unformed or acquired faith) cannot save.[33] Only faith working by love saves. St. Paul knew that as well as St. James. What St. Paul is claiming (and we must be careful not to miss his point or be thrown off by his incautious phraseology) is that Abraham merited the first grace of justification by his good works, preeminently by the good work of believing God with his unformed faith.[34]

In other words, the career of Abraham is an illustration of the theological principle which Biel cites with great regularity: "God does not deny his grace to those who do what is in them." Abraham did what was in him.[35] He was a virtuous man who struggled to love the God who had called him from Ur of the Chaldees and who grasped the promises of God with his own unformed and imperfect faith. He performed works which were good *de genere* and by them merited the infused love which would form his faith and make it saving.[36]

If Paul meant only to suggest that Abraham merited grace by his unformed faith, why did he express himself in such a careless and exaggerated way in Romans 4 and Galatians 3? The answer for Steinbach lies in the mystery of divine providence. The excessive language of Paul (not excessive, of course, if one knows how to read it properly) concerning the faith of Abraham provided the later Pelagian heretics no foundation in Paul's letter to which they could rightfully appeal in support of their ideas.[37] The theological situation of the Church in the first four centuries dictated the kind of polemical rhetoric at which Paul was master.

Now, however, that the Pelagian heresy has been met and successfully weathered by the Church, the need for more restrained and precise theological language requires the Church to rephrase the moderate intentions of Paul in forms appropriate to their real meaning. Theologians after Pelagius can, without eroding the authority of either Paul or Augustine, use language and formulations which they themselves would have rejected before the advent of the Pelagian heresy.[38]

When the text from Genesis which Paul quotes says that "Abraham believed God and it was reckoned to him for righteousness," it means that Abraham believed God with an unformed faith which earned the gift of infused love. He earned it, of course, by an act that met the standard of God's generosity and not by an act that conformed to the standard of God's justice, but merit it he did. Once having merited the gift of love, Abraham could believe God with a formed faith and be in the full sense of the term a righteous man. Indeed, one can find no better illustration of the nominalist view that sinners merit grace by their virtue than the Pauline image of Abraham.

II

There is scarcely a point which Steinbach makes which Luther does not take some pains to deny. He rejects, for example, the contention that Paul and Augustine defended exaggerated theological positions out of pastoral or polemical necessity.[39] Luther sees no need for a new hermeneutic to adjust the historically conditioned teaching of the ancient Church Fathers to modern circumstances,[40] and he certainly sees no need for a hermeneutic which can with a clear conscience interpret Abraham as the model pilgrim of nominalist soteriology. The teaching of Paul is true as it stands. The hermeneutical problem is not how to adjust or modify the modern reader's customary ways of thinking and talking about God so that he can begin to grasp the astonishing and wholly unexpected message of Paul. In Luther's view, it is scholastic theology and not the New Testament which needs to be subjected to radical hermeneutical surgery.[41]

When asked to discuss what the New Testament means by faith, Luther seizes on the language of Hebrews 11:1 as the most appropriate vocabulary for explaining its nature: "Faith is the substance of things hoped for, the evidence of things unseen." If one examines this biblical definition of faith through the lenses provided by Aristotelian philosophy, one will seriously misunderstand what is being said.[42] When the Bible talks about substance, it is not talking about the essence or quiddity of a thing.[43] It is talking about what stands under a person, about a supporting foundation on which one builds one's life.[44] Sinners have the substance of their lives in visible objects which they can see, touch, catalogue, buy, exploit, cherish, destroy, or sell.[45] The godly have their substance in things that cannot be seen, things that can only be believed or hoped for.[46] Believers build their lives on promises unsupported by empirical evidence and very probably contradicted by it.[47] Therefore, faith seems an incredibly stupid enterprise to sane and sensible people who are not (as they understand themselves) swayed by emotion or sentiment and who cling with both hands to solid and incontrovertible facts.[48]

When Luther insists that the object of faith is invisible, he does so for two reasons, neither of which has very much to do with Plato or with heavenly archetypes. The object of faith is invisible either because it is future (who of us can see next Wednesday?) or because it is hidden in the present under the form of a contrary and contradictory appearance.[49] Luther is quite certain in his own mind that the New Testament speaks of a God who is deliberately and simultaneously hidden and revealed, hidden in fact in his very revelation. This simultaneity of hiddenness and revelation makes faith a much more complex phenomenon than Steinbach ever dreamed it could be.

In other words, it is not apparent to sight that the promise to Abraham of a son is anything more than a wistful projection by a childless old man; or that Abraham's search for a new homeland is anything nobler than a quest for better pasture for his cattle and sheep; or that his abortive attempt to offer his son, Isaac, as a human sacrifice is anything other than an act of primitive and misguided religious fanaticism. Yet the Bible, against reason and common sense, claims that Abraham was justified precisely because he was not sane and sensible. He believed a promise to which no prudent and responsible man would have given credence and, by doing so, became such an object of divine

mercy and love that the angels (if they could indulge in envy) might
have been jealous of him. The presence of God was discerned by
Abraham not by sight but by hearing and trusting the word of promise
which contradicted the evidence his eyes could see all too clearly.[50]
Abraham's faith justified him because it was formed by the Word of
God, which he unreservedly and unconditionally trusted. In his scholium on Hebrews 11:8, Luther observes:

> But this is the glory of faith, simply not to know: not to know where
> you are going, not to know what you are doing, not to know what you
> must suffer, and with sense and intellect, virtue and will, all alike made
> captive, to follow the naked voice of God, to be led and driven, rather
> than to go. And thus it is clear, that Abraham with this obedience of
> faith shows the highest example of the evangelical life, because he left
> all and followed the Lord, preferring the Word of God to everything
> else and loving it above all things; of his own free will a pilgrim, and
> subject to the perils of life and death every hour of the day and night.[51]

Central to Luther's early thought is the correlation of Word and
faith. The God of the Old and New Testaments is a God who enters
into covenants and who makes promises.[52] When Scripture speaks of
the truth of.God, it has in mind the unbroken and unbreakable fidelity
of God to his promises.[53] These promises are grasped by faith. Since,
however, the promises are to a very large extent testimonies concerning matters still pending in the future, faith has more the character of
hope than the character of memory. Those people who are justified by
faith have, as Luther says, all their goods in words and promises.[54]
Their substance,[55] the ground on which they build their lives, is the
invisible reality of the "things that do not appear"—invisible either
because they are future or because they are hidden in the present
under the jarring and discordant form of a contrary appearance.

Since the promises of God touch matters which contradict reason,
sight, and common sense, Luther is willing to talk rather paradoxically
about justifying God as a way of justifying the self. Since God is just
already, he does not need to be justified by sinners. Nevertheless, God
is justified in his words when people trust his promise of grace for the
humble.[56] By conforming their judgments to the judgment of God
against the contrary evidence of reason and common sense,[57] people
confess that God is true and risk their lives on his promises.[58] By justifying God in this way, they are in turn themselves justified by God.

The proper disposition for such justification is prayer. The sinner
cries out for salvation,[59] groans like Christian before he has opened the
wicket gate, and awaits with eager expectancy on God, who is truthful
and cannot lie, to make good on his promises. The verbs which give

theological content to the old axiom about "doing what is in one" are "ask," "seek," and "knock".[60] Luther's sinners accuse themselves of sin and justify God in his judgment. It is by becoming a "real sinner" that Luther takes advantage of the good news that the only thing the sinner has to offer in exchange for grace—namely, his ingrown and besetting sin—is exactly what God asks him to give.[61] The gospel is not "give me your virtue and I will crown it with grace" but "despise your sin and I will shower you with mercy." To suggest that Abraham merited the first grace of justification by his virtuous activity and his unformed faith is to turn the gospel on its head.

Luther, who believes that justification is by naked trust in the fragile, apparently contradictory, and largely unsubstantiated promises of God, regards Abraham as an example of an "absolute believer." By "absolute believer," Luther has reference more to the scope of Abraham's faith than to its constancy. Abraham is justified not because he believes this or that promise of God but because he stands ready to believe *any* promise of God, no matter how violently it may contradict the judgments of his own prudential reason and common sense.[62] Abraham's faith is not so much an act (e.g., believing that Sarah will become pregnant in spite of her advanced years) as a disposition (e.g., believing that whatever God promises, however startling, he is able to perform). Steinbach's translation of Abraham's faith into a pious work is, on Luther's principles, a fundamental misreading of Paul.

Luther sums up his views concerning the faith of Abraham in his 1538 lectures on Genesis:

> Then what? Is the Law useless for righteousness? Yes, certainly. But does faith alone, without works, justify? Yes, certainly. Otherwise you must repudiate Moses, who declares that Abraham is righteous prior to the Law and prior to the works of the Law, not because he sacrificed his son, who had not yet been born, and not because he did this or that work, but because he believed God who gave a promise. In this passage no mention is made of any preparation for grace, of any faith formed through works, or of any preceding disposition. This, however, is mentioned: that at that time Abraham was in the midst of sins, doubts, and fears, and was exceedingly troubled in spirit. How, then, did he obtain righteousness? In this way: God speaks and Abraham believes what God is saying.[63]

III

Our last commentator will detain us only briefly. Not that Girolamo Cardinal Seripando was not important and did not write a significant commentary on Romans and Galatians, but rather, as C.S. Lewis once observed, things need to be explained at length not in proportion to their importance but in proportion to their difficulty.

Seripando accepted neither Steinbach's image of Abraham as an Occamist pilgrim who earned the first grace of justification by his unformed faith and his virtuous acts nor Luther's portrait of Abraham as the "absolute believer" who risked his life on a promise of God and so was justified by faith alone. In Seripando's opinion, Paul makes it quite clear that works which precede justifying faith are works "according to the flesh" (*secundum carnem*).[64] Fleshly works do not justify nor, as Steinbach suggested, is righteousness ever imputed to them by a merit of congruity.[65] Seripando is very sympathetic to Luther's ferocious attack on the Pelagianizing tendencies of German nominalism and agrees in the main with Luther's Augustinian protest.

But Luther's constructive alternative to Steinbach is itself seriously flawed. Abraham was not justified by faith alone[66] because St. James is adamant that faith without works is dead.[67] The faith which justified Abraham was a faith which worked by love.[68] However, such faith is not a natural endowment.[69] It is a gift of God which is bestowed without antecedent human merit. The faith with which Abraham pleased God was not something that Abraham offered to God as a pious work but a gift which God both conceded and accepted.[70]

Faith is therefore the entrance to righteousness,[71] but the believer is not justified by faith alone, since faith is perfected by love and by the virtues which flow from love. Abraham is justified by faith (which is a gift and not a natural human faculty), and this faith is in turn consummated in works of charity.[72] Faith must be living and active rather than idle and dead.[73] Faith is related to works as a beginning to the end, as a foundation to the building erected upon it, as the root of a plant to the fruit which it finally bears.[74]

When Paul uses such words as "impute" and "non-imputation," he does not have in mind the forensic doctrine of justification taught by Luther, Bucer, Calvin, and the rest of the magisterial Protestants. What he means rather is this: "To impute is to ascribe to a man what he neither has nor can have by the power of human nature, such as faith for righteousness: since faith is beyond any man, and since no one can fully merit righteousness, which does not operate according to a scheme of reward. Not to impute, however, is not to attribute to a man what he both has by a fault of nature and cannot get rid of by the powers of nature, such as sin. Concerning this, David said, 'Blessed is the man to whom the Lord does not impute sin.' "[75] In short, what Seripando is eager to revive against both the Pelagianizing tendencies of Steinbach and the far too innovative and untraditional theology of

Luther is the ancient and venerable Augustinian tradition of the interpretation of Paul, a tradition which emphasizes "grace alone" against Steinbach and "faith formed by love" against Luther.

IV

There we have it, three distinct and competing views of the meaning of Abraham's faith. Depending whether one believes Steinbach or Luther or Seripando, Paul teaches that Abraham did or did not earn grace by his works, was or was not justified by faith alone, did or did not find the perfection of his faith in works of charity. One should learn from the example of Abraham—again depending upon which reading of Paul one finds convincing—to "do what is in one" in order to merit the first grace of infused love, or to abandon all confidence in one's own good works and cling to the promises of God by faith alone, or to make sure that the faith which one professes is a faith which works by love. Three models of piety are implied by the three images of Abraham, and it is necessary for the faithful to make a discriminating choice between them. It is not possible to embrace all three at once.

That much is obvious, but there are some other aspects of this controversy which do not lie so clearly on the surface, and I should like to conclude by making a few brief observations about them.

1. There are certain Protestant interpreters of the New Testament who are inclined to believe that the meaning of any biblical text is virtually, if not altogether, identical with the original intention of the author of that text. Since Steinbach, Luther, and Seripando have not placed their interpretations of Romans 4 and Galatians 3 in the original context created by the separation of Christianity from its Jewish matrix, they have simply misunderstood Paul, and their exegesis should be quietly buried in the nearest available wastepaper basket. The meaning of a text is exhausted by the intention of the original author of that text.

That is, of course, to place a demand on the Bible which no sensible person would think of placing on any other literary text. Even granting what I am not readily prepared to grant, that it is an easy matter to recapture the original intention of an ancient author, a good literary text creates a field of meanings and associations not explicitly worked out in the mind of the author but implicitly contained in the text itself. In the interaction of reader and text, those implicit meanings are discerned and brought to expression. The meaning of a text is defined in part by the intention of the author as it is in part by the prior meanings of the words which he uses, but new experiences cast new light on old texts.

2. I do not wish to suggest that a text has no proper meaning of its own but can mean anything that an interpreter, provided his imagination is virile enough to overcome the inhibitions of his conscience, wants it to mean. There was, for example, some brave talk in the later middle ages by theologians who had been seriously frightened by Wycliffite and Hussite readings of the Bible that the Church could, under the inspiration of the Holy Spirit, choose the less grammatical meaning of a biblical text as its true theological significance. That is a hypothesis easier to embrace as an abstract principle than it is to employ in a concrete instance.

In point of fact, the Church or, perhaps I should say, Christian churches of whatever kind have found it exceedingly difficult to contend for very long against the plain historical-grammatical meaning of the words of Scripture. While no interpreter is bound to the original intention of the author as the sole meaning of a biblical text, one is bound by that intention to a limited field of possible meanings. Steinbach's interpretation of Paul was the interpretation most difficult to sustain on purely literary grounds. It did not, to speak plainly, save the appearances or give an adequate account of the phenomena. Not incidentally, it was the interpretation most difficult to justify theologically. While the interpretations of Luther and Seripando have survived in one form or another down to the present day, the interpretation of Steinbach has fallen into well-deserved obscurity and is only resurrected by scholars as a historical curiosity. Luther and Seripando represented the wave of the future in Pauline studies, not only because they were the better theologians (I would be willing to defend that proposition without reservation), but also because they were the better literary critics.

3. I hope not to be misunderstood when I say that the Bible was, in the fullest sense of the term, a sixteenth-century book. It influenced European attitudes toward war and peace, the structure of civil government and the family, the process of human growth and development, theories of child-rearing and education, as well as attitudes toward economic relations and policies of taxation. The Bible was appealed to by people who loved the Church and who hated it; who hoped to reform society and who despaired of any fundamental progress in human relations; who were members of a cultured and highly literate elite, or who were illiterate and so were motivated to action by what they had been told by others. Sixteenth-century Europeans were comforted by the Bible in bereavement, used it to sanction marriages and contracts, bolstered their own wealth and position in society by a string of appro-

priate quotations, or were moved by the Bible to astonishing acts of self-renunciation and charity. The Bible was on the lips of religious martyrs—Roman Catholic, Protestant, and Anabaptist—and on the lips of their executioners. In the judgment of sixteenth-century Europeans, the Bible was worth both the dying and the killing for.

No other ancient authority—not Plato or Seneca or Cicero or Aristotle—could compete with the Bible in general importance or motivate more "sorts and conditions of men" into pursuing courses of action which, without the sanction of the Bible, they would have been reluctant to undertake. Indeed, no sixteenth century author ever composed a book or poem or political treatise more influential in his own time than the Bible, and some of the most important sixteenth century plays, poems, political treatises, philosophical tracts, paintings, legal opinions, lists of *gravamina,* and private letters were intended—at least in part—to be extended comments on the biblical text. That was because the Bible was regarded by sixteenth-century Europeans as Scripture and not merely as an interesting and profitable book. A book which is regarded as Scripture is not, whatever one may think of it personally, just like any other book. It carries as divine revelation an *a priori* authority accorded by the community, which acknowledges it to no other literary text.

In view of the fascination of the sixteenth century with the Bible, it is astonishing that so little attention has been paid by scholars to the history of biblical interpretation in the period from the death of Henry VII of England to the accession of James VI of Scotland to the English throne. Progress may have been retarded by certain historians who can only understand the past if they attribute to unsympathetic and long-dead figures values which they themselves hold or which they can at least conceive of some of their contemporaries holding. Since the Bible is not important to them, much less Scripture, they dismiss it as a causative factor in sixteenth-century social, economic, and political life. Like nineteenth-century missionaries to the New Hebrides, they rush about replacing the grass skirts of the natives with suitable garments from the tailors of New England or New York. The past, however, remains stubbornly the past, and our ancestors continue to believe, in spite of the shift in our values, exactly what they always believed.

There is one commandment, and one only, which historians, however frequently they may violate the other nine, must scrupulously observe or surrender their credentials, and that is, "Honor thy father and thy mother." That is to say, the past must be allowed to remain the past. It may not be remolded into our own image and likeness. If Philip of Hesse, Henry VIII of England, Christopher of Württemberg, Charles V of the House of Habsburg, and Christian II of Denmark regarded the Bible as authoritative Scripture, we had better find out exactly what that meant if we want to understand the political history of early modern Europe. The history of biblical interpretation is not incidental to European cultural history but central to it. The debates between Steinbach, Luther, and Seripando, or More, Tyndale, Murner, and Henry VIII, or Melanchthon, Eck, and Contarini are not a religious sideshow or pointless argy-bargy but reveal the aspirations, values, and failings of sixteenth century Europe as nothing else can.

4. Which leads me to a final and concluding personal observation. We have slowly become aware in America that it is not possible to conduct medieval, renaissance, and reformation studies in isolation from each other and that the lines which divide the Medieval Academy from the Renaissance Society of America and the American Society for Reformation Research are dictated by the demands of the professional guilds to which we belong and not by the nature of the subject matter with which we are dealing. I am not as certain that we are fully aware that interdisciplinary approaches are not a luxury in medieval and renaissance studies but a necessity. Nowhere has this fact come home to me with more force than in my study of the history of biblical interpretation.

Literary theory, the history of philosophy and theology, cultural and social history, political theory, and iconography all intersect in the history of biblical interpretation. Ockham could move with ease from logic to metaphysics to theology to political theory to epistemology. We who are expert in only one of the fields which Ockham mastered find that we need each other's help in order to understand our own special discipline correctly. Whatever breaks down the artificial barriers dividing the disciplines from each other will enable each separate discipline to fulfill its own unique task more adequately and so advance the common good.

V

LUTHER AMONG THE ANTI-THOMISTS

Did Luther know the theology of Thomas Aquinas? Historians, particularly Roman Catholic historians, have raised serious questions about Luther's familiarity with the theological positions of St. Thomas. Joseph Lortz, for example, suggested that the tragedy of the Reformation was traceable in part to Luther's ignorance of the balanced synthesis of grace and free will in Thomas's theology. Luther lived in a time of theological unclarity, dominated by the "fundamentally uncatholic" theology of William Ockham and his disciples. Luther made a legitimate Catholic protest against the uncatholic theology of Ockham and Biel, only to press his point too far and fall into doctrinal error. Had Luther only known the Augustinian theology of Thomas Aquinas, argued Lortz, he would have found adequate Catholic resources to combat the decadent theology of the Occamists without lapsing into heresy.[1]

There is, of course, little evidence that Luther, whose theological course of study prescribed large doses of Biel and d'Ailly, ever spent much time in the direct reading of Thomas. Luther did read and annotate a *Commentary on the Sentences of Peter Lombard,* by the fifteenth century Thomist, Henry of Gorkum (d.1431), though the *Commentary* is scarcely more than a paraphrase of Lombard's own teaching and gives no insight into the world of late medieval Thomism.[2]

On the other hand, while Luther was not responsible for lecturing on Thomas Aquinas, there were two Thomists on the faculty of the University of Wittenberg when Luther arrived there from Erfurt: Martin Pollich of Mellerstadt (d.1513), a scholar better known for his writings on syphilis than for his defense of Thomism, and his mercurial junior colleague, Andreas Bodenstein of Carlstadt (1480–1541).[3] At the time of his break with Thomism in 1517, Carlstadt charged that scholastic theology (including the views of the Thomists) had capitulated to a new Pelagianism, a charge echoed by Luther several months later in his "Disputation against scholastic theology".[4]

Some historians, particularly Hennig[5] and Grane[6], have pointed out the significance for Luther of the clash in 1518–1519 with such Thomist defenders of the Roman Church as Sylvester Prierias (1456–1523) and Thomas de Vio Cardinal Cajetan (1468–1534). Hennig in particular argued that Luther had met the theology of Thomas Aquinas in Cardinal Cajetan, its best and most authoritative interpreter, and rejected it.[7] In his own day, however, Cajetan was opposed by Bartholomew Spina and Ambrosius Catherinus, both avowed Thomists, who unlike Hennig thought that Cajetan had strayed from the path of authentic Thomism.[8]

Recent historians have also been divided over the role of Cajetan as an interpreter of Thomas. Scheeben, Mandonnet, Limbourg, Grabmann, and Caro have defended the reliability of Cajetan's reading of Thomas, while Gilson, Maurer, Pesch, McSorley, Jenkins, and Janz have expressed more or less serious reservations.[9] Janz, for example, believes that Luther could not have heard the authentic voice of Thomas on grace and free will through Cardinal Cajetan, who diverged significantly from Thomas in his more optimistic assessment of the capacities of fallen human nature.[10] On those questions, John Capreolus was closer to the original spirit and intention of St. Thomas than was Cajetan.

While it seems reasonable to assume that Luther's views on the theology of Thomas Aquinas were shaped in part by his encounters with colleagues like Carlstadt and with Dominicans like Prierias and Cajetan, we should not overlook the fact that Luther's understanding of Thomistic theology had already been influenced by the interpretation given to Thomas in Occamist theology.[11] Although Luther did not read Capreolus and the Dominican commentators on Thomas, he did study the Occamist theologians, especially Gabriel Biel, who cited Thomas at least 389 times in his *Collectorium on the Sentences of Peter Lombard,* and Pierre d'Ailly, who argued with Thomas in his much shorter *Questions on the Sentences.* Indeed, it was an Occamist of sorts, the secular theologian, John Pupper of Goch, who attacked Thomas as a Pelagian long before Luther or Carlstadt were born. Whatever Luther owed to his colleagues and his enemies, it was in the school of William Ockham and not in the school of John Capreolus or Cardinal Cajetan that he first encountered the theology of Thomas Aquinas.

I want in the following essay to look at the image of Thomas Aquinas in the writings of two Occamist theologians from the 15th century, Gabriel Biel (d.1495) and John Pupper of Goch (d.1475). Although Luther read Biel at a beginning stage in his theological education, he did not read Goch until the early 1520's, after his views on the inadequacy of Thomism were already firmly fixed. But he found in him a kindred soul and praised him as a "truly German and genuine theologian".[12] Both theologians have a good deal to say about the views of Thomas Aquinas on sin and grace, and both thereby provide an indispensable context for reconsidering the question, Luther and Thomas Aquinas.

I

John Pupper of Goch was a secular priest who served as a rector of a house of Augustinian canonesses in Malines.[13] Very little is known for certain about his life. He may have studied at Cologne or Paris, though the evidence concerning his student days is sketchy at best. He wrote four theological treatises which attacked scholastic theology, especially the theology of Thomas Aquinas, in the name of a doctrine of Christian liberty.[14] The treatises were discovered and edited by two humanists, Cornelius Grapheus and Nicholas of 's-Hertogenbosch, who published them in Antwerp in 1521–1522.

Goch's main treatise on Christian liberty seems to have been occasioned by a controversy with mendicant friars, particularly with the Dominican, Engelbert Messmaker, prior of the convent in Zwolle.[15] The Dominicans had made what Goch regarded as exaggerated claims for the monastic life and buttressed their claims with citations from St. Thomas Aquinas. In response, Goch attacked monastic vows as antithetical to Christian liberty, a view hardly calculated to endear him to mendicant friars.

Goch's critique of Thomas centers on four points. Thomas errs (1) in teaching that the natural will of man cooperates with the grace of God in order to gain justification and merit eternal beatitude;[16] (2) in believing that merit is an act to which a reward is owed by a debt of justice;[17] (3) in arguing that one kind of good act—in this case an act performed as the result of a religious vow—is more meritorious than another;[18] and (4) in presupposing that an act informed by charity is an act proportionate to eternal blessedness by a debt of justice.[19] There are other differences, of course, such as Goch's blanket condemnation of Aristotelian metaphysics.[20] But these four points sum up for Goch what is fundamentally deficient in Thomas's theory of grace.

In opposing Thomas's position as he understands it, Goch appeals primarily to the Bible, St. Augustine, and certain themes out of the Occamist tradition. If we examine the first of Goch's objections to Thomas—that Thomas teaches a cooperation between the natural human will and divine grace—we discover that his criticism rests on a very curious doctrine of the human will. Goch posits not one but two wills in the Christian: a natural and a graced will.[21] The natural will, although it is freed from the weakness of concupiscence and the service of sin, is not able to cooperate with God since it has no inner principle which makes such cooperation possible. Goch compares it to a stone which will continue to fall downwards, unless thrown upward by an alien force.[22] Grace throws the natural will in a direction it could not move itself. The most the natural will can do—and then only under the alien influence of grace—is consent to the grace that moves it.[23]

The natural will is not turned into the graced will nor is it replaced by it. The graced will is a gift of God infused into the sinner. The two wills, the natural and the graced, coexist in the sinner as really distinct and mutually separable.[24] God cooperates with this graced will which he himself has bestowed as a supernatural gift and by such cooperation produces works which are good and meritorious. What Goch wants to reject is the notion that the natural free will is so healed by grace that it cooperates with God in order to merit final salvation.

At times, Goch can state his position more radically by appealing to the doctrine of divine acceptation, an idea current in Scotistic and Occamistic circles but uncongenial to Thomas. On several occasions, Goch baldly asserts that merit depends on the will and estimation of God alone, and not on the quality of the work performed or the moral and religious condition of the worker.[25] Like the Occamists, Goch emphasizes the gift of uncreated grace, the Holy Spirit who indwells the faithful, though unlike them, he denies flatly the existence of an infused habit of created grace.[26]

Objections two and four—that a work is owed a reward by a debt of justice and that there is a proportion between a good work and its reward—allow Goch to show what he considers to be the essentially unbiblical character of Thomas's theology. Thomas's fatal weakness from Goch's point of view is his understanding of the relationship between goodness (the moral value of human acts) and dignity (the religious value of those same acts).

Thomas, of course, makes a clear distinction between the ethical and the religious value of human acts.[27] While he does not deny that sinners can perform acts which are generically good, he regards them as imperfect virtues and denies all religious value to them. Human acts only have saving significance when formed by grace. There is even some debate among late medieval Thomists whether Thomas teaches the necessity of grace for all human virtue, a position affirmed by Capreolus but denied by Cajetan.

At any rate, Christians cooperate with the habit of grace and perform morally good works which God in justice regards as meritorious.

To be sure, God does not regard these works as meritorious by his justice in the strict sense of the term. God's justice is only justice in a certain sense, since the relationship between God and human beings is not a relationship between equals.[28] Furthermore, God's indebtedness to Christians is not so much indebtedness to them as it is to himself to gain glory through the morally good acts of his creatures.[29] Nevertheless, Thomas is willing to talk in a very restricted sense of "justice" in this relationship.

Goch uses the parable of the workers in the vineyard in Matthew 20 in order to refute the notion that one can talk of justice in any sense in connection with divine rewards. God gives a reward to the workers not because of their merits but only because of his promise.[30] It is not the worthiness of the workers or the kind of works performed by them but solely divine acceptation which determines merit.[31] The first workers in the vineyard who had borne the heat of the day received the wage of one denarius. But so did the last workers, who worked for scarcely an hour. The parable celebrates divine goodness and pity and overturns all human notions of justice and proportionality.

Objection three—that good works performed as the result of a religious vow are more meritorious than the same works performed without a vow—weighs rather heavily on Goch's mind. Thomas does teach, after all, in the *Summa Theologiae* II-II q.189 a.2 that good works done because of a vow are higher and more meritorious than other works. He holds this view because he believes that a vow is an *actus latriae,* an act of devotion, the highest of the moral virtues, and therefore can confer an additional dignity on good works which result because of it.[32]

Goch emphatically denies that there is any New Testament warrant for the profession of vows.[33] The exegetical evidence traditionally adduced by the mendicants to buttress their claims is examined briefly by Goch and found wanting.[34] Indeed, vows are incompatible with the Christian freedom taught by the New Testament since they introduce an element of compulsion and constraint which is foreign to it.[35] Christians have been made free by grace to conform their wills to the will of God spontaneously out of filial love and do not need the compulsion and constraint of vows and rules to induce their grudging consent.

Goch dismisses with undisguised contempt the idea of Thomas that a vow increases merit.[36] On the contrary, since vows are incompatible with Christian freedom,[37] they tend to undercut merit.[38] Can a vow, however, considered as a discrete act of self-offering to God, ever be meritorious? That is a different question from the question whether a vow confers greater merit on the acts which result from it. Goch gives a somewhat grudging and qualified yes to this question.[39] A vow can be meritorious if it springs spontaneously from the graced will. The key is that it must be free and must spring from grace.

If a vow is not automatically meritorious and even tends to undercut the merit of other acts which are performed because of it, of what use is a vow? Here Goch must tread very carefully indeed. The Church, whose absolute teaching authority he recognizes, has instituted monasticism and monastic vows. The mendicant orders were formed not against the wishes of the Church but with its explicit blessing. Can the Church be thought to have erred in this matter?

Goch is unwilling to draw that conclusion. What he does hold is that monasticism and monastic vows are a positive constitution of the Church.[40] Monasticism is not grounded in natural law nor in an explicit teaching of revelation, but in a tactical decision of the Church to establish certain structures in order to gain certain ends. Monasticism was founded not as the most exemplary form of the state of perfection but as a hospital where the spiritually weak can be supervised and assisted to make at least some progress in the Christian life.[41] The mendicant orders are the home of the spiritually infirm, not an encampment of the spiritual elite of the Church militants. With that polemical flourish, Goch deflates what he regards as the exaggerated spiritual claims of the Dominicans and their chief theological authority, St. Thomas Aquinas.[42]

II

Unlike Goch, Biel is not out to show the essential weaknesses of the theology of Thomas Aquinas and his disciples, though he regards certain aspects of Thomas's thought as fundamentally unsatisfactory. Biel has a far more irenic spirit. He wants to interpret Thomas clearly, agree with him when he can, and absorb what he regards as Thomas's positive contributions into his own theology. Even when he finds Thomas's arguments unacceptable, he still is often able to find some sense in which he can agree with the general point Thomas is attempting to make.[43]

Biel differs in that respect not only from Goch but also from Pierre d'Ailly (d. 1420). In this *Questions on the Sentences of Peter Lombard,* d'Ailly quotes Thomas fifteen times, though never on the issues of grace and free will. In ten of the fifteen quotations, d'Ailly contradicts Thomas. He is particularly concerned to refute Thomas's understanding of sacramental causality. On the whole, Thomas is not one of d'Ailly's favorite authorities; d'Ailly prefers to cite Augustine, Ockham, Gregory of Rimini, Scotus, Boethius, Bradwardine, and Holkot instead.[44]

Perhaps the most important passage in Biel's treatment of Thomas's doctrine of grace is his lengthy discussion in book II of the *Collectorium,* distinction 28.[45] What Biel is attempting to report and interpret is Thomas's teaching on the necessity for grace in order to fulfil the commandment to love God above all things. The principal text which Biel has in view is the *Summa Theologiae* I q.109 a.1, 2, 3, 4, 6, 7, 8, and 9.

Biel distinguishes between the *concursus generalis,* the primary causality of God indispensable to all human acts, and the *auxilium speciale,* the actual grace of God over and beyond the motions of nature. Does Thomas teach that the sinner needs both the *concursus generalis* and the *auxilium speciale* in order to perform actions which are morally good? It should be admitted from the outset that Thomas does not make it easy for his interpreters, since he uses the term *auxilium divinum,* divine aid, ambiguously, sometimes referring to the *concursus generalis* and sometimes to the *auxilium speciale.*[46]

It is clear to Biel that Gregory of Rimini demands both. Under the conditions which presently obtain, no sinner can perform an act which is morally good without the assistance of the special grace of God. Indeed, not only does the sinner need the *auxilium speciale,* the supernatural assistance of God, but so does the Christian. The presence of a habit of sanctifying grace is not enough to insure that the Christian will be able to avoid sin and love God supremely. Over and beyond the gift of sanctifying grace, the Christian needs the special assistance of God. Although Gregory concedes that sinners can do works which are good by nature (they can fight for their country or honor their parents), he nevertheless argues that such works are not morally good unless they are directed toward God as their end.

Biel regards Gregory's position as extreme and is happy to report that St. Thomas speaks on this question "more moderately." As Biel understands matters, Thomas argues that human beings before and after the fall were able to perform morally good works proportionate to their nature with nothing more than the concurrence of God as Prime Mover. However, even in the state of integrity before the fall, Adam and Eve needed the assistance of grace in order to be capable of meritorious works. Virtue was attainable through nature, but merit was not. In other words, even though Adam before the fall was capable of loving God supremely and so of fulfilling the law according to the substance of the deed, he was incapable of fulfilling the law in the proper manner—namely, meritoriously—apart from the infusion of sanctifying grace.

Biel is cautious in his approach to Thomas's teaching in the *Summa Theologiae* I q.109 and introduces his summary with the formula

"blessed Thomas seems to feel." Nevertheless, Biel finds five important points in this passage: (1) human nature cannot act meritoriously
without infused grace; (2) supported only by the general *concursus* of
God (i.e., his natural causality), the human faculty of free choice is
capable of works which are morally good but not meritorious; (3)
sinners can avoid both mortal and venial sins without infused grace,
though they can only do so for a limited period of time; (4) sinners can
prepare themselves to receive grace without infused grace; but (5) they
cannot rise from sin without it.

While in the strictest sense most of what Biel has reported he has
reported correctly, he has nevertheless managed to give a misleading
impression. Leaving aside the question whether Thomas posits the
necessity of grace for acts which are morally good, an issue disputed
among the Thomists themselves, there is no question that Biel slights
the importance for Thomas of the disposing grace of God which moves
the human will toward God and prepares it for the reception of sanctifying grace. Although it is true that sinners can prepare themselves for
grace without infused grace (to posit the contrary would involve the
danger of an infinite regress), it is not true that they can prepare
themselves for the reception of infused grace without the assistance of
grace.

This misleading impression is continued in lecture 59 of Biel's *Exposition of the Canon of the Mass.*[47] In this case, Biel is interpreting
question 114 of *Prima Secundae.* Again, Biel puts forward five propositions which he believes he derives from Thomas's discussion: (1) no
human work, considered in itself apart from grace, can merit eternal
blessedness; (2) no morally good work performed outside a state of
grace can merit condignly, since condign merit presupposes a certain
worthiness in the agent, and such worthiness cannot coexist with a
state of mortal sin; (3) sinners can merit grace *de congruo,* however,
since *de congruo* merits are based on the liberality of God rather than
on the worthiness of the agent, and since God is too generous a Judge
to allow any good work to go unrewarded; (4) even good works performed in a state of grace are, strictly speaking, not condign merits,
since there is no real equality between temporal works and eternal
rewards; and (5) that good works performed in a state of grace can
nevertheless be regarded as condign merits is due less to the worthiness of the human agent than (a) to the grace which cooperates with
human free choice, (b) to the Holy Spirit who moves the will of the
agent, and (c) the promise by which God ordained an eternal reward
for good works performed in a state of grace.

There is a nuanced shift, first of all, in the larger theological context
which Biel provides for Thomas's points. While both Thomas and Biel

talk about divine ordination and preordination, Biel's emphasis on promise shifts Thomas's discussion into a voluntaristic framework. Biel gives the impression that for Thomas merit rests on a fiat of the divine will which is unpredictable and defies rational scrutiny. What worries Thomas, however, is what Farthing calls "the radical ontological deficiency of any creature—whether integral or fallen—with respect to the merit of an infinite reward".[48] The ontological element in Thomas's argument is slighted by Biel, who prefers to focus on voluntary and self-limiting covenants. The word *ordinatio* thus gains a meaning for Biel which is not altogether at home in Thomas.

Furthermore, it is simply not true that Thomas teaches that sinners can merit the grace of justification, not even by merits of congruity. While Biel, following the Franciscan tradition in theology, makes a temporal distinction between merits of congruity (which rest on the generosity of God) and merits of condignity (with rest on the inherent worth of the agent's activity), Thomas does not. For Biel, good works performed in a state of mortal sin will be rewarded as merits of congruity, provided that the agent dies in a state of grace. For Thomas, good works performed in a state of mortal sin (if they can be called truly good) will never receive eternal rewards at all. For both Biel and Thomas, good works performed in a state of grace will be rewarded as condign merits. For Thomas, those same good works are merits of congruity. The difference between condign and congruous merits is whether one focuses on the unworthiness of the agent (merits of congruity) or on the work of God in the agent which confers inherent value (merits of condignity).

If we stand back from Biel and ask what he has done in his discussion of Thomas's doctrine of grace, we can say that he has for the most part reported accurately what Thomas said but that he has misunderstood him at certain important points. He has not appreciated the extent to which Thomas insists on the gracious preparation of the human will for the reception of sanctifying grace. He seems unable to grasp the fact that Thomas's acceptance of congruous merit is not an acceptance of the Occamist thesis that sinners can merit justifying grace in a congruous manner. On the question whether Thomas teaches that grace is necessary for morally good works, Biel sides with Cajetan against Capreolus. The idea that grace is necessary for virtue is associated in Biel's mind with the name of Gregory of Rimini, but not with St. Thomas, who seems to Biel to speak more moderately. The general effect of Biel's interpretation is to move Thomas in a more Pelagian, even in a more voluntaristic direction, and away from the more Augustinian, more ontological framework in which he properly belongs.

John Pupper of Goch does not take Biel's more Pelagian reinterpretation of Thomas (which he obviously did not know) as his starting point. Thomas cannot be accused of teaching that human beings, by exercising their own natural powers to the full and assuming responsibility for their status in the presence of God, are able to merit justification by a merit of congruity. Gabriel Biel teaches that, but Thomas Aquinas does not. And Goch does not waste his time trying to caricature Thomas's Augustinian view of human nature. What Goch is out to show is that at its best, the theology of Thomas Aquinas maintains certain positions which render the whole system unbiblical and Pelagian.

To call a system Pelagian is not to render a historical judgment. Goch uses Pelagianism to describe a contemporary theology which ascribes to human beings a role in their own justification which, properly speaking, belongs to God alone. In order to avoid Pelagianism on Goch's terms, one must deny: (1) that the natural will, even transformed by grace, is capable of cooperating with God; (2) that one can speak of either justice or proportionality in connection with human merit; and (3) that good works performed as the result of a religious vow are more meritorious than works which are not. Furthermore, one must affirm: (1) that human merit rests on a supernaturally infused, graced will which coexists with the natural will as really distinct and mutually separable; (2) that human acts must be accepted by God in the sense in which Scotus and Ockham use the term divine acceptation; and (3) that the activity of God in the human soul must be ascribed to uncreated rather than created grace. Finally, one must admit that the study of Aristotelian metaphysics has proven detrimental to the knowledge and love of God and to a right understanding of eternal salvation. If that is the test of Pelagianism, then Thomas is a Pelagian. It will do no good to protest the adequacy of this test or the atomistic way in which it is applied to isolated propositions in Thomas's writings. It is the only test Goch will allow, and he applies it with the rigor of St. James. Whoever offends in one point has offended in all.

III

No historian would seriously dispute the proposition that Luther's break with scholastic theology was primarily a break with the theology of his own Occamist teachers. Nevertheless, in his 1517 "Disputation against Scholastic Theology," Luther attacks all scholastic theology, including Thomistic theology.[49] He does not single Thomas out by name as he does Biel and d'Ailly, but it is clear, as Denis Janz observes, "that Luther did not regard Thomist theological anthropology as differing substantially from that of his nominalist teachers."[50]

Luther attacks the proposition that it is possible to do what is morally good or avoid sin without the help of grace. He denies that human beings can love God supremely by the exercise of their natural moral powers or prepare themselves for the reception of grace. While Luther is directly attacking the theology of Biel and d'Ailly, he has also indirectly attacked at several points the theology of Thomas Aquinas as presented by Biel. While Biel's Thomas denies the possibility of loving God supremely without infused grace, he does teach the other propositions condemned by Luther.

That Luther increasingly lumps the Thomist teaching on grace with the Scotist and Occamist is made explicit in a passage in his 1519 "Resolutions on Propositions debated at Leipzig."

> For it is certain that the *moderni* (as they are called) agree with the Scotists and Thomists in this matter (namely on grace and free will) except for one man, Gregory of Rimini, whom they all condemn, who rightly and convincingly condemns them of being worse than Pelagians. For he alone among all the scholastics agrees with Carlstadt, i.e., with Augustine and the Apostle Paul, against all the more recent scholastics. For the Pelagians, although they assert that a good work can be performed without grace, at least do not claim that heaven can be obtained without grace. The scholastics certainly say the same thing when they teach that without grace a good work can be performed, though not a meritorious one. But then they go beyond the Pelagians, saying that man has the natural dictates of right reason to which the will can naturally conform, whereas the Pelagians taught that man is helped by the law of God.[51]

In this quotation, Luther accepts the judgment of Biel that only Gregory of Rimini taught the necessity of grace for moral virtue. Ironically, he is paired with Carlstadt, who as a former Thomist and disciple of John Capreolus ought to have known that on this question Capreolus put Thomas and Gregory of Rimini in the same camp.[52] Luther admits that the scholastics teach that grace is needed for merit, but argues that they eviscerate this point when they teach that human beings can conform their wills to the natural dictates of right reason and so prepare themselves for grace. Once again, Luther appears to accept Biel's reconstruction of Thomas as a theologian who believes that free will and the *concursus dei generalis* (the natural causality of God) are all the sinner needs to prepare himself for grace and merit justification with a merit of congruity.

Luther reads Thomas with Biel's eyes rather than with the eyes of Goch. Yet, one can easily understand how Luther found confirmation for his negative judgment of Thomas's doctrine of grace in the slashing attack of this angry Flemish theologian. By 1522, Luther has abandoned all doctrine of merit and finds the radically Augustinian position of Goch too conservative for his own new theology of justification by faith alone. Nevertheless, Goch's attacks on justice and proportionality, on the cooperation of the natural will with grace, on the efficacy of religious vows, and on the negative role played by Aristotle in Christian theology help to confirm Luther's already negative judgment of Thomistic theology and to reassure him that he was on the right track when he numbered Thomas with the other modern Pelagians.

Of course, not everyone in the Protestant camp agreed with Luther. There were Thomists who were converted to the Protestant cause and who remained, to a greater or lesser degree, Thomists all their lives: theologians like Martin Bucer, Peter Martyr Vermigli, and Jerome Zanchi. Even Philip Melanchthon could read Thomas with profit when he wrote his lectures on the gospel of John. The story of Thomas Aquinas and Protestantism has yet to be written, and it is not identical with the story of Thomas and Luther. What this more modest essay has attempted to show is that the shorter theme—Thomas and Luther—cannot be told correctly without seeing that it is only a chapter in the longer story of the place of Thomas Aquinas in the Occamist theological tradition.

VI

LUTHER AND HUBMAIER ON THE FREEDOM OF THE HUMAN WILL

In 1527, Dr. Balthasar Hubmaier, a leader of the Anabaptist community in Nikolsburg, Moravia, and a former associate of Ulrich Zwingli in Zurich, wrote two attacks on the theological anthropology of Martin Luther.[1] The two pamphlets, *On the Freedom of the Will* and *The Second Booklet on Human Free Will,* were clearly written with the debate between Luther and Erasmus over the freedom of the human will in mind.[2] Apparently, the dispute between Luther and Erasmus had stimulated a similar debate in Nikolsburg. Some Anabaptists (Erasmus claims to have been buttonholed by them himself) had declared themselves for Luther and were determined to eradicate completely the doctrine of human freedom. Hubmaier saw clearly, as the Luther partisans did not, that the doctrine of the bondage of the will undercut the Anabaptist understanding of conversion, baptism, the nature of the Church, and Christian morality. Therefore, while he confessed that he had been influenced by Luther (a claim which Luther bitterly disputed), and while he conceded the importance of at least some of Luther's observations, he nevertheless dismissed Luther's teaching on the bondage of the will as a dangerous half-truth.[3]

It is not clear whether Luther read Hubmaier's pamphlets. What is clear is that Luther did not write a response to them. The Catholic polemicist Eck criticizes Hubmaier in his *Enchiridion,* while Zwingli and Oecolampadius attack him repeatedly from a Reformed point of view. But Luther adds no postscript directed against Hubmaier to his *De Servo Arbitrio.* All we have are Luther's writings on the bondage of the will prior to 1527 and Hubmaier's critique of them. Yet, these documents from a debate which never quite took place are impressive evidence that theologians in the sixteenth century who had a similar education and who started their careers with a similar theological orientation could within a very brief period of time find themselves defending antithetical positions.

The similarities between Luther and Hubmaier are marked, particularly if one compares Luther with Zwingli, Oecolampadius, Calvin, or even Melanchthon. Both Luther and Hubmaier were born in the early 1480's; both had an old-fashioned scholastic theological education, Luther at Erfurt and Wittenberg, and Hubmaier at Freiburg and Ingolstadt; both earned a theological doctorate in the same year (1512); both made a point of studying Greek and Hebrew; both served as university lecturers (though Hubmaier soon left the university to become a cathedral preacher at Regensburg); and both were associated during the early stages of their careers with the *via moderna*. Hubmaier succeeded his teacher, John Eck, as rector of Peacock Hall, the nominalist bursa at Freiburg.[4] At Freiburg and later at Ingolstadt, Hubmaier read (by his own account) not only the high scholastic doctors, Thomas Aquinas, Bonaventure, and Duns Scotus, but also such modern theologians as William Ockham, Robert Holkot, Gabriel Biel, and John Major of Haddington.[5] While Hubmaier was a secular priest and Luther an Augustinian friar under some obligation to study the teachers of his own order, Luther's teachers were (like Eck) interested primarily in the Franciscan tradition in theology. Luther was directed by them toward Occamist authors, particularly Biel and d'Ailly, though at some point—probably fairly late—he read as well the Augustinian friar, Gregory of Rimini.[6] Thomas Aquinas he knew mainly as a series of citations in the *Collectorium* of Gabriel Biel.[7]

In short, both Luther and Hubmaier were taught to view the problem of the human will from a generally Occamist orientation, though Hubmaier's teacher, Eck, qualified this Occamist vision with insights taken from Bonaventure and the Old Franciscan tradition. When the break with the medieval Church came, Luther repudiated entirely and utterly without nostalgia the anthropology of the Occamist theologians, while Hubmaier (whose break on such questions as baptism and the voluntary Church was more radical than Luther's) held on to certain tenets from his Occamist past. In order to understand the full force of this disagreement between Luther and Hubmaier, it is necessary to sketch briefly their common point of departure in late medieval Occamism.

I

It is, I think, an understatement to say that German Occamists like Biel were optimistic about human nature and its capacity to will what is good and achieve the good it willed.[8] That is not to imply that Biel overlooked the darker side of human nature or took the office of Christ as Judge lightly. The fall into sin was a catastrophic event for the human race, an event which necessitated (in the sense of an indispensable prior condition) the redeeming intervention of God in history. Still, it was an event which did not extinguish the fundamental goodness of creation. Confidence in the ineradicable goodness of creation is the theological basis for Biel's rather cheery assessment of human prospects. The toughness of creation, its resistance to damage under the repeated impact of sin, has left less for grace to repair and more for nature to do.

In spite of his optimism, Biel describes the human situation grimly enough. Human beings are *spoliatus a gratuitis et vulneratus in naturalibus,* deprived of the gracious gifts of God, particularly the gift of stabilizing grace, and wounded in their natural powers by indomitable concupiscence. Sinners not only need to be pardoned for their sins but also to be healed. They are not merely malefactors; they are victims of a contagion which no human remedies can purge. That does not mean that they have lost their reason or their free will, but only that both have suffered damage. They have also retained the use of conscience and *synderesis;* that is, they have a natural inclination away from evil and toward what is good.[9] This inclination is not a habit of the will, both because it is inalienable (as a habit would not be) and because it does not interfere with the free decisions of the will.

Biel's pessimism, however, is more apparent than real and is more than offset by his confidence that even sinful men and women are capable of heroic moral achievement. Even the infected human will, apart from all supernatural assistance (excluding, of course, the assistance of the *concursus dei generalis,* the natural cooperation of God with creation),[10] is capable of loving God supremely, at least for a flickering moment of time. That capacity for loving God more than one loves wife or family or goods or self has never been lost, though it has been impaired. Sinners are psychologically inhibited by their sin. It is now difficult to love God, whereas it was easy before the fall. Sinners must summon up their inner resources, turn a deaf ear to the voice of concupiscence, and by sheer force of will do what for Adam and Eve was a spontaneous, unforced, unselfconscious act. But, hard or easy, the act can still be done. Sinners can still produce human affection for God, which is the fulfilment of the law, even though they cannot induce in themselves the charity that justifies. This *amor dei super omnia propter deum,*[11] this unconditional love of God for his own sake, is identical in the sinner with the moment of contrition.

God, however, is under no natural obligation to pardon sinners or heal the effects of their sin simply because they have at last directed toward him the love which they have always owed. Biel supplements the good news about the residual moral capacities of fallen human nature with good news about God's covenant with the Church. This covenant can be summed up either in biblical language ("Draw near to God and he will draw near to you") (James 4:8) or in the language of the old theological axiom, *facientibus quod in se est Deus non denegat gratiam*, God does not deny his grace to those who do what is in them.[12] To use the axiom commits the user to no particular school of theology. It was sometimes used by confessors to encourage priests and religious who had grown weary of well-doing and who were alarmed that they no longer derived any spiritual sustenance from the rites and exercises in which they participated. They were urged by the axiom to persevere in the dreary round of their tasteless duties in the confidence that spiritual refreshment lay just over the horizon, on the other side of their inner desert.

Biel used it, however, in a more technical and restricted sense. God has bound himself in a covenant by an immutable oath to give saving grace, what the scholastics call *gratia gratum faciens,* to any person who will, by the heroic exercise of his or her natural moral energies, love God supremely.[13] Considered from the standpoint of his absolute power, God was under no obligation to bind himself to the Church by a covenant this generous. Considered from the standpoint of his ordained power, the obligations which God has assumed under the terms of this covenant are absolute and immutable and will never be abandoned.[14] God gives grace to men and women who use the capacities which they have (right reason, free will, conscience, and *synderesis*). Salvation is not only available on reasonable terms; it is universally accessible. Sinners cannot stand before Christ at the last judgment and plead that they could not do what was in them; they can only ruefully admit that they did not do it. Everything hangs on the free will of the sinner. Even God does not predetermine human destiny. In short, Biel teaches that sinners can earn grace by perfect obedience to the inner meaning of the law. What makes this gospel good news rather than bad is that sinners can do what they should.

The question could still legitimately be asked why sinners, who are capable of loving God supremely without the assistance of grace, need as a kind of afterthought to be infused with grace in response to their contrition. Biel seems to presuppose as a disposition for justifying grace what a more Augustinian theologian might regard as its final effect. If sinners are capable of vaulting over the barrier of their own sin, why does the Church offer them a ladder once they have landed safely on the other side?

Part of the answer is obvious. Sinners need to have their sins pardoned, their good works accepted as merits, and their souls healed. The rest of the answer, however, is more ingenious and rests on a distinction between fulfilling the law according to the substance of the deed and fulfilling it according to the intention of the lawgiver.[15] According to the substance of the deed, an act is good when it conforms to natural law or—what amounts to the same thing—the dictates of right reason. According to the intention of the lawgiver, some good acts may be restricted by special conditions over and beyond the demands of natural law. Anyone, for example, can ask a blessing on bread and wine, but only a priest can confect a valid eucharist. Sinners who love God without the infused habit of charity still love God, if one considers nothing more than the substance of the deed. But God has determined that he will accept as meritorious and reward with the gift of eternal life only those good works which are performed in cooperation with an infused habit of charity. The necessity for two kinds of love, natural affection and infused charity, does not rest on the substance of the deed itself (in that sense love of God is love of God) but on the intention of the lawgiver. No guests are admitted to the banquet without the wedding garment. This is not a subject for debate but only for obedience.

II

Luther's rejection of the optimistic anthropology of Gabriel Biel proceeds, I think, in two stages.[16] In the first stage, Luther still retains many of the old formulations of Biel, though he infuses them with new meaning and employs them in ways of which Biel would surely have disapproved. Luther is like a soldier mustered out of the army who still wears his old uniform when he putters about in his garden. In the second stage, Luther finds Occamist formulations offensive and irredeemable in themselves and launches a polemical counterattack against the *Sautheologen,* the "pig-theologians," who have misread the human situation, turned Christ into a second Moses and the gospel into a legal code. The first stage lasts through the *Dictata super Psalterium,* that is, into the year 1515; the second stage begins with the lectures on Romans and rises to a crescendo in the *De servo Arbitrio* of 1525.

The first clue that the earliest Luther has parted company with Ockham and Biel is his repeated assertion that God elects sinners to eternal life without any consideration of their antecedent merits or foreseen use of grace.[17] God is not a passive observer of the human scene (like the Epicurean God in a watchtower whom Calvin ridicules). He is a determiner of human destiny whose hidden and mysterious decisions cannot be anticipated or appealed. Unlike Biel, who interprets election as foreknowledge, Luther understands it as predetermination. It is this election or predestination which constitutes the real preparation for grace, apart from which any human activity is utterly pointless.

A second clue is Luther's very Augustinian contention that no human works are morally good without grace.[18] Staupitz, of course, had taught the same thing, and it excluded for both of them the idea that human virtue could merit first grace. Indeed, there is no human virtue without the first grace which creates it. Luther goes beyond Staupitz, however, when he argues in a 1514 sermon that good works are sins when they are not done in the fear of God.[19] Sin is not merely a moral category for Luther. Pride and unbelief can be posited just as well, sometimes even better, through human virtue than through human vice. At any rate, the notion that there is a natural virtue which can earn an infusion of charity by its own efforts is an absurd one for Luther.

Luther does not, however, abandon all Occamist formulations. He still talks about the role of *synderesis* (the natural human longing for the good), about "doing what is in one," and about *de congruo* or "fitting" dispositions for the reception of grace. His understanding of predestination and his rejection of human virtue (the indispensable basis for human merit) prior to grace force him inevitably to reject the Occamist content of the Occamist formulations. The old Occamist wineskins are filled with new Lutheran wine.

Synderesis, for example, functions very much for Luther as the "sense of divinity" does for John Calvin, not that the two terms describe an identical reality. *Synderesis* is primarily a moral term; "sense of divinity," primarily religious. *Synderesis* longs for what is good; the "sense of divinity" for what is ultimate. But the function of both is similar. Human beings know (at least in some limited sense) what is good and have an ineradicable longing for it. If they did not long for it, they would not be human. But the question for Luther, as for St. Paul, is not whether one knows the will of God but rather what one does with what one knows. Without grace, one cannot do the good which one prefers. Therefore, *synderesis*, so far from providing an anthropological resource for the return of the sinner to God, actually intensifies the sinner's predicament and increases his guilt. Because human reason is blind and the human will is deformed, *synderesis* (which is hailed by Luther at first as a residuum of health in the soul) is a mark of what Paul Tillich called "unhealthy health," an apparent health which is only a symptom of a far more serious disease.[20]

Similarly, when Luther talks about "doing what is in one" and a proper disposition for the reception of grace, he has in mind something rather different from what Biel proposed in his understanding of the covenant between God and the Church. According to Biel, God promises to give his grace to the virtuous, that is, to those men and women who use their free wills to elicit an act of unconditional love of God for his own sake. According to Luther, God promises to give his grace to what Luther calls "real sinners".[21] Real sinners are people who admit they are sinners and who justify God in his judgment when he condemns them as such. They do not present God with their virtues, much less with the virtue of unconditional love of God for his own sake, but with their sins. They pray for grace; according to Luther, they even "cry out" for it. But the proper disposition for the reception of grace is not the presence of virtue but the confession of sin. Sinners can either excuse and justify themselves and so make God out to be a liar, who judges them to be sinners; or they can accuse themselves and so justify God as true in his judgment. Only those who justify God are justified by him. Human virtue is not only insufficient to merit justifying grace; it is even irrelevant. It is not the righteous but sinners to whom the gospel is addressed.

Luther repeats these themes in his lectures on Romans (1515–1516), but with a growing sense of anger at the scholastics, particularly the Occamists, for their inadequate treatment of sin and grace. A good deal of what is the matter with the Occamist theory of justification is immediately traceable to their flawed anthropology. They have not understood that concupiscence is not merely a "tinder of sin," a highly flammable material which must be kept away from fire but is harmless when properly stored. It is not merely an inclination toward evil which is only sinful when the human free will consents to it. It is a power which corrupts the will and renders it incapable of loving God apart from the healing force of grace. The Occamists are not wrong to posit the existence of *synderesis* (Luther later changes his mind and drops this concept from his theology), but they are certainly foolish when they imagine that such a weak inclination toward the good could ever break free under its own power from the gravitational pull of concupiscence and form the basis for the unconditional love of God.[22] That is why it is utter nonsense to rest human salvation on the fragile foundation of human virtue. "Look at man as he actually is," Luther demands, and you will discover that "this life is a life of cure from sin; it is not a life of sinlessness, as if the cure were finished and health had been recovered."[23]

Coupled with this sense of the enduring power of concupiscence is a holistic understanding of the anthropological terminology of Paul.

Concupiscence is a wound in the whole person and not merely a gentle inclination in the will. Flesh and spirit are not higher and lower faculties in human nature; they are descriptions of the whole person turned in upon itself in its irrepressible egoism and its radical alienation from God.[24] Spirit is the whole person in its openness to God and its trust in God's promises. Justification, as it touches flesh and spirit, touches the whole person. The whole person trusts the promises of God and so is spirit; the whole person remains a sinner, even while justified, and so is flesh.[25] The best analogy Luther can think of is the two-natures Christology of Chalcedon.[26] As Christ was fully human and fully divine, while remaining one person, so the believer is flesh and spirit, wholly sinner and wholly just, while remaining one individual center of moral responsibility before God.

By the time of the *Disputation against Scholastic Theology* (1517), Luther is prepared to state the conclusions to which he has come in a sharp and provocative way:

> 5. It is not true that the desire is free and is able to make one choice as well as another. In actual fact it is not free at all but is in bondage. (This is spoken against the view generally held.) 6. It is not true to say that the will is able of its own volition to conform itself to that which is right (spoken against Scotus and Gabriel Biel). 7. On the contrary, without the grace of God the will produces of necessity an action which is wicked and wrong. 17. The natural man cannot want God to be God. Rather he wants himself to be God and God not to be God. 18. For the natural man to love God above all else is a fictitious figment. It is but a chimera (against almost all accepted opinion). 29. The perfectly infallible preparation for grace, the one and only valid attitude, is the eternal election and predestination of God. 30. The only contribution man makes is to resist it. In actual fact, rebellion against grace precedes any receiving of it.[27]

To which could be added from the *Heidelberg Disputation* (1518):

> 13. Free will after the Fall exists only in name and as long as a man "does what in him lies," he is committing mortal sin.[28]

There is no way to redeem Occamist anthropology by appealing to the distinction between fulfilling the law according to the substance of the deed and according to the intention of the lawgiver. Luther is on the warpath against what he regards as Judaizing tendencies in Christian theology, and the effect of this distinction is to make Christianity a more law-oriented religion than Judaism itself. Moses only expects obedience to the law codes of the Torah, summed up in the commandment to love God supremely and the neighbor as oneself. Biel, however, adds a second exaction over and beyond the law; he requires that one must love God supremely with a habit of grace that one has earned through the exercise of natural virtue. This intensification of the law is paraded as a clarification of the gospel. "O you fools," Luther exclaims, "you pig-theologians! . . . For if we can fulfil the law by our own powers, as they say, grace is not necessary for the fulfill-ment of the law but only for the fulfillment of a divinely imposed exaction that goes beyond the law. Who can tolerate such sacrilegious opinions!"[29]

III

Hubmaier understood Luther's doctrine of predestination and his denial of the freedom of the human will as another form of the Stoic assault on human freedom and responsibility. If Luther is correct, then it is impossible for Hubmaier to comprehend (1) how fallen human beings, lacking all freedom of the will, can be held responsible for their sins, or (2) how sinners, lacking all anthropological resources for the return to God, can respond to the call of God and be converted.

Hubmaier argues that a limited freedom of the will has survived the trauma of the fall and forms a natural anthropological resource for the return to God.[30] He does not accept the view of Biel that sinners are capable by the exercise of their natural powers of eliciting an act of supreme love for God. He teaches rather that human beings were created as tripartite beings: spirit, soul, and flesh. The will of the spirit was unscathed by the fall and still desires the good, though it cannot bring the soul and body back to God without the assistance of the external preaching of the Word and inner illumination by the Holy Spirit, actions deemed unnecessary by Biel, though affirmed by Bona-venture and the Old Franciscan theological tradition esteemed by John Eck.[31]

Hubmaier generally describes the fixed direction of the unfallen will toward the good by the word "conscience"—though it is, perhaps, more accurate to speak in this context of *synderesis* rather than consci-ence, since it is the inclination of the practical reason toward first principles and not the application of the practical reason which Hub-maier has principally in mind. At any rate, it is clear that reason has been more heavily damaged by the fall than has the will. The will of the spirit still desires the good, and even the will of the fallen soul would affirm it, were it not for the fact that the darkness of reason renders both impotent. The will of the spirit (what Gerson would call the *synderesis voluntatis*) is God's ally in fallen human nature. Sinners do not need a new will in their spirits, where it is intact, or in their souls, where it is only half-dead and can be revived. The will of the soul is a largely neutral entity. It is guilty, because it participated in the original act of Adam's rebellion against God, and it is under the power of the flesh, because it has lost all knowledge of the good and there-fore cannot cooperate with the will of the spirit. Only in the flesh has the will completely fallen. However, there it is not restored (since it is incorrigible), but merely overcome—penultimately in the redeemed by the alliance of the will of the soul and the will of the spirit and ulti-mately by death and resurrection.

The Occamist principle, "to those who do what is in them God does not deny his grace," operates for Hubmaier—as for Robert Holkot—on two levels: (1) the level of reason and revelation and (2) the level of grace and free will. Sinners do not need to wait for the proclamation of the gospel and illumination before some response is possible. The heathen, who have never heard the gospel, have two resources for the return to God: (1) the unfallen will of the spirit (the conscience or image of God, or *feuerlen,* or *synderesis voluntatis*) and (2) the revela-tion of God in nature. Sinners who perceive the power and divinity of God in creation and who long to know him in the strength of their natural inclination toward the good dispose themselves for the recep-tion of God's further revelation of himself through the gospel. God does not reveal himself to sinners through private revelation. The *vo-catio,* the invitation to salvation, comes to sinners through the external proclamation of the Word. If God cannot find ordinary messengers to proclaim the gospel to sinners who hunger and thirst after piety, he will use extraordinary messengers—even angels, if need be. Hubmaier does not retreat to the doctrine of the inner Word, promulgated by Hans Denck. Faith comes by hearing.

Sometimes the Word is preached but not understood. Hubmaier seems to regard preaching and illumination as coincidental events. Nevertheless, it is possible for the Word to be preached externally without internal comprehension. In such a situation, the sinner still retains the possibility of taking further initiative. Once again, the sin-ner may do what is in him, this time by praying for the illumination which he does not have.

"Doing what is in one" on the level of reason and revelation is not the starting point for the return to God for every sinner. The invitation to salvation through preaching and the illumination of reason by the Holy Spirit may be granted to the sinner by grace alone. The initiative of God may in fact render the initiative of the sinner superfluous, at least on this level. What is important to see, however, is that the sinner is not utterly dependent on the initiative of God for gaining that knowledge of the gospel which will make salvation possible.

If "doing what is in one" is optional on the level of reason and revelation, it is not optional on the level of grace and free will. Fallen human beings cannot assume full responsibility for their status in the presence of God, cannot prepare themselves for the reception of grace, until their reason is illuminated by the preaching of the Word and the action of the Holy Spirit. Once illuminated, however, sinners are granted the possibility of further response. Since the will of the spirit has not fallen but only has its freedom circumscribed by ignorance, sinners are fully capable of taking the necessary preparatory steps for the reception of grace.

The link between the unlimited freedom of God and limited human freedom is the doctrine of the covenant. By making use of their limited freedom, sinners dispose their wills for the reception of grace, which cannot be given to them without their free and uncoerced consent. When sinners respond to the offer of the gospel, God *must* regenerate them, not because of the quality of their response but because God has bound himself by his promises to justify everyone who responds to the gospel.[32] God is a captive of his own covenant; the freedom of the absolute will has been imprisoned by his ordained will. The God of Hubmaier no less than the God of Biel is a God who manifests fidelity to his covenant.

When Hubmaier thinks of a covenant between God and the Church, he thinks of two-sided covenant in which there are mutual obligations and to which human response provides the key. While God has taken the initiative in establishing the structure in which human beings may be saved, his act of regenerating sinners is itself a response to the human act of fulfilling the condition of the covenant. God draws sinners to salvation or permits them to be damned, if they will not be saved. But in neither case does he act the part of the free sovereign of Augustinian theology. In the last analysis, it is human choice and not divine sovereignty which is decisive. The ordained will of God is the guarantee of the reliability of the gospel, but not of its ultimate triumph.

The harsh things which St. Paul has to say in the ninth chapter of Romans about the sovereignty of God and the ability of God to deal with human beings as the potter does with clay should be referred to the hidden or absolute will of God.[33] Hubmaier does not deny that God could deal with human beings in such an arbitrary fashion, but he clearly regards it as a hypothetical possibility which God has chosen not to actualize. The revealed will of God emphasizes the universal offer of salvation. Whosoever will may come. God neither compels sinners to enter his kingdom nor places any obstacles in their path. In Hubmaier's theology as in Biel's, sinners cannot plead that they could not come to God. They can only admit that they did not come. Since free human decision is essential as preparation for regeneration, and regeneration is essential as a precondition for the reception of baptism, it follows that baptism cannot be administered to infants.[34] The Church does not embrace the whole community but is rather a society of men and women baptized as adults and living in conscious tension with the world.[35] Hubmaier does not make the tension between the Church and the world as fierce as some of the other Anabaptist thinkers who teach non-resistance and the total renunciation of the sword,[36] but it is nonetheless fairly severe. The Church must be a voluntary association of believers or it is not the Church of the New Testament. At this point, Hubmaier's Anabaptist convictions and his scholarly heritage coincide. Affirm freedom of the will, and the Anabaptist vision of redemption can be affirmed with it. Deny freedom of the will (as Luther has done), and the Anabaptist position becomes impossible to maintain. The two stand or fall together for Hubmaier.

IV

While Luther did not write a response to Hubmaier, there is no reason for us to protest that we have no inkling what direction that response would have taken. It is true, of course, that Hubmaier did not try to revive what were from Luther's point of view the worst features of Occamism. He was as offended as Luther was by the notion that fallen human nature could love God supremely without the assistance of grace. Nevertheless, in his defense of a limited freedom of the will that had survived the fall, in his retention of a disposition for the reception of grace, and in his rejection of predestination, Hubmaier showed himself to be a fellow traveler with Ockham and Biel. Hubmaier understood himself, I think, to be following a middle way between the Pelagianism of the late scholastics and what he regarded as the Stoicism of Luther, retaining the best features of each and avoiding the mistakes of both. He saw no reason to reject a theme from late medieval nominalism simply because it had been put to bad use in Catholic theology. His defense of human freedom, which became a fundamental motif in early Free Church ideology, contains arguments quite shamelessly borrowed from his theological studies at Freiburg and Ingolstadt.

Luther also retained ideas from his Occamist past, but on the subject of anthropology he made a radical break with Ockham and Biel. There was no way in Luther's view to extricate the doctrine of the freedom of the will from what he regarded as an unacceptable Judaizing tendency in Christian theology. Occamists had transformed the gospel into a new law, more difficult than the law of Moses, and in a certain sense more arbitrary. This transformation of the gospel into law was only possible because of an incredibly optimistic faith in the perfectibility of human nature. Luther attacked his teachers by embracing an Augustinianism more thoroughgoing and severe than the position of Augustine himself. I have not spent much time in this chapter discussing the positive alternative of Luther to Biel, his doctrine of justification by faith alone. But it should be said that Luther's pessimism, like Augustine's, was set against the background of hope. The gospel is good news because it is utterly realistic about the frailty of human virtue and the ambiguity of human motives. It points to a mercy which swallows up human vanity and wickedness and is never deceived by them. The precondition for the reception of grace is not heroic virtue but faith. Of course, the faith with which one believes is itself a gift of God. But that is a topic we have discussed already.

VII

SCRIPTURE AND THE LORD'S SUPPER IN LUTHER'S THEOLOGY

Students who read Reformation documents for the first time are frequently surprised by the vehemence of the debate between Luther and his opponents over the meaning of the eucharist.[1] For many Protestants, the sacraments play such a subsidiary role in their faith and piety that they are astonished to see the sixteenth century reformers attacking one another over what appear to the modern eye to be fairly minor differences in eucharistic theology. "Dear Lord God!" writes Luther in 1527 to Oecolampadius, the reformer of Basel, "who asked you about your notion? Who wants you to tell what you regard as certain? . . . But when you are under obligation to speak . . . then you gush and gabble."[2] Luther's views of Zwingli are hardly more flattering. They range from his 1527 characterization of Zwingli as a "clumsy carpenter" who "hacks rough chips"[3] to his 1528 judgment that Zwingli was an "un-Christian" theologian who "holds and teaches no part of the Christian faith rightly."[4] Luther for his part earned the nickname "Dr. Pussyfoot" (*Doktor Leisetritt*) among Protestants who regarded his break with medieval Catholic tradition as half-hearted or even insincere.

Because Protestants believed it was possible to write dogmatic theology that was wholly biblical in its source and norm, the battle over the eucharist quickly became a battle over biblical texts. Luther's eucharistic treatises, particularly the two long treatises against Zwingli of 1527 and 1528, are filled with allusions to the Bible. Some of the texts which Luther cites were chosen by Luther himself; others were forced on him by his opponents. The most important texts for Luther can be organized into four clusters: (1) texts which Luther believes support the argument that the eucharist *is* the body of Christ, (2) texts which define "flesh" and explain the puzzling statement of John that the "flesh profits nothing;" (3) texts which deal with the nature of communion and distinguish worthy from unworthy reception; and, finally, (4) texts evoked by the debate over the article of the creed which asserts that Jesus Christ is "seated at the right hand of God."

I

Of all the clusters of texts which Luther uses, the most important by far for him is the series of texts which appears to support his contention that the eucharist is the body of Christ (Matthew 26:26, Luke 22:19, I Corinthians 11:24), a series which Luther usually cites in the conflated form: "He took bread, and gave thanks and broke it, and gave it to his disciples and said, 'Take, eat; this is my body which is given for you.' "

Since the Fourth Lateran Council in 1215, medieval Catholic theologians had defended an official explanation of the real presence of Christ in the eucharist by an appeal to a theory called transubstantiation. The doctrine rests on a philosophical distinction between the substance of a thing (what a thing really is) and its accidents (how it appears to our senses). According to this theory, when a priest consecrates the elements of bread and wine, the accidents of bread remain the same but the substance is miraculously changed by the power of God into the body and blood of Christ. The bread and wine still feel, smell, taste, and look like bread and wine, but appearances in this case are deceiving. The reality which is present is Christ himself.

Luther retained the doctrine of real presence but rejected the theory of transubstantiation which had been used to explain the manner of that presence. In part, Luther rejected the philosophical explanation because of a deeply held conviction that the use of Aristotelian philosophy by scholastic theologians had seriously impeded their efforts to understand the mind of the New Testament.[5] Aristotle's views of felicity, justice, the eternity of the world, and the mortality of the human soul could not, in Luther's view, be reconciled with elementary Christian doctrine. The pagan Aristotle was not only unbaptized but unbaptizable. Luther was therefore skeptical of any philosophical explanation of the eucharistic presence of Christ. His skepticism did not, however, prevent him from appealing to philosophy in his own later quarrel with Zwingli.

Moreover, the doctrine of transubstantiation provided an explanation of real presence which multiplied entities beyond necessity. The real miracle of the eucharist is that Christ is present, not that the substance of bread and wine are absent. Late medieval theology requires two miracles, whereas the New Testament knows only one. Christ is present in the eucharist but so are the bread and wine in their full reality.[6] That is the point Luther intends to make when he speaks about the presence of Christ "in, with, and under" the elements of bread and wine.

Luther's rejection of transubstantiation found a sympathetic echo in other circles of reform. Protestant leaders from other parts of Europe agreed with Luther that the Lord's Supper was not a sacrifice offered to God but a benefit offered to the Church. A consensus quickly formed which interpreted the eucharist in the new context of Word and faith rather than in the older context of sacrifice and priest. The eucharist was a visible Word of God, a promise attached to bread and wine and directed toward the Church. The focus of interest shifted from the sacrificing priesthood to the communing congregation.

Not all Protestant leaders, however, agreed with Luther's retention of the doctrine of the real presence of Christ in the eucharist. Zwingli, for example, interpreted the words, "this is my body," in line with certain exegetical suggestions made by the Dutch humanist, Cornelius Hoen. Hoen made the grammatical point that the verb "to be" is sometimes used in a metaphorical sense, as, for instance, in the "I am" sayings of the Gospel of John. When Jesus calls himself the True Vine, the Gate of the Sheepfold, the Good Shepherd, the Resurrection and the Life, and the Bread of Life, no one takes him to mean these predications in a literal sense. In this context, Jesus is speaking metaphorically and using the verb "to be" in the sense of "to signify." There is a relationship of similarity, not identity between the subject and the predicate of the "I am" sayings.

One should interpret the words of institution, "this is my body," in exactly the same way. To insist, as Luther does, that the bread and wine *are* the body and blood of Christ is to commit idolatry, to ascribe to the creature (namely, bread and wine) the glory that belongs only to the Creator (Romans 1:23). When Jesus says, "this is my body," he means, "this signifies my body," just as a wedding ring signifies a marriage but is not identical with the human relationship.[7] Oecolampadius agreed in the main with Zwingli and appealed to the early Fathers in support of his position, especially to Tertullian, who used words like *figura* to describe the eucharist.[8] The bread and wine are a figure or type or sign of the body of Christ just as a bride is a type or figure of the Church. Schwenckfeld rejected the identification of "to be" with "to signify," though he accepted the necessity for a symbolic interpretation of the words of institution. Otherwise Judas, who was present at the Last Supper, would have eaten the body and blood of Christ. He suggested that the words of institution, "this is my body," should be reversed and interpreted to mean, "my body is this: namely, the spiritual food and drink of John 6."[9] Carlstadt gave the most eccentric and least widely accepted interpretation of Matthew 26:26 when he proposed that, as Jesus uttered the words, "this is my body," he pointed to himself rather than to the bread and wine.[10]

Luther rejected all symbolic or metaphorical interpretations of the words of institution, but not because he thought all such interpretations impossible or absurd. Of course, the words, "this is my body," could be read metaphorically, and there are precedents for such metaphorical readings elsewhere in the Bible. What the Swiss theologians and their radical allies failed to demonstrate was not the possibility of such a reading but its necessity.

The central message of the Bible is that God is found in dust, that the Second Person of the Trinity has taken humanity in Jesus of Nazareth. God always comes to men and women in creaturely elements that they can see, touch, and handle. That does not mean that his saving presence is self-evident to human reason or that his glory is visible. Just as the flesh of Jesus Christ is the *figura* or form under which the divine nature is hidden, so too are the bread and wine *figurae* or forms under which the body and blood are hidden. The reality of the divine presence is always hidden under the form of a contrary appearance. In that sense, the incarnation and the eucharist are exactly parallel. No objection can be alleged against the doctrine of the real presence which cannot be alleged equally well against the incarnation itself. To say "this signifies my body" is to obscure the reality of the incarnational principle. The bread and wine are not a sign of the body of Christ (*figura* in Oecolampadius' sense) but the form under and through which the body is offered to the communicant.[11]

II

A second cluster of texts centers on John 6 and the meaning of the word "flesh," especially in the difficult sixty-third verse: "it is the Spirit that makes alive; the flesh profits nothing." Zwingli's exegesis of this text depended, at least in part, on his dualistic understanding of human nature. Every human being has a soul or immaterial nature and a body or physical nature. While both soul and body have been created by God and as created are good, the soul is higher than the body and in certain important respects transcends it. The spiritual nature of a human being cannot be nourished by the body or by the physical objects which the body sees, smells, hears, tastes, and touches. Spiritual goods are communicated immediately to the human spirit by the action of God rather than mediately through physical objects. The human body or flesh is nourished by eating bread and wine. The human soul or spirit is nourished by the invisible and incorporeal activity of the Holy Spirit. That is what John 6:63 means. It is the Holy Spirit acting immediately on the human spirit which makes the human being spiritually alive. The flesh—that is, the human body and the creaturely elements of bread and wine which it ingests—cannot communicate spiritual life to the human soul. When the human soul has been quickened and nourished by the Holy Spirit, then it is appropriate for the human being to eat the bread and drink the wine as a eucharist or act of thanksgiving for an invisible work of grace already completed. Bread and wine belong to the public confession and response of the Church. They cannot, however, be viewed as a means of grace without lapsing into idolatry.[12]

Luther reads the anthropological terminology of the New Testament in such a way as to stress the psychosomatic unity of the human person. "Soul," "body," "spirit," and "flesh" are understood to refer to the whole human being, the *totus homo,* in its various relationships to God, the neighbor, and the self. The flesh is, from Luther's perspective, either a designation for men and women in their weakness and mortality ("all flesh is grass") or a description of the self-centered self in its alienation from the ground of its true being ("the fleshly mind is enmity against God"). While flesh may in certain contexts be a designation for the body, it is certainly not used in that sense in John 6:63. "The flesh profits nothing" simply means that the self-centered self is unable to reconstitute its broken relationship to God or become the principle of its own spiritual renewal.[13] Spiritual life is communicated by the Holy Spirit alone, though John does not mean to imply that this communication of grace takes place apart from physical means of grace. In short, the text has nothing whatever to do with the eucharist and should never have been cited by the Swiss theologians in the first place.

III

Other texts, particularly I Corinthians 10:16–33 and 11:26–34, deal with the question of the unworthy reception of the eucharist. Zwingli is especially interested in the effect of the activity of the Holy Spirit on the congregation during the celebration of the eucharist. It is not the elements of bread and wine which become the body of Christ during the eucharistic service but rather the congregation which is gathered around the elements. Modern Zwingli scholarship has spoken of a transubstantiation of the worshipping congregation into the body of Christ through the invisible activity of the Spirit.[14] The individual members of the congregation form one loaf which by the Spirit of God is transformed into one body. The congregation, not the elements, becomes for Zwingli the focus of the eucharistic action.

Faith as a response to the activity of the Spirit becomes crucial for Zwingli's doctrine of the eucharist. The work of grace is received by faith prior to the reception of bread and wine. One eats the bread and drinks the wine as an outward and visible sign of an inward and spiritual grace already present. The Church, which is the body of Christ, confesses itself to be that body when it shares the eucharistic elements.[15] By so doing, it remembers the cross and resurrection of Jesus, give thanks for the presence of Christ and his Spirit in the Church, and anticipates the heavenly banquet which will take place in a renewed heaven and earth. However, to eat the bread and drink the wine without faith is to engage in an empty ritual. There is for Zwingli no unworthy eating of the body and blood of Christ, no *manducatio infidelium*. Without faith, there is no communion in the body of Christ.

Luther is afraid that Zwingli's rejection of *manducatio infidelium* has had the subtle effect of transforming faith into a work and has undermined the utterly gracious character of the gifts which God gives the Church through the sacraments. For Luther, the Lord's Supper is a testament, a one-sided covenant in which God both sets the terms by which he will be gracious to the Church and fulfils those terms himself. The condition for putting the testament into effect is the death of the testator, not the faith of the beneficiary.[16] A sacrament is constituted by God's will, testament, and promise. The promise creates faith because the death of the testator has rendered it effective. Faith grasps the effective promise; it does not make the promise effective. Christ gives himself to men and women in the eucharist whether they believe it or not. Otherwise faith would be a work, a sacrifice, something offered to God in order to induce him to be gracious. Unless one affirms that even unbelievers eat the body and blood of Christ, one will lapse into a new form of works-righteousness, all the more insidious because it marches under the banner of faith alone. "The cup of blessing which we bless" *is* "the blood of Christ." It does not merely signify the blood of Christ, and it does not wait on the faith of the recipient to become what it is.[17]

That does not mean that faith plays no role whatever in the eucharist or that it makes no difference whether one communes worthily or unworthily. I Corinthians 11:27–29 speaks in chilling terms of the consequences of unworthy participation in the sacrament. Faith does not make Christ present; Christ is present whether greeted with faith or unbelief.[18] But faith grasps the benefits which Christ is present in the eucharist to give, while unbelief only increases the liabilities for which it will have to answer at the Last Judgment. All unbelievers are "guilty of the body and blood of the Lord" and "eat and drink damnation" for themselves.

IV

The fourth debate is not about a biblical text at all but about an article of the creed which is looked upon as the summary of many biblical texts, the article concerning the session of Christ at the right hand of God. Zwingli takes as his starting point the confession that Christ has assumed finite human nature.[19] The incarnation did not divinize the humanity which was assumed. While the human nature of Jesus was without sin, there is no other difference between it and the humanity of Peter or Mary Magdalene. Even the resurrection does not remove finite limitations from the human nature of Jesus. Indeed, so far as Zwingli is concerned, there is a soteriological necessity that Christ assumed, bore, and continues to bear finite human nature. Only finite human nature is authentic human nature. Unless human nature remains finite in the hypostatic union (that is, remains one with us in our finitude), the redemptive significance of the incarnation, crucifixion, resurrection, and perpetual intercession at the right hand of God will be undermined. Christ cannot be our Redeemer unless he is one of us. There is, therefore, no real communication of attributes, only a metaphorical ascription to the whole person of Christ of attributes which belong properly to one nature or the other. That is what the later Reformed theology means when it talks about *communicatio idiomatum in concreto sed non in abstracto*.[20]

If the humanity of Christ continues to be finite, even after the resurrection, then the "right hand of God" must be a place where this finite humanity can be found.[21] One should quickly add that Zwingli has no idea where the "right hand of God" is located and does not speculate about it. It is sufficient for him that the finite humanity of Christ is not found in the space and time which we inhabit. However, if the finite humanity of Christ is at the right hand of God, then it cannot be in the eucharistic elements. Christ stands at the right hand of God to intercede for the Church. But if he is *there,* he cannot be *here.* It is not possible for a finite body to be in two places at the same time. Finitude implies and demands a single location.

Christ, however, promised his continual presence with the Church (Matthew 28:20) and not merely his continual intercession on its behalf

(Hebrews 7:25). In part, Zwingli explains this presence by an appeal to the Johannine promise of another comforter (John 14:16), the Holy Spirit, who is the Spirit of the Son as well as of the Father. In part, he explains this presence by an appeal to a doctrine which the later Lutherans call derisively the *extra-Calvinisticum*.[22] The *extra-Calvinisticum* rests on a sharp distinction between the two natures of Christ. While the human nature remains finite in the hypostatic union, the divine nature remains in that same union infinite and unbounded. Christ can be present with the Church in the power of his divine nature. Indeed, it is the presence of Christ by his Spirit and in the power of his divine nature which transforms a congregation of individual believers into the eucharistic body of Christ. The divine nature which is present is hypostatically united to a finite human nature which must be absent. Both the presence of the divine nature and the absence of the human nature are soteriologically essential to the being and well-being of the Church.

Luther's rejection of Zwingli's position on the ascension of Christ and the session at the right hand of God is absolute. To begin with, Zwingli has approached the question of the mode of Christ's presence in a philosophically unsophisticated and naive way. Luther returns in his argument to the Occamist distinction between circumscriptive, definitive, and repletive presence: (1) "an object is circumscriptively or locally in a place, i.e., in a circumscribed manner, if the space and the object occupying it exactly correspond and fit into the same measurements, such as wine or water in a cask, where the wine occupies no more space and the cask yields no more space than the volume of the wine;"[23] (2) "an object is in a place definitively, i.e., in an uncircumscribed manner, if the object or body is not palpably in one place and is not measurable according to the dimensions of the place where it is, but can occupy either more room or less. . . . This I call an uncircumscribed presence in a given place, since we cannot circumscribe or measure it as we measure a body, and yet it is obviously present in the place. This was the mode in which the body of Christ was present when he came out of the closed grave, and came to the disciples through a closed door, as the gospels show;"[24] (3) "an object occupies space repletively, i.e., supernaturally, if it is simultaneously present in all places whole and entire, and fills all places, yet without being measured or circumscribed by any place, in terms of the space it occupied. This mode of existence belongs to God alone, as he says in the prophet Jeremiah, 'I am a God at hand and not afar off. I fill heaven and earth.' This mode is altogether incomprehensible, beyond our reason, and can be maintained only with faith, in the Word."[25]

While the philosophical argument is not the most important one from Luther's point of view, it is nevertheless clear that Zwingli and

his followers have committed what Luther considers a philosophical
error. They regard the resurrected body of Christ circumscriptively or
locally when they should regard it definitively or uncircumscriptively.
The resurrected Christ is no longer subject to the limitations of space
and time. He can appear in a circumscriptive or measurable mode
when he pleases, as in his post-resurrection appearances to the disciples (Matthew 28:2, John 20:19). But he passes through the stone
which sealed him in the tomb and through the door which locked in
the disciples in order to do so. Zwingli and Oecolampadius in their
fascination with circumscriptive presence are unable to give a satisfac-
tory exegetical account of the unnerving ability of the risen Christ to
appear exactly when and where he pleases, no matter the physical
barriers. But if Christ can pass definitively, uncircumscriptively,
through stone and wood, he can pass into the eucharistic elements of
bread and wine. For a brief period of time, Christ was in the stone and
wood, though he was not measurable according to their dimensions. If
the body of Christ "does not have to be in a given place circumscriptively or corporeally, occupying and filling space according to its
size,"[26] and if it was present, however fleetingly, in the stone and wood
"without space and place proportionate to its size,"[27] then there is no
reason why it cannot similarly be in the eucharistic bread and wine.
Grant the reality of the post-resurrection appearances, and you must
concede the possibility of the eucharistic presence. You cannot swallow the camel of the resurrection and choke on the gnat of the real
presence.

Zwingli and his followers also seem to be unaware, Luther argues,
that the "right hand of God" is a metaphorical expression for the place
of favor from which God rules. That Christ is at the right hand of God
means that he is the favored one through whom God exercises his rule
(Psalm 8:6, Luke 10:22). Since God exercises his rule everywhere,
even in hell, the right hand of God is found everywhere. The very
expression which Zwingli regards as circumscriptive and local, the
Bible itself proves to be uncircumscribed and incorporeal. Since the
right hand of God is found everywhere, and since the body of Christ is
as the right hand of God (Luther is in these circumstances prepared to
concede that point), then the body of Christ is ubiquitous. It is not
limited by space and time but is present wherever God rules.[28] That
does not mean that he is savingly present for me whenever and however I choose; he is savingly present only through the means of grace
which he has chosen. "There is a difference," Luther says, "between
his being present and your touching."[29]

The body can be ubiquitous because there is a communication of
attributes in the risen Christ. The glorified humanity of Christ has

taken on certain divine attributes, such as the property of ubiquity. The important thing for Luther, however, is to see the doctrine of the ubiquity of the body of Christ in the context of the divine will and Word. It is the will of God which makes the difference between presence (*da*) and saving presence (*dir da*); it is the Word of God which makes the saving presence in the bread and wine accessible.

> So, too, since Christ's humanity is at the right hand of God, and also is in all and above all things according to the nature of the divine right hand, you will not eat or drink him like the cabbage and soup on your table, unless he wills it. He also now exceeds any grasp, and you will not catch him by groping about, even though he is in your bread, unless he binds himself to you and summons you to a particular table by his Word, bidding you to eat him. This he does in the Supper, saying, "This is my body," . . . [30]

Behind the disagreement between Luther and Zwingli over the right hand of God is a disagreement over the nature of the ascension itself. Zwingli looks upon the ascension as the final stage of a drama which begins and ends in heaven. The creed outlines the stages of this drama when it lists the incarnation, crucifixion, resurrection, and ascension as successive acts in the history of the Word become flesh. The Word comes from heaven to assume human flesh, lives a life of active and passive obedience to God, dies, is raised from the dead, and returns to the heaven from which he has come. The ascension means that the humanity of Christ is no longer accessible to me in my space and time.[31]

Luther looks upon the ascension as a quite different sort of event. Once having come to us in the incarnation, Christ does not go away. He remains in our space and time. What changes in the ascension is not the fact of Christ's presence but solely the mode of that presence. Prior to the ascension, he was accessible in a circumscriptive way to sight; after the ascension, he is invisibly accessible to us in the means of grace. Before, he could be arrested by his enemies and flogged; after, he can only be found where he has bound himself by his Word to be: in bread and wine and water. The ascension does not point to the absence of the humanity of Christ at the right hand of God. Rather, it celebrates the ubiquitous presence of the God-man, Jesus Christ, and the universal accessibility of that saving presence through preaching and the sacraments. After citing Matthew 17:5, Luke 3:22 and 24:36, John 20:14, Acts 7:55 and 22:17, Luther remarks:

> These and similar appearances which were granted to the prophets, apostles, and saints many, many times, show indeed that both God and

Christ are not far away but near, and it is only a matter of revealing themselves; they do not move up and down or back and forth, for God is immutable, and Christ also sits at the right hand of God and does not move hither and yon.[32]

V

There are very few theologians in the twentieth century who would accept without qualification Luther's eucharistic theology or the exegesis which underlies it. Even in Luther's own day, serious questions were raised in Lutheran circles about the doctrine of the ubiquity of the body of Christ. Nevertheless, Luther's defense of the real presence of Christ in the eucharist has important implications for Protestant theology in the present.

1. Both Zwingli and Luther perceive that the eucharist cannot be discussed for very long without turning to Christological issues. Luther, however, is suspicious of what he considers to be an excessive spiritualizing tendency on Zwingli's part. Christianity, after all, is not a Gnostic religion. It is a historical religion which stresses the activity of God in time and space. The central message of the New Testament in Luther's view is that God has assumed humanity in Jesus of Nazareth; he has identified himself with the fragile elements of the earth. Christianity glories in a God found in dust. Therefore, for Luther a realistic understanding of the incarnation and a realistic doctrine of the eucharist imply and demand each other. A theology which seeks refuge in the calm and unverifiable realm of the spirit, which appeals too quickly to sign, symbol, saga, myth, and legend, is a theology which is unwilling to face the utter humiliation of God in the eucharist. "Signifies" is a fitting description of the eucharist only if it is an appropriate designation for the incarnation as well, for a Jesus who is a sign or symbol or myth of God's presence but not the presence itself.

2. There is no objection to the eucharist as a means of grace which cannot be lodged equally well against preaching. When Zwingli (in an attempt to underscore the once-for-all character of the cross) protested against Roman Catholic and Lutheran doctrines of the eucharist by citing John 6:63, he took hold of a sword that cuts both ways. Preaching itself is a physical act; speaking and listening, no less than eating and drinking, involve biological processes. One could as easily say of preaching as of the eucharist: "the flesh profits nothing." Zwingli, however, is not willing to downgrade the public reading and interpretation of Scripture. But if in fact physical acts are unable to convey spirtual nourishment to the soul, there is no reason to hold the preach-

ing office in more esteem than the celebration of the eucharist. A preacher can be a witness to the Word of God ("signifies") but not a bearer of that Word ("is"). Futhermore, the only Word that could possibly matter would be the inaudible Word spoken by the Holy Spirit, without the medium of human language, to the human spirit. In short, to attack the eucharist as a physical act is to leave the Christian nothing but mental prayer and wordless contemplation. The parishioner who hangs on the words of the preacher stands in the same peril of idolatry as the communicant who relies on the visible elements of bread and wine.

3. The offer of the saving presence of God is irrelevant unless there is a reliable place where it may be encountered. No theologian before or after Luther has celebrated the universal presence of God more than Luther has. At times, Luther appears in his unguarded statements to veer toward pantheism. Both the doctrine of the ascension and of the ubiquity of the body of Christ are interpreted in such a way as to emphasize the immediate presence of God "in, with, and under" all human experience. Immanence and transcendence are interpreted by Luther not in terms of "up and down" but in terms of nearness and accessibility. God is near; that is his immanence. God's presence is inaccessible apart from his Word and sacraments; that is his transcendence. The eucharist is important as a place where God has attached the promise of his saving and accessible presence. Wherever I turn, God is there; but he is only there for me where he has bound himself to accessibility by his promise. The eucharist overcomes the nearness of God in which I live and move and have my being and renders his presence accessible and saving.

4. Finally, while both God's gift and the human response to it are in a certain sense equally important, the gift is primary, and the response secondary. That may seem, of course, like a perfectly obvious conclusion, hardly worthy of mention, but there is a tendency in Protestantism to think of faith more highly than one should. By stressing the primacy of the Word, Luther wants to emphasize the responsive rather than the causative character of faith. God gives himself to us in baptism, in preaching, and in the eucharist whether or not we greet his gift with faith. Indeed, the very faith we have is itself a gift of God. God cannot be anticipated or outmanuevered, only enjoyed. The eucharist is a sign of the primacy of God's promise, that God is always there first, that he is already doing his work in the world. Both the gift of God's presence and the human receptive faculty are effects of a goodness which envelopes and anticipates us. We are invited to join something already underway, which will happen whether we believe it or not, whether we participate in it or not, whether we enjoy it or not.

The eucharist gives us access to a redemptive event which is already happening, which we have not yet missed, but could miss all too easily. That is why Luther greets the eucharist with the "is" of the concrete and present event. God is not conjured into the eucharist by human piety. Faith has a proper object only if God is already savingly present. The eucharist is an announcement of the saving presence of God and an invitation into that presence. Faith is essential to the enjoyment of that presence precisely because it is not its precondition. That is why all of Luther's eucharistic arguments return finally to the text from which they began: "Take, eat; this is my body."

VIII

LUTHER AND CALVIN ON CHURCH AND TRADITION

Luther and Calvin never met, though they had friends in common, particularly Philip Melanchthon, whose affection for Calvin was regarded with suspicion by Luther's stricter disciples (though not by Luther himself), and Martin Bucer, whom Luther had won for his cause at the Heidelberg Disputation of 1518. In the ordinary course of events, there would have been no reason to expect Luther and Calvin to meet, separated as they were by age, culture, and education. Calvin was born in the year that Luther first lectured on the *Sentences* of Peter Lombard. By the time Calvin was converted to the Protestant faith, Zwingli, Oecolampadius, and Hubmaier were already dead, and Luther had just turned fifty. Unlike Luther, who had received a scholastic theological education at Erfurt and Wittenberg, Calvin studied the classics at Paris and read law at Orleans and Bourges. Since Calvin understood no German (a fact which, the Zurich theologians hinted darkly, contributed to Calvin's inordinate respect for Luther), he was restricted to the Latin writings of Luther and Zwingli or to the works which had appeared in Latin or French translation. Only Calvin's swift rise to prominence in the evangelical movement brought him to Luther's attention, and then not before 1539, when Luther was fifty-five and Calvin thirty.

We have far more evidence about Calvin's attitude toward Luther than about Luther's attitude toward Calvin. Not everything Calvin had to say about Luther was complimentary. Calvin deprecated Luther's tendency to find an edifying point in biblical texts without first subjecting those texts to hard and critical analysis.[1] While Calvin agreed with Luther that the defense of the truth required theologians to engage in polemical discussions (it was Calvin, after all, who called the relatively inoffensive and reform-minded Albert Pighius "that dead dog"), he could not agree with the ferocity of Luther's attacks on other Protestant reformers—even reformers with whom Calvin disagreed—or overlook the self-indulgent character of Luther's piques and rages.[2] Futhermore, while Calvin disagreed with Zwingli, whom he regarded as a theological second-rater, on questions relating to the eucharist, he was nevertheless forced to side with Zwingli against Luther on such sensitive issues as the importance of the session of Christ at the right hand of the Father or the impossibility of an unbeliever's receiving in the eucharistic service more than the mere signs of bread and wine.[3] Indeed, as Brian Gerrish has persuasively argued, Calvin saw Luther in historical perspective as an important, even decisive, theological teacher, but a teacher who had historical antecedents and who initiated but did not culminate a theological development.[4] The Lutherans were not wrong to venerate Luther; they were only mistaken in their inordinate veneration, a veneration which excluded historical change and development, which took the living Word of a prophet and codified it into inflexible law. The Reformation is about *sola fides, sola gratia, solus Christus* (faith alone, grace alone, Christ alone). It is in Calvin's view untrue to itself when it rejects the succession of authentic teachers in the Church and appeals (against Luther's own self-understanding) to Luther alone. The reformed churches learn from Luther as they learn from any truly evangelical theologian, but they remain independent of him. *Sola scriptura* not *solus Lutherus,* the Bible and not Luther's teaching, is the only standard to which the evangelical theologian is bound.

Calvin is notorious, however, not for his negative but for his positive judgments of Luther. Karl Holl called Calvin Luther's best disciple, and there are historical reasons for that judgment. Calvin signed the Augsburg Confession[5] and in the controversy with Zwingli and the Zurich theologians sided instinctively with Luther on the question of the real presence of Christ in the sacrament. He was impatient with Protestant theologians like Bullinger and the Zurich pastors who were unwilling to acknowledge the deep and unrepayable debt which all evangelical theologians owed to the pioneering work of Luther. He was tolerant of Luther's polemical outbursts, though he disapproved of them and urged Melanchthon to exercise his best offices to encourage Luther to offer his arguments in a more moderate and conciliatory tone of voice. In a letter of November 25, 1544, Calvin wrote to Bullinger:

> I often say that even if he should call me a devil, I should still pay him the honor of acknowledging him as an illustrious servant of God, who yet, as he is rich in virtues, so also labors under serious faults. . . . It is our task so to reprehend whatever is bad in him that we make some allowance for those splendid gifts.[6]

For Luther's opinion of Calvin, we have two principal sources, one written and one oral. The written source is a letter from Luther to Bucer dated October 14, 1539. In it, Luther writes: "Farewell and please greet reverently Mr. John Sturm and John Calvin. I have read their books with special pleasure."[7] The oral source is an anecdote which Melanchthon reported by messenger to Calvin and which Calvin repeats in a letter to Farel:

> Certain persons, to irritate Martin, pointed out to him the aversion with which he and his followers were alluded to by me. So he examined the passage in question and felt that he was there, beyond doubt, under attack. After a while, he said: "I certainly hope that he will one day think better of us. Still, it is right for us to be a little tolerant toward such a gifted man." We are surely made of stone if we are not overcome by such moderation! I, certainly, am overcome, and I have written an apology for insertion into my preface to the Epistle to the Romans.[8]

If we ask what writing inclined Luther to be so favorably disposed toward Calvin, the only clue we have is the allusion to Cardinal Sadoleto in the 1539 letter to Bucer. Apparently, the work which impressed Luther and which restrained him from attacking what he regarded as inadequacies in Calvin's position was Calvin's *Reply to Sadoleto,* an open letter addressed to the bishop of Carpentras and published in Strassburg by Wendelin Rihel in September, 1539.[9]

The *Reply to Sadoleto* deals with the doctrine of the Church and the question of the relation of the authority of Scripture to the authority of the fathers and councils. Luther himself had written just a few months earlier a German treatise on the same subject entitled *On the Councils and the Church.*[10] Luther finished his treatise in March and was therefore unaware of Calvin's opinions. Calvin, though deeply indebted to Luther, did not read German and so was unable to consult Luther's essay. There is, therefore, in these essays no direct dependence on one author on the other. Nevertheless, Luther saw in Calvin a spokesman for the whole Protestant movement and regarded his *Reply to Sadoleto* as the articulation of a position with which Luther wanted to identify himself. Indeed, he was so impressed with Calvin's treatment of the very questions with which he had struggled himself that he was unwilling to criticize Calvin or listen to the criticism of others. For a brief period of time in 1539, Luther and Calvin, the aging reformer and the young French theologian, represented a common front against Rome on the central disputed issue of religious authority.

I want in what follows to compare Luther's *On the Councils and the Church* with Calvin's *Reply to Sadoleto,* noting the similarities and differences in their historical settings, their arguments, and their styles. The two treatises give a glimpse of what we might call an ecumenically Protestant position on the authority of Church, magisterium, Scripture, and tradition. They sum up the best Protestant thinking prior to the convocation of the Council of Trent. They are important not only as a clue to the deep affinity between Luther and Calvin but also to the self-understanding of Protestantism at the end of its second decade.

I

Luther's treatise was prompted by the decision of Pope Paul III to convoke a general council at Mantua in May, 1537. After a series of delays and postponements and the naming of Vicenza as a new site for the council, the outbreak of war between Francis I and Charles V forced the pope on May 21, 1539, to postpone the council indefinitely. Though many early Protestants, Luther among them, had called for a free council on German soil to settle the religious questions which divided western Christendom, the Protestant League of Schmalkalden rejected the proposed council when it was finally offered to them. In the end, the Protestant princes decided that the "Council convoked by Paul III was not the free Christian council in German lands demanded by the Estates and promised by the Emperor" but a papally dominated assembly that was prepared to condemn Lutheran teachings without a hearing. "How could we feel safe at a Council held in Italy," the princes demanded, "where the Pope wields so much power and where our enemies are so many?"[11]

During this period of increased interest in a council, Luther began to read extensively in the history of the early and medieval Church, particularly the *Historia Tripartita* by Cassiodorus Senator, the *Lives of the Popes* by Bartolomeo Platina, the newly published (1538) *Complete Councils* of Peter Crabbe, and the *Ecclesiastical History* of Eusebius of Caesarea together with the supplement to Eusebius composed by Rufinus.[12] Luther wanted to approach the question of Church councils from the perspective of history as well as from the standpoint of theology and exegesis. He wanted to examine concretely how councils in the past had functioned, what authority had been ascribed to them, and whether they offered a viable instrument for the further reform and reconstitution of the Church. Because he became skeptical of the reliability of medieval historical sources during the course of his studies, he restricted his analysis to the Council of Jerusalem and the first four ecumenical councils, Nicaea, Constantinople, Ephesus, and Chalcedon. *On the Councils and the Church* is divided into three main sections.

The first section is largely negative.[13] By the application of a somewhat roughly hewn historical method, Luther sets out to demonstrate that on many issues the fathers and councils so contradicted themselves that it was impossible to find a doctrinal consensus. Of course, scholastic theologians and canon lawyers had always known that there were tensions and antinomies within the tradition. Late medieval theologians and lawyers attempted programmatically to reconcile and harmonize tensions and contradictions within the theological and legal traditions, confident that in the one Church led by the Holy Spirit into a unified vision of truth all such disagreements must be more apparent than real. Luther argues that this theological confidence is historically unfounded and cites numerous examples of conciliar decrees which are no longer followed in the Roman Church or which were contradicted by later councils. No one would dream of forbidding German Catholics from eating *Blutwurst* or rabbits trapped in snares, though the Council of Jerusalem (attended, as Luther gleefully points out, by apostles and not merely by bishops in apostolic succession) forbade the eating of blood and required a limited Kosher observance by Gentile Christians. No Catholic prince (including the late Pope Julius II) would welcome the enforcement of the ancient conciliar restrictions on the participation of Christians in war, and no Catholic bishop would think of invoking the opinions of Cyprian on the baptism of heretics or the readmission of apostates to communion. There is no way to harmonize these ancient decrees and opinions with modern theology and practice, to which they stand in absolute contradiction, and all attempts to do so since Gratian and Lombard have only made matters worse.

In the second section, Luther attempted to define more narrowly the nature and task of a council.[14] After a lengthy discussion in which he scrutinized the records of the councils of Jerusalem, Nicaea, Constantinople, Ephesus, and Chalcedon, he concluded that a council could not, and had never been expected to, establish new articles of belief beyond the articles contained in Holy Scripture. Councils defend and explain teaching which the prophets and apostles have already articulated. Therefore, there is nothing valid in the teaching of a council which is not first and more powerfully stated in Scripture itself. A council, then, "is nothing but a consistory, a royal court, a supreme court or the like, in which the judges, after hearing the parties, pronounce sentence, but with this humility, 'For the sake of the law.'"[15] The law which Luther had in mind is the Bible. The bishops in a council pass judgment on heresy, but only as that heresy can be proven to be heresy out of Holy Scripture. A judgment is not valid merely because it has been made by properly constituted and legally competent persons. However much Luther emphasizes the importance of offices in the Church, he does not simply invest those offices with the charism of truth. The decision of a council is valid not because it has been made by the proper persons under the proper conditions in a duly constituted assembly but because that decision is in harmony with the teaching of Holy Scripture. In that sense, the authority of a council does not differ at all from the authority of any capable pastor or teacher. All three are servants of the Word.

The last section of the treatise shifts from the problem of councils and their authority to the larger question of the doctrine of the Church.[16] Because of his doctrine of justification by faith alone and his stress on the invisibility of the Church, Luther had been accused of holding a kind of "Platonic" ecclesiology, an idealized and utopian doctrine of the Church, which had no fixed place in space and time and therefore lacked the rootedness in this world which marks the corporation of the medieval Catholic Church. This chapter focuses on the historical character of the Christian Church as Luther understands it and the visible signs by which it can be recognized. The discussion, therefore, is very practical and down to earth. The Church is an assembly of holy Christian people, holy because their sins have been forgiven and are now being mortified through Christ. Unlike other assemblies gathered for other purposes, the Church preaches and hears the Word of God, baptizes, celebrates the eucharist, administers discipline, calls and ordained ministers, prays, and bears the cross. While faith is invisible and election is a mystery, the characteristic activities which identify this society are public ceremonies which anyone can attend. The most important mark, however, is possession of the Word of God: " . . . even if there were no other sign than this alone, it would still suffice to prove that a Christain, holy people must exist there, for God's Word cannot be without God's people, and conversely, God's people cannot be without God's Word."[17]

II

Unlike Luther, who took a question that was troubling all of Germany, Calvin was prompted to write by what started out to be a purely local matter. In March, 1539, Jacopo Cardinal Sadoleto, bishop of Carpentras in southern France, sent a letter to Geneva, asking it to return to the Catholic faith. Sadoleto was one of the more illustrious members of the Sacred College of Cardinals, a prelate who had served every pope since 1513 except Hadrian VI in one important office or another. Sadoleto returned to Carpentras from Rome in 1538 at almost the same time that Calvin and Farel had lost a political struggle in

Geneva and had been expelled from the city by the triumphant party. It seemed an opportune time for the Catholic Church to attempt to recall Geneva to the ancient faith of its ancestors, and Sadoleto was quick to seize it. Whether Sadoleto acted on his own initiative or was commissioned to write by a conference of Catholic bishops in Lyons is unclear. What is clear is that he wrote an eloquent and persuasive appeal for reunion.

Geneva sent a copy of Sadoleto's letter to Bern. After mutual consultations which stretched over several months, the city councils of Bern and Geneva finally decided in late July to ask Calvin to draft a response on their behalf. Calvin, however, was living happily in Strassburg, where he was minister to the French refugee congregation. Bern, therefore, sent Simon Sulzer, hat in hand, to Strassburg to ask Calvin to swallow past resentments against both Geneva and Bern and compose the kind of reasoned response to Sadoleto which Sadoleto's reasoned and moderate letter deserved. After some hesitation (the Calvin family did not find it easy to swallow resentments) and at the urging of his friends, Calvin agreed.

Calvin begins his *Response to Sadoleto* by making an assertion which is absolutely essential for understanding not only Calvin and the Reformed tradition but Luther as well. Calvin claims to have held both the office of doctor and of pastor in the church at Geneva and to have a legitimate Christian calling within the larger Christian community.[18] Calvin did not merely go to Geneva; he was divinely sent. Like Luther, who appeals again and again to the office which he holds in the Church as the legitimation for his reform activity, Calvin rejects the notion that he is merely exercising his own right of private judgment or pursuing a vocation which has no public authorization. He is an office-bearer in the Church, standing in that valid succession which derives its legitimacy from faithful transmission of the ancient apostolic message. It is the Word that is transmitted that gives validity to the office of pastor and teacher and not the office that gives authority and form to the Word.

Calvin does not accept Sadoleto's point that the Catholic Church was united on the eve of the Reformation and that the Reformation is a disruption of the harmony and peace of the Church.[19] Actually, the Catholic Church was broken when Luther's Reformation began, riven by dissension between pope and council, Franciscans and Dominicans, Scotists and Albertists, scholastics and humanists. Indeed, it was the brokeness of the Church, its loss of that unity in doctrine which the Church of Christ must have, which prompted the Protestant Reformation. Sadoleto is correct to believe that truth is one and that error disrupts unity. His only fault is failing to recognize that the Protestant

Reformation, by recovering the true teaching of Scripture, is restoring unity to the badly fragmented Church of the later middle ages.

The charge of theological innovation is also beside the point. A doctrine is an innovation (and therefore a departure from the teaching of the apostles) when it is genuinely new; it is not an innovation simply because it is new to Cardinal Sadoleto. A more accurate reading of Church history must acknowledge that the late medieval Church has introduced doctrines and practices not known to the ancient Church. Hence, the attempt of the Protestant reformers to recapture ancient doctrine and discipline is labeled innovation by a Church which has lost contact with its own past and which identifies modern belief and practice with the faith and discipline of the early Church.[20] One searches in vain in the early fathers and councils for the doctrine of transubstantiation, for the practice of private confession and absolution, for purgatory and the intercession of the saints. In other words, while Sadoleto has appealed to antiquity, his appeal was formal and without theological content. If theologians study the ancient fathers, they will discover that the fathers support the Protestant reformers far more often than they support Sadoleto. In point of fact, the Protestant reformers are attempting to keep faith with the ancient teaching of the apostles as understood by the fathers against the later unwarranted innovations and novelties introduced by the medieval Catholic Church. The papists teach doctrines "sprung from the human brain."[21] They have leaders who neither understand the Word nor care greatly for it. The laity in the old Church venerate the Word but do not read or obey it. This de-emphasis on the Word has led to the "supine state of the pastors" and the "stupidity of the people."[22] While Calvin is keen to find support for Protestant teaching in the fathers and early councils, he does not regard them as more than venerable interpreters of Holy Scripture. The Bible is superior to both fathers and councils, though fathers and councils are indispensable aids for the proper understanding of Scripture.

> For although we hold that the Word of God alone lies beyond the sphere of our judgment, and that fathers and councils are of authority only in so far as they accord with the rule of the Word, we still give to councils and fathers such rank and honor as it is meet for them to hold under Christ.[23]

Calvin contrasts the passive, implicit faith recommended by Sadoleto with the active spirit of *docilitas* or learning readiness which characterizes true Christian faith. Real humility is submission to the Word of God and not passive submission to every opinion uttered by the Catholic Church or its hierarchy. "Sadoleto," Calvin complains, "you have too indolent a theology. . . . all that you leave to the faithful is to shut their own eyes and submit implicitly to their teachers."[24] Implicit faith undercuts the theological responsibility of the people of God, while the active docility which follows conversion prompts men and women to study Holy Scripture in the sphere of the Church and in association with the fathers and councils. The Church has instrumental authority since "we cannot fly without wings." It leads believers to the sources of truth and life. But the Church is not merely mother; it is also school. Even simple believers have a theological responsibility which they must assume. Like Clement of Alexandria, Calvin believes that every stage of the Christian life is justified only in so far as one is pressing on, however hesitatingly and ineptly, to the next stage. The faith that justifies is never static.

Vincent of Lerins had argued that Catholic truth is the doctrine taught everywhere (*ubique*), always (*semper*), and by all (*ab omnibus*). Sadoleto institutionalizes this ancient test of truth and makes it a test of the true Church. While Calvin admires and accepts Sadoleto's use of the Vincentian canon in his definition of the Church, he cannot accept the definition itself. Sadoleto's definition refers to the Church and the Holy Spirit, but omits all reference to the Word by which the Spirit of Christ forms and governs the Church. Yet a Church which is governed by the Spirit without the formative and restraining function of the Word is nothing more than a sect, a charismatic assembly which has lost touch with the historically grounded Word uttered in space and time.[25] The Word preserves the government of the Church from vagueness and instability. Therefore, Calvin offers his own corrected definition of the Church modeled on the Vincentian canon:

> Now, if you can bear to receive a truer definition of the Church than your own, say, in future, that it is a society of all the saints, a society which, spread over the whole world, and existing in all ages, and bound together by the one doctrine and the one Spirit of Christ, cultivates and observes unity of faith and brotherly concord. With this Church we deny that we have any disagreement. Nay, rather, as we revere her as our mother, so we desire to remain in her bosom.[26]

Calvin also answers what he regards as Sadoleto's caricature of the evangelical understanding of justification by faith alone.[27] Faith is not mere credulity, not a mere assent of the mind to true doctrine, but a committal of the whole self to God. To be justified by faith means to be united to Christ in a bond of mystical union (Luther had spoken of being baked into one cake with Christ). Naturally, anyone so possessing Christ and so possessed by him will perform good works. What is at stake is not the existence of good works but their status. Protestants deny only that these works contribute to justification or form even the partial basis for God's acceptance of the sinner. Good works are not merits in the Catholic sense, but only the fruits of faith.

Calvin ends his treatise with what appears to be an autobiographical confession of faith. He indicates that he was prevented from embracing Protestantism by his reverence for the Church in which he had been raised and that only after a long struggle did he suddenly embrace the faith which first struck him (as it now strikes Sadoleto) as an innovation.[28] Sadoleto, of course, has recommended against such conversion and has assured the Genevese that God would not condemn a man or woman who remained with the Church in which they had been baptized, even though they were convinced that that Church had erred and sinned against its own true nature. The difficulty with Sadoleto's position on conversion is that it could be embraced by Jews, Turks, and Saracens as a justification for their rejection of Christianity.[29] It is the perfect anti-missionary argument. Still, in all, Calvin prefers to end on a positive note and concludes his *Reply to Sadoleto* with a prayer for Christian unity.

III

I observed at the beginning of this chapter that Luther and Calvin make a common ecumenical front in 1539 against Rome on the question of the Church and its teaching authority. That is not to say that there are no differences between them. There are certainly differences in style. While Calvin is painfully direct in his criticisms of the old Church and is not above occasional *ad hominem* thrusts at his opponent (particularly if he can disguise them in what appear at first glance to be compliments), he nevertheless maintains a fairly restrained and moderate tone, at least as moderate as the tone of Sadoleto himself. Luther, on the other hand, can never resist for very long the temptation to be a kind of theological Peck's Bad Boy, merrily ripping out the shirttails of his enemies and setting fire to them. Furthermore, while Calvin is content to outline a general theology of history and avoid the discussion of specific historical cases, Luther builds his argument on the examination of specific historical texts and demonstrates the validity of his position on the basis of concrete examples. But these differences, and others like them, only serve to underscore the fundamental similarity of their arguments.

1. *Fathers and councils.* Both Luther and Calvin agree that the authority of fathers and councils is subordinate to the authority of Holy Scripture. Luther takes the negative side of the argument and stresses

the contradictions and tensions within the Church's theological traditions, while Calvin stresses the positive agreement of the best of the
fathers with Protestant teaching. The Catholic Church, in other words,
appeals to a tradition which is in part contradictory and uncertain (for
instance, the Council of Jerusalem on dietary laws or Cyprian on the
baptism of heretics) and which in part undercuts the very positions
which the Catholic Church seeks to establish (such as the doctrine of
transubstantiation or the discipline of auricular confession). So far
from dreading an encounter with the Church's tradition, Luther and
Calvin seem to relish the prospect, confident that a fair-minded reading of history will demonstrate the utter necessity of the Protestant
appeal to Scripture alone as the authoritative source and norm of
Christian doctrine.

2. *Vision of History.* Both Luther and Calvin reject the notion that
Protestant reformers are theological innovators who have disrupted a
1500–year-old consensus in Christian doctrine. Innovations have been
introduced by the Catholic Church during the middle ages which were
not found in the earliest Church. The patristic age was more successful
than later Christian eras in avoiding the introduction of theological
novelties, though even the fathers were not altogether successful in
suppressing theological innovation. Nevertheless, those fathers and
councils are authoritative which succeeded best in explaining and defending biblical truth. While Luther seems more skeptical of the value
of patristic authors than does Calvin (though they share some of the
same likes and dislikes), both agree on the importance of the fathers as
exegetical guides to the interpretation of Scripture. What the Protestants are attempting to do (at least as they understand it) is to persuade the Church to abandon its fascination with the theological and
disciplinary innovations of the later middle ages and return to Scripture and the fathers, Scripture as the authoritative text and the fathers
as helpful interpreters (not infallible but better far than the scholastics). In short, the Catholic charge of theological innovation has been
met by a counter-charge of "*tu quoque!*" The defenders of the old
Church have in the opinion of Luther and Calvin too restricted a vision
of Christian history and invest the customs and doctrines of the relatively recent past with the dignity and authority which belong to the
ancient apostolic tradition alone—all with the result that what is truly
ancient, such as the Pauline doctrine of justification by faith, seems to
them to be a theological novelty.

3. *Office and magisterium.* While both Luther and Calvin agree in
stressing the importance of offices in the Church, they also agree in
subordinating the authority of the office to its proper functioning in a
new and untraditional way. Traditional Catholic teaching tied the au-

thority of the office-bearer to the office itself. A bishop has certain powers granted by God which are inherent in his office. Whether he uses those powers wisely or abuses them shamelessly, the powers inhere in the office. The same is true of priest or pope or council. Luther and Calvin place authority in the Word of which pastors, teachers, and councils are servants. That does not mean that Luther and Calvin have embraced Donatism. The efficacy of Word and sacrament is not dependent on the personal faith or holiness of the minister. But the authority and legitimacy of the pastoral and teaching offices are derived from the Word which is proclaimed and taught and not from the society or corporation that proclaims it.

Luther and Calvin, in other words, are not conciliarists. They do not believe that a council, properly assembled and constituted, will necessarily be led by the Holy Spirit to an infallible definition of the truth. Councils have come to decisions which were nothing more than human, historically conditioned acts. If that is not so, then the Church is obligated to enforce the dietary laws of the Council of Jerusalem. The council is a court required to render judgment on the basis of an authority which is external to its own will and of which it is not the author. It is a useful court, but it is not the source of the law by which it judges. Its decisions are authoritative and binding on the Christian community to the extent that they are in agreement with Holy Scripture. To the extent that they are not, they are invalid and bear no authority whatever. The same is true of the decisions of priests, bishops, theologians, and popes.

4. *Exegetical optimism.* Both Luther and Calvin reflect the exegetical optimism which marked early Protestantism. For a brief period of time, Protestants thought it would be possible to write a theology which was wholly biblical and excluded all philosophical and speculative questions. It became clear within a decade that such hope was not well-founded. Nevertheless, Protestants remained optimistic about the clarity of Scripture and the simplicity and persuasive power of the truth which it contained. Protestants were not well-prepared for the internal disagreements within Protestantism when the careful exegesis of one group of godly and learned men clashed with the exegesis of another group equally learned and godly. On the whole, Luther and Calvin seem to believe that good exegesis will drive out bad and do not provide a great deal of help in suggesting a practical mechanism for the reconciliation of conflicts. All we have in these two documents is the suggestion of Luther that a council can serve as a useful, though not infallible, court of judgment on disputed questions. The later history of Protestantism confirms that Protestants have tended to rely on synods, presbyteries, conferences, councils, and assemblies for the resolution

of differences. But Luther and Calvin in these two treatises appear to leave the question hanging. It is the superiority of Scripture to tradition which is on their minds as they face Rome. Luther and Calvin are confident that in every generation the lively and living Word of God will create communities of obedient hearers and doers of that Word. The unity which the Church seeks beyond all theological and doctrinal strife is the unity which the Word itself creates through the action of the Holy Spirit: " . . . for God's Word cannot be without God's people, and conversely, God's people cannot be without God's Word." On that point, Luther and Calvin make common cause.

IX

LUTHER AND THE
DRUNKENNESS OF NOAH

The study of Luther's hermeneutics has focused in recent years on the study of Luther's earliest exegetical writings, especially his *Dictata super Psalterium* (1513–1515). This fascination with Luther's earliest writings is not difficult to explain. It is, after all, hard to match the excitement and sense of discovery which characterize Luther's writings at the beginning of his career. New ideas, many with revolutionary potential, begin to take form as he struggles to write his first lectures on Paul and the Psalms. Again and again, even when he is trying to cite precedents for his ideas in Augustine or Lyra, he proves to be a very unconventional interpreter, filling the old theological wineskins with a new and not altogether familiar vintage. Tracking these new themes through the young Luther's successive exegetical lectures and commentaries has proven to be a fascinating occupation for a whole generation of Luther scholars.

On the other hand, historians, who tend by nature to have more curiosity about the origins than the consolidation of movements, have been put off by the technical difficulties surrounding the chief work of Luther's later years, his massive commentary on Genesis. Though the first edition of the commentary was published in Wittenberg before Luther's death, Luther himself did not see this work through the press. The commentary we have was compiled and edited by Veit Dietrich from student lecture notes.[1] Unfortunately, Dietrich's understanding of his responsibilities as an editor did not exclude, as it would for a modern editor, the interpolation of his own views and comments in Luther's text. Without any compunction, Dietrich refers to events which happened after Luther's death, adds references which Luther did not supply, and even makes Luther sound on occasion more Melanchthonian than Melanchthon himself. Still, the editors of the American edition of Luther's works are surely correct when they argue that "the main body of his commentary . . . could have come from no one but Martin Luther."² Dietrich has altered and "improved" Luther at certain points, but he had not supplanted Luther's commentary with a commentary of his own.

Because the commentary on Genesis is so large and unwieldy, it is difficult to know where to begin in a study of it. Rather than attempt to examine every aspect of the hermeneutical approach of the old Luther to the biblical text, I propose to do a case study, to examine in detail Luther's treatment of a limited part of the Genesis narrative. I have chosen for consideration one of the most puzzling and at the same time one of the most familiar episodes from the early chapters of Genesis, the story of the drunkenness of Noah (Genesis 9:18–29). Luther comments on this text at three different periods in his career: (1) his earliest comments are found in a sermon preached on St. Martin's day, November 11, 1519, and in a brief scholium prepared at about the same time; (2) a second set of comments comes from a series of sermons preached in 1523–24 and published in 1527; (3) Luther's final and most extensive comments were delivered as lectures in November, 1536, and included in the edition published by Veit Dietrich in 1544.

In order to provide a context for Luther's commentary on Genesis 9, I want to compare his exegesis with the interpretation of one of the most popular fifteenth century commentators, Denis the Carthusian, also known as the Ecstatic Doctor. Although Denis died in 1471, his commentaries remained popular throughout the sixteenth and seventeenth centuries. There is no evidence that Luther consulted Denis when he wrote his own lecture notes on Genesis 9, and I have not selected him because of his influence on Luther's exegesis. If we wished to compare Luther with one of his sources, it would be far better to choose Nicholas of Lyra or even St. Augustine. Denis is important not as a source for Luther but as a near contemporary, a man who inhabits the theological world in which Luther is raised, who reads many of the same books, and who inherits most of the same exegetical traditions. By comparing Luther's treatment of the Noah story with the exegesis of a man who like Luther stands at the end of the middle ages, we are in a better position to assess what is new and what traditional in the biblical interpretation of old Luther.

I

The story of the drunken Noah is a very simple one. After the great flood is over, Noah tills the earth and plants a vineyard. He drinks rather too freely of the wine which the vineyard yields and becomes intoxicated. As a result, he falls asleep whith his sexual organs un-covered. His youngest son, Ham, discovers Noah lying in a drunken stupor and tells his two brothers, Shem and Japheth. Shem and Japh-eth take a garment and, by walking backwards, cover their father without seeing his nakedness. When Noah wakes, he pronounces a blessing on Shem and Japheth and a curse on Canaan, the son of Ham.

While the narrative is a spare and simple one, it leaves the reader with many unanswered questions. Did Noah, for example, have any experience of vineyards or of wine before the great flood? If not, was his intoxication merely accidental? Is Noah in any sense culpable for his act? Why does Noah's curse fall on Canaan, Ham's son, and not on Ham himself? Is Ham guilty because he saw his father's nakedness, when the narrative seems to imply that Ham came upon his father accidentally? Is Ham guilty for telling his brothers? What exactly did he tell his brothers? Or is Ham's guilt related to some action on his part which has been suppressed by the narrator? Was Canaan a silent, but unmentioned, actor in the story? Why does Noah bless the Lord God of Shem rather than Shem himself? What does Noah mean in his blessing of Japheth, that "Japheth shall dwell in the tents of Shem?" Why was the story told at all? What purpose does it serve in the larger framework of salvation history? As Erich Auerbach has pointed out so memorably, if the story were a Greek epic poem or drama, a chorus would be waiting in the wings to answer these questions and tell us whatever the actors themselves neglected to explain. The biblical nar-rative, however, cries out for an interpreter to fill in the missing pieces and supply the larger framework of meaning.

Modern scholarship, of which the commentary on Genesis by Ger-hard von Rad is typical,[3] regards the account as a composite narrative in which the J or Yahwistic primal history is combined with a Priestly account written several centuries later. The final editor of the text has taken a story which had a universal framework and explained the origins of all nations and has given it a local, Palestinian frame of reference. That is why the curse is pronounced on Canaan, who lives in Palestine, rather than on Ham, who is the father of such remote nations as the Egyptians and the Hittites. The story alludes to the three peoples inhabiting Palestine: the Jews (the children of Shem), the original inhabitants of the land who were conquered by the Jews (the Canaanites or children of Ham), and friendly non-Jewish tribes, perhaps the Philistines, who shared occupation of Palestine and as-sisted in the subjugation of the Canaanites (the children of Japheth).

The story helps to explain why Israel did not completely occupy the land of Canaan as Yahweh had promised Moses. One might conclude

that Yahweh did not have sufficient power to carry out his promise to
the Jews to give them the entire land of Canaan as their heritage. That
is, of course, an unwarranted conclusion. The story of the drunkenness
of Noah makes it plain that it was never the intention of Yahweh to
give Canaan to the Jews to the exclusion of other, non-Jewish peoples,
the so-called children of Japheth. From the very beginning, it was the
openly declared intention of Yahweh for Jew and non-Jew to occupy
Palestine in peace and to rule jointly over the conquered Canaanites.
The promises of Yahweh to Israel through Moses did not and could
not set aside Noah's ancient blessing of Shem and Japheth. The *de
facto* multiple occupation of Palestine expresses rather than violates
the will of God in salvation history.

The Yahwist regards the cultivation of vineyards and the production
of wine as a postdiluvian activity. It represents an amelioration of the
curse on the land which was pronounced at the time of the expulsion of
Adam and Eve from the garden of Eden. As the Old Testament makes
plain again and again, the vine is the noblest of all plants (Psalm
104:15), and there is no greater earthly happiness than to own a vineyard and enjoy its harvest (Genesis 49:11–12, I Kings 4:25, II Kings
18:31, Hosea 2:15, Micah 4:4, Amos 9:13). Noah, however, has no
prior experience with vineyards or winemaking and so places himself
unwittingly in the power of the wine he has made. His drunkenness is
an accident and should not be viewed as a voluntary abuse of this new,
good gift of God.

There is a hint in 9:24 that the narrator has suppressed part of the
story. It is possible that Ham was no innocent observer of his father's
nakedness but may rather have performed some illicit sexual act with
his drunken and therefore vulnerable father. Robert Alter suggests
that the language, "to uncover the nakedness of" or "to see the nakedness of," is not only explicitly sexual, but also the language usually
employed by the Old Testament in cases of incest.[4] If so, the character
of Ham would certainly correspond to the character of the Canaanites,
whose worship involved ritualized sexual acts and cultic prostitution.
At any rate, whatever Ham has done, he is cursed for his immodesty
and disrespect for his father. This is in sharp contrast to the modesty of
Shem and Japheth, who refuse to look at their naked father and cover
him with a garment used as a blanket.

The text, therefore, provides a justification of the subjugation of the
Canaanites, the children of Ham, who continue to demonstrate the
moral depravity of their ancient ancestor. It also provides a satisfying
theological explanation for the failure of the Jews to occupy the promised land as the sole conquerors of Palestine. Other non-Jewish tribes,
the children of Japheth, also have a right to live within the boundaries

of the lands promised to Israel. Their rights are guaranteed in the blessing pronounced by Noah on his son, Japheth, rights guaranteed prior to the exodus and the giving of the Law to Moses.

II

Denis the Carthusian offers three interpretations of the story: a literal, an allegorical, and a tropological one. Denis does not mean by the literal sense of the Bible what modern scholarship means. When modern scholarship talks about the literal sense of the text, it has in mind the historical events which lie behind the text and to which the text in its present form provides clues. When Denis speaks about the literal meaning of the story of Noah, he is interested exclusively in the narrative as its presents itself to the reader without probing behind that narrative to an earlier form of the tradition or to an underlying set of historical events which are not explicitly mentioned in the text itself.

On the level of the literal sense, Denis suggests, following Alcuin, that Noah's drunkenness was accidental.[5] The human race did not have the use of the vine prior to the flood, and so Noah was innocent of the effect that wine would have on him. While Denis is certain that Noah's lower body was uncovered, there is no hint in Denis's interpretation that Ham had sexually abused his father. Ham's crime was his derision of Noah as a silly old fool who had acted shamefully. Although Noah was in fact not guilty of any conscious wrongdoing, Ham ascribed guilt to him. This attitude stands in sharp contrast to the charity, reverence, and modesty which Shem and Japheth showed to Noah.

The text calls Ham Noah's youngest son not because Ham was the last born but because he was Noah's youngest son in grace and virtue. Denis accepts the order in which the sons' names are listed as the order of their birth. Japheth is therefore the youngest son, though he is senior to Ham in filial piety and wisdom. Denis rejects, however, as inept the suggestion of some that the curse falls on Canaan because Canaan first saw the drunken Noah and reported what he saw to his father, Ham. Noah's sons had no children of their own before the deluge. Since the planting and maturation of Noah's vineyard seem to have happened very soon after the ending of the flood, Canaan can only have been a very small child when his grandfather became intoxicated.

All of this raises for Denis the theological question posed by the prophet Ezekiel, when he asserts (Ezekiel 18:20) that a son shall not bear the iniquity of his father. Denis responds that a father can be cursed in and through his son and that God visits the iniquities of fathers on their children up to the third and fourth generations (Exodus 20:5, Number 14:18). Because a son is derived from the material substance of his father, he can be punished with corporal penalties for the sins of his parents. The soul, however, is a different matter, since the soul is not derived from one's parents but created immediately by God. Children are not punished for the mortal sins of their parents but bear the guilt of their own transgressions alone. No one ever lost grace because of the indiscretion of one's great-grandfather, Adam only excepted.

Denis regards the curse of Canaan as a physical rather than a spiritual matter. Although Ham had committed mortal sin and was deserving of eternal punishment, Noah did not mention the spiritual consequences of Ham's sin, but pronounced a temporal punishment on Canaan instead. Actually, neither Ham nor Canaan ever lived to see the fulfilment of Noah's prophecy, which only found its fulfilment centuries later in the subjugation of the Canaanites by the twelve tribes of Israel. Denis suggests that the physical punishment of the Canaanites was intended as a kind of medicine for the spirit and draws a parallel between the children of Ham and modern Jews without demonstrating that the expulsion and subjugation of the Canaanites (or of the modern Jews) ever resulted in a positive spiritual benefit for the involuntary recipients of this subjugation. Nevertheless, it is an important point for Denis that Noah cursed members of his own family not out of ill will but out of love and a zeal for justice. It is Noah's fondest hope that the curse of Canaan will bring the children of Ham to repentance and a reinstatement in grace.

Similarly, Noah blessed God for the gifts of grace which would be shown to Shem and his children, who would serve as the chief agents for the preservation of the worship of the true God. Japheth would be "englarged" in the sense that his posterity would be numerous; he would dwell in the tents of Shem in the sense that many Gentiles would be converted to Judaism and to the Church which is older than Shem, the Church which stretches from Adam to Christ. These believing Gentiles, these so-called children of Japheth, would take the place of Jews, the proper children of Shem, who like Ham and Canaan were unbelieving. The story of the drunken Noah is not for Denis, as it is for modern scholarship, an explanation of the multiple titles to the land of Palestine but rather a celebration of the multiple titles to the gifts of grace. From the very beginning, Jew and Gentile were destined by God to share in the same salvation, even if the Gentiles can participate only by "dwelling in the tents of Shem."

In his allegorical interpretation, Denis follows a tradition which goes back at least to Cyprian and which regards Noah the peasant farmer as a type of Christ.[6] Strictly speaking, of course, the whole Trinity is the farmer (John 15:1) who cultivates the human heart by infusing grace and bearing away every obstacle to spiritual growth. However, it is appropriate in this context to speak of Christ, the Second Person of the Trinity, as the farmer, who through his incarnation tills the earth—namely, the synagogue—by preaching to it. He plants a vine, which Denis interprets as both the primitive Church and the synagogue (Isaiah 5:7, Hosea 10:1). Intoxicated with the fervor of love, Christ like Noah drinks the cup, in this case the cup of his suffering and death. He is naked in his tabernacle; that is, he is suspended on the cross in the midst of his own people, the synagogue. Ham, who stands for the unbelieving Jews, seeing the nakedness—that is, the mortality and fragility of the human flesh—of Christ, the Creator, provokes both Jews and Gentiles to derision of the crucified Savior, saying, "He saved others, but he cannot save himself!" Shem and Japheth, who represent converts to Christ from Judaism and paganism, explain the apparent "nakedness" of Christ and defend him from all attacks and aspersions of his enemies. Christ became incarnate and was crucified not out of necessity nor because of his own guilt but out of love and for the salvation of the whole world. The garment which covers the naked and vulnerable Christ is the sacrament; the shoulders which bear that garment represent the Church's memory of the past. Christ wakes from the sleep of death, condemns the unbelief of Ham, and commends the faithfulness of Shem and Japheth. Denis rejects the exegesis of Jerome, who argues that Gentiles dwell in the tents of Shem after the original occupants, the Jews, have been evicted. The point of the story seems rather to be that God creates a new Church out of two peoples, believing Jews and Gentiles alike.

In his tropological or moral interpretation, Denis compares Noah to a prelate who becomes vainglorious or whose moral life is stained by some carnal act.[7] While his subordinate, represented in this case by Ham, owes his prelate reverence and obedience, he is in fact ungrateful and indiscreet. The moment he finds out about his superior's moral lapse, he rushes off to tell whoever will listen and to expose the weakness of his superior to the widest possible unsympathetic audience. The good subjects of that prelate, represented by Shem and Japheth, suppress any urge to gossip about the human weaknesses of their bishop. Like Noah's good sons, they cover with the mantle of charity the faults of others and so are blessed by God. That does not mean that priests ought not to discuss the faults of their bishop when the common good is at stake, but only that they should do so at the proper time and place and in the spirit of charity and godly fear. The story of Noah interdicts malicious gossip, not ecclesiastical reform.

III

Luther's first exegesis of the drunkenness of Noah is very similar to Denis's allegorical interpretation.[8] In his 1519 sermon and again in the brief scholium which dates from the same period, Luther identifies Noah as a type of Christ and makes many, though not all, of the same points make by Denis. Noah is the crucified Christ, drunk with love and exposed to shame and derision by the faithless Jews, who are typified by Noah's son, Ham. Shem represents the Jews who believe in Christ and Japheth the believing Gentiles. Believing Jews and Gentiles do not see the cross as shame but as the highest glory. Luther has no real interest in the fate of the Canaanites. The descendants of Ham are the faithless Jews; the descendants of Shem are the faithful Jews, from whom come the earliest disciples and apostles of Christ. Japheth dwells in the tents of Shem because both the Bible and the first beginnings of Christianity were nurtured in the circle of faithful Jews. Noah curses Canaan rather than Ham because Ham had, on the ark, been a trusted servant beloved by God. While there are some nuanced differences between Luther's earliest interpretation of the drunkenness of Noah and the allegorical exegesis offered by Denis, those differences are hardly worth mentioning.

Luther's second attempt, on July 12, 1523, to interpret the story is more original and demonstrates some of his characteristic theological insights.[9] Although Luther still identifies Noah with Christ, he shifts his main interest from the story of the passion and resurrection of Christ, typified by Noah's drunkenness, to the all too human experiences of Noah himself, who is now viewed as an archetypal believer. Noah is a holy man, and yet he becomes drunk. Luther is unwilling to offer Noah the excuse that he had had no prior experience with vineyards or wine. Although drunkenness is a sin (even if, as Luther makes clear, not the worst sin), Noah is not regarded as a sinner because of his drunkenness. The patriarchs frequently did things which, if we should do them, would be sin for us. In the wisdom of God, the patriarchs are held to a different standard. Through the drunkenness of Noah, God wanted to teach all Christians, but especially German Christians, that Noah was justified by his faith, not his works, and that if we fix our attention on the works of the saints rather than on their faith, we shall be badly mislead. God does not call on us to imitate the works of the saints but their faith, a point which the Franciscans and Dominicans can never seem to grasp. Noah's drunkenness was good for him but would harm us.

Ham, however, is not similarly excused for ridiculing his father.

Luther sees Ham as a tragic figure. If Ham had not been a holy and faithful man, he would not have been able to live through the horrors of the deluge. But even an excellent man can fall and bring the world tumbling around his ears. Ham provides a warning that no one should think that he is so secure in grace that he could not fall. Still, the curse on Ham and Canaan was not fulfilled immediately. In fact, the sons of Ham, the Egyptians, even succeed in enslaving the sons of Shem, the Israelites, before God turns the tables, destroys Pharaoh and his armies, and conquers the land of Canaan. It is characteristic of the true Word of God, Luther observes, that it first appears to be false, and that all its prophets appear to be liars.

While Luther accepts the allegorical reading of the story and stresses the literal, he rejects any tropological interpretation which identifies Noah with a bishop or magistrate or which brings down the curse of Canaan on the head of ecclesiastical reformers. By using a tropological interpretation of the drunkenness of Noah, wicked bishops see to it that no one acts against them, even if they are seriously at fault. Luther willingly concedes that no Christian should uncover or expose to public ridicule the secret fault of the Christian brother or sister. But public faults call for public remedies. Preachers cannot be silent in the face of public wrongdoing. Bishops who defile their public office and yet have the temerity to lay claim to the comfort of Noah's blanket must remember that Noah was a holy man and guiltless of any abuse of public trust.

In his final treatment of Noah in 1536, Luther portrays drunken Noah as a man who is not only the head of the family but the supreme magistrate and bishop of the postdiluvian world.[10] As in his earlier exegesis, Luther rejects the suggestion of Lyra that Noah was not at fault because he did not know the effect wine would have on him. If one is determined to find an excuse for Noah's lapse (as Luther is not), it would be far better to argue that Noah was an old man who was exhausted by overwork and who was therefore intoxicated by a draught of wine that would not have bothered him, had he been fresher and less tired. But even this "better" excuse is swept aside by Luther, who also drops his earlier double standard for Noah as a guiltless patriarch. Noah has committed an act for which he is morally culpable. The tragic story of his drunkenness is included in the Pentateuch to show that "even the greatest saints sometimes fall" and to provide comfort for the godly who learn through Noah to recognize their own weakness.

Luther is still fascinated with the figure of Ham, though he no longer portrays him as a tragically fallen saint (that role has been shifted to Noah). Nor is Ham's ridicule of his drunken father in any sense comparable to the laughter of children who make sport of a drunken peasant. Like Absalom, Ham is convinced in his heart that he could rule church, state, and household better than his father, whose actions have frequently not met with Ham's approval. Ham only needs an opportunity to demonstrate his superiority to the world and to expose the incompetence of his father. What better opportunity could there be than to stumble on drunken Noah lying naked in his tent! There at his feet lay irrefutable evidence that it was time for a change of leadership, time for a younger man to pick up the burdens which old age could no longer bear. He therefore declines to perform for his father the courtesy which anyone would perform for a drunken and naked stranger lying beside the road. Rather than cover his father's body, he rushes off to inform his brothers, savoring his father's disgrace as though it were good news.

> Thus Ham appeared wise and holy to himself, and in his own judgment he regarded many things that his father had done as evil or foolish. This points to a heart that despises not only its parent but also the commands of God. Therefore nothing is left for the wicked son except to wait for an opportunity he could use as evidence to bring his father's foolishness to public attention. Hence he does not laugh at his drunken father like a child, nor does he summon his brothers as for some laughable sight. He wants this to be conclusive evidence that God has forsaken this father and has accepted Ham.[11]

Shem and Japheth, however, have not driven from their hearts the reverence and affection which they owe Noah as their father, magistrate, and bishop. Although they see Noah's offense as clearly as Ham does, they overcome it. They recognize that God has let Noah fall in order to teach them not to despair when they, too, are overcome by a similar weakness. They know only too well that human nature is weak and undependable and that the sins of others grant no one a license to judge. The proper response to Noah's drunkenness is to extenuate and excuse it. And so the brothers perform the office Ham should have performed and cover Noah's naked body with a garment.

Awakening from his sleep, Noah is filled with the Holy Spirit and announces in prophetic majesty the shape of things to come. The wrath of the Holy Spirit against Ham is so severe that Noah is not allowed to call Ham by name but pronounces the curse on his grandson, Canaan. Noah repeats the curse three times to show how much God hates the sin of disrespect for parents. However, since the curse does not take effect immediately, Ham laughs at the prophecies of Noah just as he laughed at his drunkenness. If he took those prophecies seriously, he would cry for mercy. Instead, he leaves his father's home for Babylon, where in time he becomes involved in the construction of a tower that will reach from earth to heaven.

The prophecies of Noah cannot be understood with the senses but can only be grasped by faith and hope. In the short run, it is Ham who is blessed and Shem and Japheth who are forced to serve Ham. God delays his true blessing and curse in order to give the ungodly an opportunity to repent and the godly a time to learn the discipline of patience. Shem and Japheth cling to the promises of God by faith, while Ham builds a city and an empire.

The blessing on Shem is so great that Noah expresses it in the form of a prayer. Shem has been designated the heir of the Messianic promise in Genesis 3:15. However, Shem is not the eldest son. By right of primogeniture, the blessing ought to have been extended to Japheth. Luther appeals to a philological discussion to support his view that the "enlargement" of Japheth refers to the "persuasion" of Japheth not to begrudge his brother Shem the honor of bearing the Messianic promise. Japheth, too, will share in salvation through Shem. This prophecy was fulfilled through Paul, himself a son of Shem, who almost single-handedly taught the children of Japheth the fundamentals of the gospel.

IV

If we compare Luther's interpretation of the Noah story with the interpretation offered by modern scholarship, we find very little in the way of common interests. Luther accepts the story of Noah's drunkenness as it is offered to him in the book of Genesis. He is not interested in the historical setting and provenance of the story, either as originally told or as amended by later editors in the retelling. He even rejects the modest historical suggestion of Lyra that "Japheth" is a reference to the non-Jewish peoples who surrounded Jerusalem and who were admitted to the Temple and its worship.[12] Japheth stands for the Gentiles who will be grafted into Christ and who receive a promise of salvation through the believing Jews that is older than the promises to Moses and to David. When Luther professes principal interest in the historical sense, he is not using "history" or "historical" in the modern sense. He seems to mean by "history" something like the plain narrative, theologically understood and interpreted.

It may, therefore, not be surprising that it is precisely in their theological observations on the text that Luther and modern scholarship come closest together. Both Luther and von Rad, for example, believe that Genesis 9 raises the theological question whether God is able to do what he promises, though for Luther the question is raised by the curse of Canaan, while for von Rad it is posed by the continued presence of Gentiles in the promised land. Still, both believe that the story of the drunkenness of Noah makes the point that the Gentiles have a role to play in the plan of God and that the author (or editor) of Genesis wanted very much to establish the ancient origins of that role.

If there is a greater distance between Luther and modern scholarship than one might have anticipated, there is less distance between Luther and Denis than one might have been led to expect. In 1519 and again in 1523, Luther repeats the traditional allegorical identification of Noah with Christ, a theme celebrated in art as well as in exegesis. Even though Luther does not retain that exegesis in his later interpretation of the drunkenness of Noah, he does make place for a restricted use of allegory and tropology.[13] On the traditional tropological interpretation of the drunkenness of Noah, Luther does an exegetical flipflop. While he rejects in 1523–24 the tropological identification of Noah with a bishop who has committed a serious fault, he incorporates exactly that point in his 1536 lectures on the "historical" sense.

Perhaps this incorporation of what had been a tropological point for Denis into the historical sense for Luther signifies one of the more important differences between Denis and Luther. The difference is not that Denis slights the literal sense of the text. Indeed, at certain points Denis seems more interested in ancient Jews and Gentiles than Luther does, though neither is inclined to treat the Bible as nothing more than an ancient historical source. Both regard the Bible as holy scripture. Therefore, they believe that the book of Genesis was written as an instrument of divine self-revelation. Its purpose is to call the human race to redemption rather than to inform it about the migrations of ancient Semitic tribes. Luther's new hermeneutical problem is that he must now find in the literal sense many of the valid theological and ethical points which older exegesis reserved for the allegorical and tropological senses.[14] The question is whether the literal sense can bear that weight and still be regarded as the literal sense. At any event, Luther's move away from the older medieval division of letter and spirit did not dispense with the problems which that hermeneutic was constructed to resolve;[15] it only recast them in a new form.

Still, the principal difference between Luther and Denis or, for that matter, Luther and modern scholarship lies less in their understanding of the meaning of the literal sense than in Luther's use of narrative imagination. Luther takes the bare narrative of the characters and incidents in Genesis and fills it out with imaginative detail. He examines Ham's motives, which at best are only hinted at in the text of

Genesis 9, and gives the story fresh life by making it psychologically understandable. Ham is not cursed for finding his father but for his unnatural ambition. Ham represents all the sons who ever conspired to push their fathers out of the path of their own advancement. He is the pure opportunist who capitalizes on the misfortunes and follies of others, who is so convinced of the rightness of his own cause that he has no natural feeling or compassion for others. The drunkenness of Noah is the opportunity, the moment for which Ham has been waiting all his life. The deep background for this story is not the presence of non-Jews in Palestine but the inner moral and psychological life of Noah's son, Ham.

Luther, of course, does not go as far as André Maurois or Gamaliel Bradford, who used the techniques of the novelist to recreate as a three-dimensional human event a moment of history at which they were not personally present and for which the remaining evidence is maddeningly incomplete. And yet, it does seem to me that Luther is attempting something of the kind. He is not interpreting the story only by his theological and historical observations on the text, which have the effect of breaking down the text into its component parts. He moderates his analysis with sections of imaginative synthesis. He interprets the story of Noah by expanding it, by putting it in a new context undreamed of by its original author or subsequent editors, by showing the events (otherwise so mysterious) as the logical projection of the character of the main protagonists. He does this by drawing on his rich imagination and his sensitive observation of human nature at work. Even if one differs with his interpretations, one must admit that he succeeds in re-creating characters whom we all recognize.

The book of Genesis, after all, is full of stories. Stories are connected narratives which pass through a succession of events to an anticipated resolution in time. It is this connected passage through time which gives the narrative life and movement and, provided that the narrative is a credible reflection of the character of its protagonists, the power to convince. By offering to his students his imaginative insights into the character of Noah and Ham, by moving from event to event to resolution, Luther is attempting to provide an exegesis which is appropriate to the nature of the material that he is interpreting. He is not lecturing on Paul's epistles, which are short on narrative and long on doctrine. He is dealing with characters who pass through time to the ends to which their own decisions and the secret purposes of God carry them.

The usual appeals to the Reformation principle of *sola scriptura* do not cover what Luther is doing in his interpretation of Noah, not even when they are qualified by a consideration of the role of tradition in the biblical interpretation of the older Luther. The vehicle which Luther uses to convey theological truth is the composition of theological fiction. Indeed, it is Luther's narrative imagination, his intuitive response to the Bible as a work of art, which sets off his interpretation of Noah and gives it such power over his readers, even readers who disagree with his interpretations or find them outmoded. Luther grasps his readers not only at the level of their discursive reason but also at the level of their imaginative participation in their common humanity. For the purpose of interpreting the biblical narratives, that may be the level that counts most.

X

LUTHER AND THE TWO KINGDOMS

> Fortunately there have always been judges who have never heard of this doctrine of justification by faith and who have therefore been prompted by a sensitive conscience to apply the law as justly as possible.[1]

This sentence summarizes very nicely what Reinhold Niebuhr finds objectionable in Luther's political theory. Luther's doctrine of justification by faith alone, with its stress on the total sinfulness of the believer before God and with its disregard for the subtle shadings of less and more which belong to any conception of human justice, heightens "the religious tension to the point where it breaks the moral tension, from which all decent action flows."[2] If all the options for action which confront human beings are tainted by sin, and if "divine forgiveness will hallow and sanctify what is really unholy," then uneasy human consciences are, in Niebuhr's opinion, prematurely comforted.[3] The notion that Christians are simultaneously wholly sinners and wholly just before God undercuts the quest for that more tolerable justice which human societies can achieve in history, even under the conditions of finitude and selfishness. Niebuhr fears that Luther's theology leads to the conclusion that since all human achievements are sinful, the moral distinctions between them are finally unimportant.

That is not to say that Niebuhr wants to deny that all structures of justice are tainted by human sin. Niebuhr agrees with Luther that human virtues as well as human vices must be the objects of divine pity and compasssion. Ironic evil is the evil which men and women bring about because of their virtues and in spite of their good intentions. The absolute justice of the kingdom of God is not a simple human possibility, and history is littered with the failed Utopian dreams of men and women who thought that it was. But relative justice—the form which love of neighbor takes outside direct, personal relationships—is achievable to an indeterminately greater degree. Christians are freed by grace for all forms of love, including that imperfect and incomplete form of love called justice. Niebuhr is very much concerned that the freedom which Luther commends is a freedom which dispenses with human justice.[4]

Luther's "defeatist"[5] or even "quietist"[6] social ethic (the terms are Niebuhr's) is reinforced by his doctrine of the two kingdoms, a dualistic social philosophy which splits the spiritual life of Christians from their life as citizens. As Niebuhr understands it, the two-kingdoms doctrine allows Luther to distinguish a private morality which is identifiably Christian from a cynical public morality which is not.[7] Indeed, the Peasants' War presents Niebuhr with the unedifying spectacle of Luther urging the peasants to live in accordance with the private morality of the Sermon on the Mount, while sanctioning the custodians of public morality, the secular princes, to reestablish order over anarchy by any violent means at their disposal.

Niebuhr's criticisms of Luther are so telling, and the eloquence with which he states them so persuasive, that one hesitates to come to Luther's defense, especially when many of Luther's political judgments were blameworthy, even in the eyes of his contemporaries. Luther's stance in the Peasants' War, his sanction of the bigamy of Philip of Hesse, and his appeal to the German princes to become "emergency bishops" represent decisions that found relatively few defenders in Luther's day and would find even fewer in our own.

On the other hand, as Harry Haile has pointed out in his marvelous biography of the old Luther, there is a Machiavellian side to Luther that is frequently overlooked by historians who are preoccupied with the events of 1525. It was Luther, after all, who attacked the judicial murder of Hans Schönitz by Cardinal Albrecht of Mainz[8] and defended the rights of the exiled Wolf Hornung, whose wife and family had been stolen by the notorious womanizer, Joachim I of Brandenburg.[9] It was Luther who dressed like an Italian Renaissance dandy in order to disguise his age when he shared breakfast with the papal ambassador, Pietro Paulo Vergerio.[10] Even such an experienced ecclesiastical politician as Martin Bucer could be reduced to putty when Luther turned on the full force of his personality.[11] A man who numbered among his personal enemies half a dozen heads of state—including Henry VIII of England, Duke George of Saxony, and Duke Henry of Brunswick—and who could wring concessions out of the most seasoned diplomat cannot, I think, be dismissed as a political "quietist" or "defeatist".

I want, however, in this essay to bracket out the question of Luther's political judgments, which is a story in itself, and focus exclusively on Luther's political theory. I think we can only judge Luther's political theory correctly if we judge it by the goals which Luther hoped to achieve and not by the goals which are appropriate to a modern democratic state. Luther's goals, I think, are clear. Luther wanted to establish (1) that Christian ethics, though not all human morality, is grounded in justification by faith alone; (2) that all Christians have a civic and social responsibility to discharge and that some Christians may discharge that duty by assuming public office in the state; (3) that the Sermon on the Mount is not merely a monastic ethic or an ethic for the future Kingdom of God but applies to the life of every Christian, even if its moral demands are not applicable to every decision which Christians must make as public persons; (4) that the state has been established by God to achieve divinely willed ends that the Church cannot and should not attempt to achieve; and (5) that God, who rules the Church through the gospel, rules this disordered world through the instruments available to the state—namely, human reason, wisdom, natural law, and the application of violent coercion.

It is important to remember that Luther is not a political philosopher.[12] One searches his writings in vain for a hint of the contract theory of government or for the first, faltering articulation of the theory of natural rights. Luther does not agree with Aristotle that the state and social order are natural to human beings or that human beings are incapable of achieving their full potential outside the state. The state has been established by God as a response to human sin and in order to contain human wickedness. Luther makes no provision for tyrannicide or revolution, preferring oppression to anarchy, while meekly giving ground to neither.

Niebuhr's charge that Luther "does not define consistent criteria for the achievement of relative justice," while partly true, is beside the point.[13] Luther does not define the criteria of relative justice because he believes that he has no obligation to define them. He regards himself as a preacher and not as a statesman. The criteria of relative justice will be defined by the prince in accordance with the principles of natural law. Of course, far more important for the prince and his advisors than a mere knowledge of the principles of natural law, is "judgment," insight into those principles as they bear on the practical decisions of statecraft. Luther speaks of this "judgment" in his exposition of Psalm 101 (1534) as though it were a natural charism granted to the *Wunderleute,* the miracle workers who administer the well-run state.[14] That does not mean that preachers have nothing to say to the prince, especially when the prince exceeds his authority and meddles in theological matters which are not his responsibility. It does mean that the state, even the state run by a non-Christian, has its own independent integrity and authority.

I

At the heart of Luther's ethical theory is a distinction between two kingdoms (*Zwei-Reiche-Lehre*) and two governments (*Zwei-Regimente-Lehre*).[15] The two kingdoms refer primarily to the two overlapping spheres of Christian existence, the life of the Christian before God and the life of the Christian in society. The two governments refer to the two ways in which God governs the world. God governs the Church through the gospel, a government from which all modes of coercion are excluded; and he governs the world through law and coercion, a government which cannot achieve its ends through the persuasive preaching of love. These two spheres of existence and two modes of government must be distinguished, even though they intersect in every Christian believer.

The relationship to God is, of course, fundamental. The soul, the inner nature of the human person, needs righteousness and freedom.[16] This righteousness cannot be conferred by eating certain foods or abstaining from others. There are no ritual or liturgical acts which will grant spiritual freedom or take it away once it has been obtained. Neither hunger nor thirst nor poor health nor imprisonment nor external misfortunes of any kind can damage the soul or destroy a wholesome and right relationship to God.

Righteousness and freedom are conferred on the soul by the Word of God.[17] The Word of God which confers this proper relationship on the sinner is the good news of Jesus Christ.[18] Luther draws a distinction between two kinds of words in order to make clear what the Bible means when it speaks of the Word of God. There is, of course the *Heissel-Wort,* the Call-Word, the word which people use when they apply names to things which already exist. The biblical story of Adam in the garden is a fine example of this. He names all the biblical creatures. He does not create them; he only sorts them out and gives them labels.

But there is a second kind of word, the *Thettel-Wort* or Deed-Word, which not only names but effects what it signifies. Adams looks around him and says, "There is a cow and an owl and a horse and a mosquito." But God looks around him and says, "Let there be light," and there is light.

God's Word, according to Luther, is a Deed-Word. It creates new possibilities where no possibilities existed before. The Word of God is a Word which enriches the poor, releases the captives, gives sight to the blind, and sets at liberty those who are oppressed. The Word which the Church proclaims is a Deed-Word. It is a Word which meets men and women at the point of their greatest need and sets them free.

A Church which has become modest about the proclamation of the gospel is not a Church which has become more relevant to the human situation, but less so.

Preeminently for Luther it is Jesus Christ who is the Deed-Word of God. It is he and no one else—certainly no decretal or indulgence—who has been anointed to set at liberty those who are oppressed. The Church has been commissioned not to occupy itself with Aristotle but to witness to him. Therefore, it is a terrible catastrophe, far worse than any natural disaster, when the Church experiences a famine of the hearing of the Word of God.[19] Christ has no other ministry than the ministry of the Word. All apostles, bishops, and priests are called to that same ministry.

> I refrain from saying anything about the utterly stupid and incompetent persons whom bishops and abbots nowadays promote everywhere to the pulpit. We really cannot say that they are called and sent, even if we wanted to, because in this case incompetent and unworthy men are given the call. This is the work of God's wrath, for it is he who withdraws his word from us on account of our sins and he increases the number of vacuous talkers and verbose babblers.[20]

The appropriate response to the Word of God is faith, not works.[21] While works have a role to play in the relationship to the neighbor, the relationship to God calls for a response of faith alone. Faith is not a natural human capacity. All men and women are alienated from God. They have placed their ultimate trust in something which is not God. God must break them down in their self-trust, in their false worship of what is not ultimate, in order to teach them trust in the gospel. Only faith in the gospel can restore health and freedom to the soul and overcome the alienation from God which is the universal predicament of mankind.

Scripture, therefore, has two parts, corresponding to the double work which God must do in order to teach faith. There are the commandments and the promises.[22] The commandments show men and women what they ought to do, but cannot give them the power to do it. When people examine themselves in light of the commandments or law of God, they discover that they are sinful and helpless and are reduced to humility by this discovery. God breaks the self-righteous down through the law in order to teach them what it means to trust in his promises. God does his strange work of wrath through the law in order to do his proper work of restoring life through the gospel.

The promises of God give sinners as a free gift all that the law commands but was powerless to effect.[23] The only response appropriate to a promise is trust. If a king promises a robber, to use an illustration which Luther employs in his early lectures on the Psalms, that he will give him ten thousand dollars on the sole condition that the robber appear at a certain place on a certain day and claim it, then it is clear that the robber, if he wishes the reward, must appear at the designated place and time. He does not receive the gift because he merits it.[24] Indeed, he is a robber and deserves punishment. The gift is given because of the king's promise irrespective of merit or demerit. All one can do with a promise is accept it or turn it down.

God promises righteousness and freedom to sinners. That promise contradicts ordinary human expectation. Sinners ought to receive punishment rather than pardon, incarceration rather than freedom. But by the double work of his law and gospel, God teaches sinners to close their eyes to ordinary human expectations and the conclusions of common sense and to open their ears to the promise which offers life and freedom. Faith comes by hearing and hearing by the Word of God. God always acts in a way which is contrary to ordinary human expectation. He vindicates his wisdom in ways that sensible people regard as foolish.

> The believer thus makes God truthful and himself a liar. For he disbelieves his own mind as something false in order to believe the word of God as the truth, even through it goes utterly against all that he thinks in his own mind.[25] Hence, we must do nothing else but listen to the word with all our mind and all our strength, simply keeping our eyes closed and directing all our prudence only to it. And whether it enjoins somethings foolish or bad, something large or small, we must do it, judging what we do in terms of the word and not the word in terms of what we do.[26]

Luther uses three analogies to demonstrate the way in which God communicates righteousness and freedom to the soul by means of faith. The first analogy is natural. A heated iron glows because of the union of fire with it.[27] So, too, the Word, like fire, communicates its properties to the soul. A soul united to the Word has all that God has promised to give and does not need to rely on good works in order to gain justification.

The second analogy is drawn from personal relations and was developed by Luther in his early commentary of the Psalms. God justifies the sinner when the sinner justifies God.[28] Sinners justify God when they ascribe to him the honor that is due him; that is, when they regard him as truthful in his promises. Faith in God's promises is the act by which sinners ascribe truthfulness, wisdom, and fidelity to God. When sinners consider God truthful in his promises, God considers them righteous because of their faith. "Those who honor me," says I Samuel 2:30 of

God, "I will honor." Paul has reference to the same principle when he argues that Abraham's faith was reckoned to him for righteousness.

The final analogy is drawn from the marriage relationship and rests on a distinction made in Roman law between property, which implies ownership, and possession, which implies right of usage. In marriage, two people who have their own property in the eyes of the law enter into possession and use of the property of their partner. The same phenomenon holds true in justification.[29] The Christians' property is their sin; Christ's property is his righteousness. When Christians are united to Christ by the wedding ring of faith, Christ's property—that is, his righteousness—becomes their possession. At the same time, their property—that is, their sin—becomes the possession of Christ. In one decisive act, Christ takes it over and takes it away. But the benefits of the relationship are inseparable from the relationship itself. There is no exchange of properties without faith.

II

While Christians are justified by faith alone apart from any reliance, however slight, on their own good works, their faith expresses itself toward their fellow human beings in spontaneous works of love. The first realm of Christian existence, the relationship to God, is, of course, primary and antecedent; the second, the relationship to society, remains secondary and consequent. But while Luther assigns good works to a secondary place, he does not slight them. Living faith towards God issues in moral activity directed toward the neighbor. These works are not reluctantly extracted from the Christian by the forceps of the law, but spontaneously overflow in unstinting measure.[30]

Luther uses three analogies to try to explain what he means when he affirms that good works do not make a good man, but a good man does good works. The first analogy is based on the creation story in Genesis.[31] Adam was not made righteous by tilling and planting the garden of Eden, since he was righteous already. But because he was a good and righteous man, he worked in the garden in order to please God and express his love and gratitude.

A bishop is not made a bishop by performing episcopal activities, such as confirming children or dedicating churches.[32] If an actor performed these actions in a play, or if a prankster did them during a festival, they would have no validity at all. The confirmation of children does not make a person into a bishop, but because a person is a bishop by valid ordination, he can confirm children and ordain priests. The office precedes the function as being precedes doing.

Similarly, a tree bears apples only if it is an apple tree.[33] One can take a botany book to the orchard and read it to the apple trees, telling them what kind of blossoms to bear and when, and what varieties of apples to yield and how, but it will make no difference to the trees. If the trees are apple trees, they will bear apples apart from our exposition of their duties and even, perhaps, in spite of it. We may congratulate ourselves when the harvest comes on our eloquent exposition of the law in the orchard, but our exhortations were irrelevant. The nature of the tree dictates the kind and quantity of fruit.

If we should try the following spring to demonstrate our rhetorical skills by reading information about cherry trees to the apple orchard, we shall see how pointless our exposition of duties has become. No exhortation, however moving, will ever persuade an apple tree to yield cherries. Similarly, no exposition of the law will ever bring good works out of an evil person. What we are precedes what we do, and what we do proceeds from what we are. Works are good if they are done in faith, that is, if the agent fulfils the first commandment by faith alone. Works do not make Christians; faith does. But faith is lively and active and is endlessly busy in good works.

Luther does not reject good works except as the basis for justification. On the contrary, Luther wishes to stress as much as possible the importance of good works in the life of faith.[34] Christ does not free men and women from good works but from false opinions concerning them. Christians are called to live in Christ by faith alone and in the neighbor by works of love. They do not perform good works in order to be justified but because they already are.

Since Christians do not need works for their own justification, they should give their works to their neighbor who does in fact desperately need them.[35] The pattern for this selfless renunciation of works and the unself-regarding bestowal of them on the neighbor is Christ. Christ put on our human condition; he clothed himself in our humanity, laying aside all his priviliges and prerogatives. He was rich by nature, but for our sake he became poor.[36]

Christians, too, are rich—by faith if not by nature. All that belongs to Christ belongs to the Christian because of the spiritual marriage which has occurred in faith. Christians are called, like Christ, to empty themselves, to put on their neighbor as Christ put on their humanity, and to give themselves as a Christ to the neighbor just as Christ offered himself freely and without reservation to them.[37] Luther summarizes the moral goal of the Christian life with these radical words: "I will do nothing in this life except what I see is necessary, profitable and salutary to my neighbor, since through faith I have an abundance of all good things in Christ."[38]

Luther describes the love of God as a *verlorene Liebe,* a lost love which pours itself out shamelessly on the just and unjust alike. That is the kind of love which the Christian, who is justified by faith alone, freely offers to the neighbor. It is a love which takes no account of gratitude or ingratitude, worthiness or unworthiness, friends or enemies, praise or blame, gain or loss. It does not attempt to place other people under obligation to itself or engage in any kind of subtle spiritual blackmail. It considers no good work wasted, even when it is despised by the recipient. Indeed, it is only as Christians pour out their lives in the world that their fellowship and bond with each other is renewed. Philippians 2 contains the pattern for the renewal of the Church. It is as the rich become poor for the sake of the poor that God makes both rich.

Luther has by this time tied the two kingdoms tightly together. Good works are the spontaneous response of Christians to the need of the neighbor, as perceived by those who, following the mind of Christ, have put on their neighbor's situation. Good works spring from true and genuine love. Love is true and genuine where there is faith and confidence in the promises of God. Confidence in God is created by the proclamation of the Word of God, the good news of what God has done for the salvation of men and women in Jesus Christ. It is the Word of God which is the essential foundation and precondition for an authentic moral life.

The Christian life, as Luther sees it, is a life of freedom. All Christians are free from sin because they have received the righteousness of Christ through faith. Christians are similarly free from anxiety that suffering or physical calamities of any kind will be able to destroy their relationship to God. They are free to bear the Word of God's judgment and grace to other Christians and to intercede on their behalf in prayer. They are free to identify with the situation of their neighbor and to pour out works of love on persons in need, because they know that they cannot hoard these works in order to justify their lives in the presence of God. They are free from the law, whether the law of God or any prescription of merely human origin which attempts to bind the Word of God. Indeed, they are free to chuckle with the angels over the rich joke that the commandments of God, no less than the promises of the gospel, can only be fulfilled by faith. Christians are free in faith and therefore free to serve. Luther grounds Christian ethics in faith alone. He is not apologetic about that fact. There is simply no place else where they can be grounded.

Luther warns against people who cannot get their minds around Christian freedom and who think that Christians can never be liberated until they drive out from the Church all ceremonies, traditions, and human laws.[39] Some Protestants feel that they can only be authentic Christians if they reject all ceremonies associated with the Roman Catholic Church, even though, by asserting their freedom in this respect, they harm the faith of simpler people. Luther advocates a middle ground.[40] Christians are, of course, free to adopt habits or styles of life which are not forbidden in Scripture. But the overriding rule is love. Christians must have respect for the conscience of the weak, even while not letting the conscience of the weak become a law for the Church.

God makes men and women free in order that they may serve their neighbor. Where the gospel is preached, communities of love are created. Such communities of love, in which authentic human freedom is realized, cannot be formed or sustained in any other way. Luther sums up his teaching in these words:

> We conclude, therefore, that a Christian lives not in himself but in Christ and in his neighbor. Otherwise he is not a Christian. He lives in Christ through faith, in his neighbor through love. By faith he is caught up beyond himself into God. By love he descends beneath himself into his neighbor. Yet he always remains in God and in his love. . . . [41]

III

It is precisely at this point that Luther's discussion of the two kingdoms or realms of Christian existence raises serious political questions. If the Christian is free from all law, including in a certain sense the law of God, what obligation does the Christian have to obey the laws of the state, particularly any laws that seem to tamper with or inhibit that freedom? What loyalty does the Christian owe the state? Does the fact that Christians are made free to love mean that they are prohibited from serving in any public office which might entail exacting the sometimes bloody penalties which the law requires? In order to answer these questions, we have to shift our attention from Luther's doctrine of the two kingdoms to his doctrine of the two governments.

The Church, which should be a community of freedom and love, is ruled by God through the gospel.[42] There is no place in this community for coercion of any kind. Indeed, the medieval Catholic Church with its decretals and canons and with its coercive judicial system has destroyed the freedom which the gospel creates and so has forfeited its claim to be the true Church of Christ. There is no place in the Church for canon law or canon lawyers, even granting that the Church must have some form of polity in order to organize its life in the world.[43] No

particular Church polity is prescribed in the Bible, though any polity
should provide for the ordered administration of the sacraments and
the proclamation of the Word. Luther is perfectly willing to have a
pope, provided that the pope is evangelical (that is, that he teaches
justification by faith alone). What cannot be tolerated is any cumber-
some system of ecclesiastical regulations which inhibits Christian freedom or any ecclesiastical bureaucracy which claims to be essential to
the spiritual life of the people of God.

Unfortunately, the great masses of baptized Germans are not true
Christians. The world is a place where wickedness thrives. Therefore,
in order to preserve the lives and property of law-abiding citizens and
to defend them against the unwarranted and unjustified aggression of
their neighbors, God has ordained a second government, the government of the state.[44] This government, no less than the government of
the Church, is God's government. He has established it, and in its
continuous proper functioning his rule and reign are at stake. Unlike
the Church, however, the state rules through law, reason, human wisdom, and coercion. The magistrate may use the sword to enforce the
law, not because violence is better than love but because human wickedness can be contained in no other way.[45] Were it not for the fact of
human sin, there would be no need for political order.

May Christians serve the state as public officials? Luther gives an
unqualified yes to this question. That yes has, I think, two parts. First
of all, Christians may serve the state because it is God who has established political order and who contains human wickedness by means of
it. To serve the state is to serve God's second goverment. God calls
Christians to that service as surely as he calls Christians to the ministry
of Word and sacrament or to other secular vocations. The restraint of
wickedness is God's work, and Christians may do it with a good
conscience.[46]

Luther finds a second sanction for life as a public official in his
interpretation of the Sermon on the Mount. The Sermon on the Mount
is not an ethic for the future kingdom of God. It provides an ethic
which is applicable to the life of the Christian in the world. No Christian may seek justice for any wrong which is done against his or her
own private person. Nonviolence and the renunciation of any form of
vengeance lie at the heart of Christian ethics. But so does neighbor
love and identification with the weak and powerless. Christians must
allow personal wrongs to pass unavenged, but they cannot allow injus-
tices perpetrated against the poor and weak of this world to remain
unopposed. The state is a vehicle for the expression of responsibility
for the neighbor and for the pursuit of justice for the oppressed.
Therefore, Christians may assume public office not only because the

state is God's government (a powerful reason in and of itself) but also because it provides a legitimate outlet for that love of neighbor which is awakened in everyone who is justified by faith alone.[47]

> He serves the State as he performs all other works of love, which he himself does not need. He visits the sick, not that he may be made well; feeds no one because he himself needs food: so he also serves the State not because he needs it, but because others need it,—that they may be protected and that the wicked may not become worse. He loses nothing by this, and such service in no way harms him, and yet it is of great profit to the world. If he did not do it, he would be acting not as a Christian but contrary even to love. . . . [48]

By the same token, Christians obey the state in all matters that do not conflict with their obligations toward God, not only because the state has been ordained by God to preserve order in the society to which they belong but also because of the Sermon on the Mount. Christians live by a higher law than the laws that govern the state. Nevertheless, they submit to the laws of the state out of love and concern for the well-being of their neighbors.[49]

Luther does not believe that any particular form of state polity has been ordained by God, though he personally favors monarchy.[50] Monarchy is certainly preferable to the democratic rule of Mr. Omnes, who is unable to set a stable and consistent course for the state. While Luther thinks (at least on Tuesdays, Thursdays, and Saturdays) that Christians make better magistrates than non-Christians because they recognize a judge higher than themselves, he does not believe that magistrates must be Christian in order for the state to function properly.[51] God governs the state through natural law and human wisdom. Luther is not interested in theocratic government, which finds the law code of the state in the Bible and insists on the rule of the elect. Unlike his great contemporary, Martin Bucer, Luther is a religious reformer who defends the legitimate rights of the secular state, even while he understands such states as instruments of divine government.[52]

Luther's opposition to the role of law and canon lawyers in the Church carries over in a curious way to his view of the state. While natural law and human reason provide the guidance which the prince needs to govern wisely and well, the prince must beware of governing the state from law books or of paying too much attention to the advice of lawyers.[53] Justice frequently contradicts written regulations. Luther is therefore very interested in the idea of *epieikeia,* the principle of equity which suspends rules in order to obtain the justice which the rules were originally written to preserve.[54] Princes need, as I indicated earlier, "judgment", an insight into justice which cuts through the regulations and positive laws of the state and renders prudent and necessary decisions. Luther has more confidence in one enlightened prince than in battalions of lawyers.

That does not mean that princes can burn Luther's translations of the New Testament with impunity, steal another man's wife, attempt to define Christian doctrine, murder advisors who have fallen out of favor, or suspend the principles of due process. Preachers have a responsibility to preach to princes—especially inconvenient messages they do not want to hear—and all Christians have the right to resist unlawful commands passively. But Christians cannot become revolutionaries. They cannot overthrow God's second government, even when it has fallen into the hands of tyrants. In such cases, they can only witness, pray, and suffer.

IV

A historian reading Luther's discussion of the two kingdoms for the first time might be tempted to remark that it all sounds more like pastoral advice than like political philosophy. And, of course, pastoral advice is exactly what it is. By linking the two kingdoms tightly together, Luther is advising Christians on the nature and character of Christian existence. Only incidentally is he interested in advising statesmen on the discharge of their public office. His motivation throughout is, it seems to me, primarily religious.

It is the tight linkage in Luther's theology between the two kingdoms that Niebuhr does not seem to see. For Luther, the vertical relationship to God and the horizontal relationship to the neighbor are so inseparably joined in the act of faith that one is unthinkable without the other. In principle, if not always in practice, there is no place in Luther's conception of the gospel for that variety of evangelical Christianity—all too common in America—which cultivates individual piety but is utterly unable to identify with the weak, the poor, and the oppressed, with whom Christ is identified. On the other hand, Luther has no patience with a social gospel which lacks religious depth and which substitutes ethical analysis and moral obligation for inner liberation and joy. Freedom in faith and freedom to love can only be isolated from each other with disastrous results for both.

At the same time, Luther's distinction between the two kingdoms is a real distinction. Because the distinction is real, Luther rejects the theocratic state and the notion that Christian magistrates are essential to the proper functioning of the political order. Reason and natural law provide adequate norms for a well-run state. There is no need for a divine political polity revealed in the Bible, a polity which can only be interpreted correctly by true believers. The state has its own dignity and authority. It is an independent sphere of God's government, and Christians may serve it with a good conscience.

That is why Niebuhr's criticism seems to miss the real weaknesses in Luther's social and political views. Justification by faith alone does not undercut the search for social justice. On the contrary, it furthers that search by making the protection of the weak and innocent through the power of the state a function of that love of neighbor which faith spontaneously awakens. Luther's acute sense of the pervasiveness of human sin does not plunge him into political quietism. On the contrary, he seems at times to be boundlessly optimistic about the power of faith to unleash human moral energies and about the competence of human reason and wisdom to govern the monarchical state. Indeed, if anything, Luther seems rather too optimistic about the triumph of grace and reason over human self-interest and the perennial recalcitrance of human sin. The political illusions that he cherishes seem to be the illusions generated by an ebullient theological cheerfulness rather than by a paralyzing theological pessimism. After all, as the later Calvinist tradition was only too happy to point out, saints (even Lutheran saints) need moral instruction and discipline, and princes (even extremely wise Saxon princes) need constitutional checks and balances. There are never enough *Wunderleute*—either of grace or of nature—to go around.

XI

LUTHER AND
FORMATION IN FAITH

The first generation of Protestant leaders faced a task that was in large measure unprecedented. It was their task, not merely to form a younger generation in the Christian faith, but to re-form an older generation that had in their estimation been formed in the Christian faith incorrectly. The proponents of the new measures agreed that children had to be taught the Creed and the Lord's Prayer as their parents and grandparents had been taught before them. But parents and grandparents also had new lessons to learn. They had to be taught to take communion in both kinds (like the heretical Hussites in Bohemia) and to do it at least four times annually (the de facto medieval norm was once a year). Furthermore, they were encouraged to abandon the recitation of the Ave Maria (a prayer particularly comforting to women in childbirth) and to leave their private devotions to the privacy of their own home. Church was no longer regarded as the appropriate place for the audible recitation of private prayers, especially prayers for the dead. Audible private prayer should not be offered during the celebration of the new ritual and certainly not while the pastor was consecrating the bread and wine. The list of holidays was shortened, and the colorful processions of the consecrated host on Corpus Christi and the relics of the saints on appropriate feast days were cancelled. Masses for the dead were abruptly stopped, and the endowments that supported them were put to other uses. The celebration of the eucharist, much less frequent under the new regulations than in the old Church, was no longer a rite to be observed by the laity, who remained prayerful spectators, but a communal meal in which all the laity were expected to participate. In short, the early years of the Protestant Reformation marked a very disorienting time for a great number of people who had always thought of themselves as good Christians and had difficulty understanding the new order that put their old status in doubt.

Ignatius Loyola, Luther's contemporary and one of the principal founders of the Society of Jesus, conceived of his task as the conversion of Christendom to Christianity. What Ignatius hoped to assist was the process by which ordinary parishioners, many of whom were only half-committed to the Church and the Christian faith, could become better followers of Jesus Christ. Although Luther did not think of his task as the conversion of Christendom to Christianity, he could have affirmed it as an appropriate goal. What set him off from Ignatius was his radical rethinking of the principles according to which such a conversion could and should occur. Before Christendom could become truly Christian, it had to abandon old habits of thinking and acting and embrace a new vision of what being an authentic Christian implied. In Luther's view the late medieval Church suffered, not so much from a failure to implement its own traditional principles (as Ignatius thought), but from a misguided and uncritical commitment to the wrong principles.

I

The Lutheran program for the re-formation of Christendom began with an appeal to Christian antiquity.[1] There was, of course, nothing in the sixteenth century less revolutionary and more traditional than an appeal to the past. Sixteenth-century Christians, both Protestant and Catholic, shared a strong cultural assumption that what is older is better than what is new. That assumption applied not only to religion but to civic and cultural relations, art and architecture, law and custom, economic and agricultural practices—in short, to the whole range of activities and beliefs that gives human society its character. The modern notion that new things are generally better and ought, in a well-ordered society, to supplant what is older was, on the whole, an idea that had not yet found a home in sixteenth-century Europe. The cultural bias was in favor of what was sound, tested, ancient, and rooted in the collective experience of generations.[2]

An appeal to Christian antiquity had been a strong motif in reform movements throughout the Middle Ages. When the mendicant orders (the Franciscans, Dominicans, Carmelites, and Augustinians) were founded, their apologists could point to what they regarded as a more ancient form of the religious life than the cloister: namely, the circle of disciples around Jesus, who had abandoned their small properties in order to follow a leader who had nowhere to lay his head. The mendicants called such a life of poverty and itinerant preaching the *vita apostolica*. Who can forget the picture of Saint Francis of Assisi stripping himself of his possessions in order to marry the widow, Lady Poverty, and to take for his cloister the highways of the world? *Nudus nudum Christum sequens.*

When Christian humanists suggested that scholars return *ad fontes* to the oldest and best manuscripts of ancient Christian and pagan writings rather than rely, as earlier scholars had, on later translations or adaptations, they were stating as a philological principle a theme deeply embedded in Christian consciousness. The water of a stream is purest near its source. Like a mountain spring, Christian antiquity represents a purer form of Christianity than its contemporary manifestations. If this is true, then the cry of Christian reformers must always be "back to the past," to the purer form of ancient Christianity that can serve as the norm and inspiration for the reform of Church and society in the present.

The Lutheran form of the appeal to the past rested on the conviction that many so-called ancient traditions of the Catholic church were not ancient at all but represented innovations introduced into Catholic life and thought at a later—often a much later—stage of the church's history. Like old English customs that cannot on closer inspection be traced back beyond the reign of Queen Victoria, the church promulgated as ancient, customs and ideas that could not be traced in unbroken succession to a period earlier than, say, the pontificate of Gregory VII or the codification of canon law by Gratian or the introduction of scholastic theology by Peter Lombard (to mention three possible turning points suggested by different Protestant authors).

When the bishop of Carpentras, Jacopo Cardinal Sadoleto, accused Calvin and the reformers of Geneva of introducing innovations and novelties into the communities they reformed, Calvin turned Sadoleto's argument on its head.[3] The Catholic claim to antiquity, argued Calvin, was a formal claim without material justification. The Catholic church was riddled with innovations introduced over centuries of inattention and theological laxity. By submitting themselves to Scripture and the writings of the ancient fathers, the Protestant communities were purging themselves of such unwanted innovations and returning to a more ancient and therefore purer form of ecclesiastical life and thought. Luther, who seems to have read and admired Calvin's letter, was in fundamental agreement with its argument.[4]

It may be important to point out that Luther and Calvin did not think the church had died. There were undoubtedly some scattered sectarians who hinted darkly at the demise of true Christianity in the Middle Ages, but such a notion was repudiated by the larger bodies of Lutheran and Reformed Christians. God had remained faithful to his promise not to forsake the Church. The gospel had been preached and heard by faithful souls from the time of the apostles until the present day, even in a church that in recent centuries had proven to be unreformed and resistant to change. If it was no longer obvious to the naked eye that the Church of Rome was still the body of Christ, one could nevertheless be assured that even this church contained *vestigia ecclesiae,* traces of the true church.[5]

The goal of the reformers was not to supplant a dead or dying church with a new Christianity, as though God had written Ichabod over a moribund Christendom and repudiated his covenant. The goal of the reformers was a reformed catholic church, built upon the foundation of the prophets and apostles, purged of the medieval innovations that had distorted the gospel, subordinate to the authority of Scripture and the ancient Christian writers, and continuous with what was best in the old church. As they saw it, it was this evangelical church, this reformed and chastened church, that was the church catholic. It was the innovators in Rome who could no longer pretend to be genuinely catholic and whose claim to be the custodians of a greater and unbroken tradition was patently false. What the Protestants thought they offered was a genuine antiquity, one that stretched back to Peter and Paul and not merely to Lombard and Gratian.

The slogan later generations of Protestants used to describe this reform was the battle cry *sola scriptura,* Scripture alone![6] While it is true that the reformers were at first optimistic that it would be possible to teach and preach a theology that was wholly biblical, they rarely intended to exclude theological sources that were non-biblical. *Sola scriptura* generally meant *prima scriptura,* Scripture as the final source and norm by which all theological sources and arguments were to be judged, not Scripture as the sole source of theological wisdom.

For Melanchthon and Calvin, though less so for Luther, the Reformation was almost as much an argument over the writings of the early Christian fathers as it was an argument over the meaning of Scripture. Typical of the level of interest in early Christian authors, even among reformers who did not edit or translate ancient Christian writings, are Luther's marginal annotations on Augustine and Jerome, and Calvin's marginal annotations on a Latin edition of Chrysostom.[7] Even internal Protestant controversies, like the bitter dispute over the eucharist between John Calvin and the Lutheran theologian Tileman Hesshusen, often had a large patristic component in them.[8] In short, the Protestant appeal to antiquity included the early Christian writers as well as the Bible, even if the Protestant reformers felt that patristic teaching could not have the last word. What the fathers taught should always be judged in the light of the clear and unchangeable teaching of Scripture. Still, when all was said and done, Luther and Calvin were optimistic that the greater weight of patristic teaching supported their reform, or, at the very least, the greater weight of the teaching of the better fathers. For his part Luther was content to leave Origen and Jerome, whose exegesis he mistrusted, to Erasmus, if he could have Augustine.

II

The Reformation was not a wholesale attack on Christian tradition and Luther was not inclined to quarrel with every traditional doctrine taught by the late medieval Catholic Church. In the Smalcald Articles (1537) Luther confessed that his reform movement accepted the teaching of Nicaea on the Trinity and of Chalcedon on the two natures of Christ. Of course, he thought such teachings were true, not because they were promulgated by general councils of the Church and so inspired by the Holy Spirit (as some Catholic theologians might have argued), but because he believed the ancient councils had clarified the true meaning of Holy Scripture. Since Luther was convinced that the weight of sound exegesis supported the fathers, he was as energetic in his rejection of the radical antitrinitarianism of the Protestant left as any conservative Catholic apologist. Luther differed with Rome over a long series of important theological issues; among them, penance, preaching, justification by faith, the meaning of baptism and the mode of Christ's presence in the eucharist. But he acknowledged that there were important issues on which they did not disagree at all. The medieval Catholic Church did not need to be recalled, corrected, and reformed on every point of doctrine. In the merciful providence of God, the Catholic Church had provided on some issues a constant witness to the truth. On such issues the Lutheran laity needed to be formed in the Christian faith as it had traditionally been taught.

There were, of course, some issues on which no agreement was possible. For example, while Luther honored Mary as the mother of the Lord (the *theotokos* or *Dei parens*) and as an outstanding example of faith, he was unwilling to accord her any honor as an intercessor for the Church. She was not for him the sympathetic Queen of Heaven whose compassion softened the harsh judgments of her unsympathetic son. Accordingly, he dropped the Ave Maria from the prayers Lutheran laity were taught. Mary did not, of course, disappear from the Lutheran Bible, and Conrad Porta, pastor of Eisleben, exalted the biblical image of Mary as a model for young girls in his

Jungfrawenspiegel (1580).[9] But any hint that Mary should be regarded as intercessor or, even worse, coredemptrix was ruthlessly excised from Lutheran theology. No more prayers to Mary were authorized for women in childbirth, and no more catechetical instruction was offered in Marian devotion. A true Christian prays the Paternoster but not the Ave Maria.

Luther also broke with medieval asceticism and the ethic that exalted virginity over chaste sexual practice in marriage. Lutheran laity were no longer instructed that a faithful monogamous marriage was an inferior state for a Christian (more of a compromise to accommodate human weakness than an ideal to which Christians should aspire) or that monastic life and rigorous ascetic practices were pleasing to God. One can take as an example of the new antiascetic spirit the Lutheran reconsideration of the question of clerical marriage.[10]

Although priests in the Eastern Orthodox churches were permitted to marry prior to ordination and priests in Western Catholic churches had married in the earlier middle ages (in England until the Norman invasion), the ban on clerical marriage was total by the sixteenth century.[11] Unfortunately, many clerics (how many is unclear) found themselves unable or unwilling to live up to the lofty rhetoric of clerical celibacy. The archbishop of York, Thomas Cardinal Wolsey, had an illegitimate son, Thomas Wynter, whose existence he did not deny. Indeed, while his son was still a schoolboy, Wolsey made him Dean of Wells, Provost of Beverly, Archdeacon of York, Archdeacon of Richmond, Chancellor of Salisbury, Prebendary of Wells, York, Salisbury, Lincoln, and Southwell, and rector of Rudby in Yorkshire and of St. Matthew's, Ipswich.

In central Europe, clerics who found the celibate life too demanding were permitted to live in a sexual relationship with a housekeeper, contingent on the payment of an annual tax to the bishop.[12] Heinrich Bullinger, the Protestant reformer of Zurich, was the child of such an informal clerical family. Nevertheless, in spite of the fact that such arrangements were given a quasi-official sanction, the housekeeper was still regarded by the townspeople as the priest's whore. Canonically, the priest and his unofficial wife were living in a state of mortal sin. In a particularly poignant exchange of documents, Ulrich Zwingli, who had slept with a young woman in a former parish, petitioned his ordinary, Bishop Hugo von Hohenlandenberg of Constance, for permission to marry.[13] The application of Zwingli was, of course, denied, even though many knew Zwingli was already secretly married to a widow, Anna Reinhart.[14]

Protestants attempted to correct the problem of clerical celibacy by denying the theoretical foundation on which it stood. Luther and his followers attacked the celibate ethic with its distinction between commands and counsels and its preference for virginity over matrimony. They insisted that celibacy was a charism, a gift given to some but denied to others, and therefore could not be made a general law. They authorized clerical marriage and encouraged the integration of the pastor into normal family life. In place of saints who were models of sexual self-denial and asceticism, the Protestants substituted the minister's family as a model of the Christian home.

There were, of course, difficulties. Upstanding middle-class families were not always willing to marry their daughters to former priests and permit them to inherit the beds so lately occupied by the priest's whore.[15] It was not uncommon for former priests and nuns to marry each other and for the children of such clerical families to intermarry as well. But the trend was, in any case, clear. The attack on the theoretical foundations of clerical celibacy allowed the Protestants to replace an off-again, on-again institution of clerical celibacy with a married order of ministers, whose marriage and family life were integral to their ministry. The Protestants ended what they regarded as the embarrassment of the erratic enforcement of clerical celibacy by abolishing the institution. The institution could no longer be maintained when the theological foundation that supported it was repudiated.

III

However, the relation of the Lutheran movement to the medieval Catholic Church was not merely a relationship of affirmation and denial. In many instances the Lutherans retained traditional practices and institutions but radically revised the underlying ideology. The pastoral office of preaching provides a sterling example of a traditional activity with a non-traditional intellectual foundation. What gave new force to the reconceived office of preaching for the Lutherans was Luther's new theology of the Word of God.

Luther's Reformation was not just a movement dedicated to the study of the Bible; it was a movement dedicated to the spoken Word of God. It was not the Word of God written but the Word of God preached that formed the center of a renewed Christianity as early Protestants conceived it. When Heinrich Bullinger of Zurich wrote in the Second Helvetic Confession of 1566, "The preaching of the Word of God is the Word of God," he was speaking for a broad ecumenical front of early Protestantism, Lutheran as well as Reformed.[16] The words were Bullinger's, but the underlying theology was in substantial harmony with Luther's. Christianity is not, as both Thomas Müntzer and Martin Luther asserted (though on different occasions and in different senses), a scribal religion, and the self-revelation of God is speech before it is text.

Luther's emphasis on the spoken word had, of course, some parallels in late medieval thought. Recent scholarship has shown how important was the spoken word in the rhetorical traditions of Italian civic humanism. The humanists understood that human beings are more than calculating reason, as scholastic theology seemed to them to assume. To be human is to have a will and emotions as well as an intellect. Many humanists, therefore, looked upon the spoken word as an instrument to move human beings, to inspire them to action, and thereby to shape public policy.[17]

The mendicant orders, of course, had always laid heavy emphasis on the spoken word in preaching and teaching. "Preach the Word" was as much a Dominican or Augustinian slogan as it was Lutheran or Reformed. While one ought not to make too much of the relationship of early Protestantism to the mendicant orders, a good number of early converts to Protestantism came from mendicant orders, including Robert Barnes, O.E.S.A, Martin Bucer, O.P., Bernardino Ochino, O.F.M.Cap., John Bale, O.Carm., and Conrad Pellikan, O.F.M.

Equally important as a late medieval parallel was the renewed emphasis on preaching in the free imperial cities. The laity in several late medieval cities in the Holy Roman Empire had laid aside funds to pay for a *Leutpriester,* a priest whose principal function was to preach on Sundays and feast days, leaving the ordinary liturgical services to the parochial clergy. The most famous *Leutpriester* in the sixteenth century was the preacher in Strasbourg, John Geiler of Kaysersberg, who died before the Reformation began.[18] The most famous *Leutpriester* to identify himself with the Reformation was the Swiss preacher Ulrich Zwingli. Like the humanists, these publicly funded preachers laid emphasis on the spoken word; like the mendicants, they laid emphasis on the spoken Word of God.

And yet there were differences. However important the preached Word was to the mendicants and the late medieval princes of the pulpit, it was still ancillary to the sacraments. In the nature of the case, the sermon could be nothing more than an invitation to baptism, penance, and eucharist, where alone saving grace was dispensed. It was not the preacher in the pulpit, however eloquent, but the priest at the altar, however inarticulate, who stood at the center of medieval worship.[19] It was not by the foolishness of preaching but by the Word joined to the elements of bread and wine and water that God saved the faithful of every generation. The sermon moves sinners to the sacraments but is not itself a sacrament.

For Luther there was one means of grace, the voice of the living God. This voice once spoke by the prophets and apostles and now speaks again in the proclamation of the Church. Preaching became for him a third sacrament, coordinate with baptism and the eucharist and largely replacing the sacrament of penance. The power of the keys, the power to bind and loose from sin, was exercised through the preaching of the gospel. No sacramental power as such was thought by him to reside in ordination or in ecclesiastical offices. Office bearers were authorized by the Word they carried. They had no authority that was not the authority of the gospel they preached. It was through the preached Word that God justifies sinners and pardons sin. Even the sacraments of baptism and eucharist were redefined as the visible Word of God.

In the face of this radical theology of the Word of God, the old hierarchical distinctions of *potestas ordinis* and *potestas iurisdictionis* simply collapsed for Luther. There is no order higher than the order of the preacher of the Word of God; there is no jurisdiction greater than the jurisdiction exercised by the pastor of a local congregation. Apostolic succession is succession in apostolic teaching. Christians in the present are linked to the first generation of apostles, not by an unbroken succession of bishops, but by an unbroken succession of preachers of apostolic doctrine. Lutheran ministers are not priests forever after the order of Melchizedek. That is a priesthood that belongs to Christ alone. Lutheran ministers belong to an *ordo praedicatorum,* an order of preachers that stretches from the patriarchs to the present. For them it is the pulpit, not the altar, that is the throne of God and the sermon, not the eucharist, that is the ladder that links heaven and earth.

While it would be a serious error to underestimate the role of the liturgy and of the redefined sacraments of baptism and the eucharist in the formation and re-formation of Lutheran faith and piety, it would be an even more serious error to underestimate the importance of the sermon. The Lutheran sermon was the principal instrument for the swift and effective reeducation of the laity; it augmented, supported, and reinforced the catechisms, pamphlets, and broadsides that poured from the evangelical presses. But the reconceived sermon was not regarded as mere instruction in faith and morals, however edifying. The sermon was never reducible to the sum of its teaching. What Luther had in mind was not a homily in the old sense but preaching as the *viva vox Dei.* Preachers have nothing to offer but human speech. However, through their voices, all too quickly stilled, God speaks an eternal Word that will never pass away. The sermon, as Luther understood it, was a *Thettel-Wort,* or Deed-Word, rather than a *Heißel-Wort,* or Naming Word. It does not merely call existing things by their correct names, like Adam naming all the beasts in Paradise; it calls new things into existence, like God on the first day of creation. Preaching of the Word of God is never mere speech, any more than baptism is mere water or the eucharist mere bread and wine. In preaching as in the eucharist the operative word is *est* and not *significat.* The preacher does not merely point to a God who is distant; God is not distant but present in, with, and under the material elements of human language.

The pastor who absolves sinners from their sins in private confession is only exercising the preaching office in an individual rather than a corporate setting.[20] In both settings it is the promise of God, whether proclaimed from the pulpit or whispered in conversation, that binds and looses from sin. Of course, the pastor and only the pastor may exercise the power of the keys in public through preaching, just as the pastor and only the pastor may preside at the eucharist. However, any baptized Christian may exercise the power of the keys in private conversation, since all Christians have the right and obligation to bear God's Word of judgment and grace to each other. Luther is unwilling to make private confession a clerical monopoly, though he regards the confession of one's sins to a pastor a good and wholesome practice so long as it is not turned into a binding law (a position with which Calvin agrees).

IV

All three strategies—the reaffirmation, the denial, and the reinterpretation of earlier Christian tradition—are evident in Luther's catechetical writings. In 1529, after a visitation to parish churches that convinced Luther of the depth of the educational crisis that faced him, he wrote a short catechism for use in both the home and local churches. Although catechetical instruction was nothing new in the history of the Church, the development of printing technology in the late fifteenth century made it possible for catechetical manuals to be widely distributed to clergy and laity at a comparatively small cost. Over the forty years following the first printing of Luther's catechism, more than 100,000 copies were printed and sold. The catechism was eventually included in the *Book of Concord* as one of the fundamental confessional documents of the Lutheran churches.[21]

However, Luther's catechism was not the first to be written and published in German. The first German catechism, called *A Fruitful*

Mirror or Small Handbook for Christians, was written in 1470 and
revised in 1480 by the Observant Franciscan friar, Dietrich Kolde of
Münster.²² Kolde had written the book less as a manual of instruction
for the young than as a handbook for mature Christians who were
preparing themselves for the annual confession of their sins that must
precede their obligatory participation in Easter communion. It was a
mirror, as the title suggests, into which Catholics could look in order
to aid them in an honest and informed self-examination.

To be sure, laity were urged to confess and commune more frequently than once a year (four times a year was the widely admired
but seldom achieved ideal), though twice-yearly communion (at, say,
the beginning and end of Lent) met the minimal standards of late
medieval Europeans for "frequent" communion. Weekly lay communion, the norm of pre-Vatican II Catholicism, was unheard of in
the fifteenth century and would have required special permission from
a bishop before it would have been allowed, as the career of the
perennial English pilgrim, Margery Kempe, clearly demonstrates.

Kolde's catechism, like Luther's, was a popular manual. It went
through nineteen editions in the fifteenth century and at least twenty-
eight thereafter. It was also translated into several early modern ver-
nacular languages. It may very well have been the single most popular catechism in late medieval Europe; it was certainly the most
popular in German-speaking lands.

There are, of course, a number of formal similarities between the
two catechisms. Both offer text and explanations of the Creed, the
Our Father, and the Ten Commandments. But Kolde offers a great
deal more: the Ave Maria together with other Marian prayers and
devotions (though without the ascription to her of the title of
theotokos and omitting the request for her intercession in the hour
of death), five ecclesiastical rules, seven deadly sins, nine alien sins,
six sins against the Holy Spirit, several open and mute sins, the great
sins of the tongue, six conditions for forgiveness, seven signs of the
state of grace, lessons on how to confess and hear mass, seven works
of corporal mercy, seven works of spiritual mercy, seven gifts of the
Holy Spirit, seven points for daily reflection, nine conditions that lead
to sin, three things that astonish the devil, five signs of a good Christian, reflections on how women should carry infants during pregnancy
and how parents should rear their children as Christians, and some
concluding considerations of the art of dying well. Although Luther
affirms with Kolde the Creed, the Ten Commandments, and the Our
Father, he omits the Ave Maria, discusses baptism, and adds a small
collection of prayers and duties. His difference from Kolde can easily
be illustrated by considering what he has to say about confession. At

first glance it may appear that Luther has kept in unaltered form the medieval sacrament of penance, commending the private confession of sins to one's pastor. On closer inspection, however, it becomes apparent that the old sacrament has not escaped significant alteration by Luther, since it rests for him on a new ideological foundation. Luther distinguishes two kinds of confession in the Small Catechism and three kinds in the Large Catechism. The two kinds, repeated in both catechisms, are secret confession to God and private confession to a pastor. The third kind, mentioned only in the Large Catechism, is confession to another Christian brother or sister. The absolutely fundamental and indispensable confession each Christian must make is to God alone. In such a confession Christians lament their particular sins and ask for a renewal of grace, as they do in general when they pray the Lord's Prayer. Confession in private to another Christian or to a pastor is not required, since Christians cannot be governed by any law in this matter and must use such confession voluntarily. At the same time Luther deplores what he regards as the abuse of Christian freedom by some slovenly Christians (his actual term for them is "pigs") who never take advantage of the opportunity to confess their sins in private to their pastor.

Luther's formula for confession to a pastor or fellow Christian is fairly simple. It is not necessary to list all the sins one has committed since one's last confession or to indicate the number of times and describe the circumstances of each offense. It is enough to confess generally that one is a sinner in constant need of God's grace and to provide a few specific examples of the kinds of sins one has in fact committed, especially the sins that trouble one's conscience. The obligation to recount one's sins in detail and to omit nothing turns what ought to be a joyous moment of absolution and reconciliation into a legal obligation that terrifies sinners.

The best preparation Christians can make for confession is to reflect on the Ten Commandments and to reexamine the conduct of their lives in the light of each precept. If after such a careful review one is still unaware of any particular sin that should be confessed (a state of affairs that Luther regarded as highly unlikely), it will still be sufficient for penitent Christians to offer only a general confession of their sins. After all, what matters in confession is not the length or detail of the confession itself but the word of absolution offered to faith. Better that sinners make only a general confession than that they concoct sins they did not commit in order to satisfy their confessor. The confessor, after asking whether the penitent believes the promise of forgiveness in the gospel, should declare the penitent forgiven in the name of the Holy Trinity. The absolution will be effective, not because the pastor shares a common priesthood with Christ, but because the Word of God binds and looses from sin.

Unlike Kolde, Luther did not regard his catechism primarily as a manual for the penitent to prepare them for participation in the modified rite of confession he still retained. The catechism was rather a handbook of mere Christianity. It retained and continued the medieval tradition of the instruction of the laity in the Creed, the Lord's Prayer, and the Ten Commandments, adding a section not found in Kolde on baptism and the Lord's Supper and omitting the Ave Maria. The Small Catechism represented what Luther regarded as the proper and essential knowledge for every Christian, stripped down to its bare fundamentals and elucidated clearly and concisely. In his *A Simple Way to Pray: for Master Peter the Barber* (1535), Luther demonstrated how such a basic catechetical knowledge could provide the foundation for a rich life of prayer, not only for Peter Beskendorf the barber but also for Martin Luther himself.[23] In matters catechetical, all Christians remain beginners. As one cannot grow beyond Christ, so one cannot grow beyond the catechism. In the Christian life progress is made by clinging ever more tightly to the fundamentals.

Kolde, who died in 1515 in Cologne, never read Luther's catechism or had any reason to anticipate the religious and theological upheaval that would divide Catholic Europe in the decade after his death. But the teaching of his catechism on confession moves in a fundamentally different direction from Luther's. For example, Kolde was not satisfied to restrict the preparation of sinners prior to confession to a review of their lives in the light of the Ten Commandments, important as the Ten Commandments undoubtedly were. Kolde wanted penitents to consider as well the seven deadly sins, the six sins against the Holy Spirit, the sins of the tongue, the five ecclesiastical rules, and the nine alien sins. The need for detail derives from the nature of the sacrament itself. Penitents must list in detail the mortal sins they have committed since their last confession, because what is not confessed cannot be forgiven. Christians who want their sins pardoned must make a thorough and probing confession of their faults. While God will not hold sinners accountable to confess sins they have genuinely forgotten, he will not forgive sins they have concealed. Detailed confession is not optional, as Luther later suggested, but obligatory for all Christians at least once a year.

It is unthinkable to Kolde and his contemporaries that confession to a layperson could result in the pardon of one's mortal sins. Only persons who share in the priesthood of Christ through the sacrament of ordination have the authority to absolve from sin. The power to absolve is conferred by ordination and not by baptism. Even the authorizing force of the gospel is not enough to sanction lay confession, if ordination by a bishop in apostolic succession is missing. A good, or effective, confession is priestly, detailed, and obligatory.

Kolde warns his readers how important it is to find a competent confessor. Not every priest was authorized by his bishop to hear confession of every sin. There were what the late medieval Church called "reserved sins," whose absolution lay beyond the competence of the ordinary parish priest. Adultery, for example, was reserved to the bishop to absolve by himself or by such deputies as he chose to authorize. Certain crimes against Church property, such as arson, could only be forgiven by the pope or his deputies. Kolde was therefore desperately concerned that penitents understand these limitations on the authority of the parochial clergy and make a good confession to a competent priest. Mortal sins absolved by a priest who had no authority over them remain unforgiven on the heads of the sinners who committed them.

While there is a good deal in Kolde's catechism with which Luther could agree and still other matters about which he would have been indifferent, it is nevertheless clear that the change of theological vision necessitated a change of penitential practice. Lutheran laity were still encouraged as they had always been when they were members of the old Church to confess their sins to their pastor three or four times a year, if possible. They were no longer required to detail their sins in confession or to worry whether their confessor was competent to absolve them. Moreover, they were permitted to confess their sins to each other and to offer to each other the Word of the gospel that binds and looses from sins. The new theology required the institution of new practices appropriate to it and the writing of new catechisms to explain both theology and practice to a laity formed in the old habits of thought and action. The Lutheran clergy affirmed the creed, denied the Ave Maria, and reinterpreted the keys. They taught the laity to do the same thing.

At the same time it is important to remember that Luther was reluctant to specify the ideal shape of the Christian life in too great detail. He could even oppose the *imitatio Christi* piety of the later Middle Ages, noting sarcastically that a successful imitation would require Christians to be born of a virgin, have brown eyes, and walk on water. Such an imitation piety is the antithesis of what Luther regards as a proper theology of vocation; namely, his conviction that Christians are called to serve God in their own space and time and not in the space and time of the apostles. He was also passionately opposed to any attempt to turn the Bible into a hagiography, a Hebraic *Lives of the Saints* that offers perfect models to the aspiring perfectible. An afternoon spent reading and contemplating the dysfunctional families in Genesis and Judges should put an end forever to the elevation of the all-too-human characters of the Bible into the company of the morally unflawed. Luther confessed that he drew far more comfort from the failings of the biblical characters than from their virtues. If God could save heroic sinners like Jacob and Samson and David, he could certainly save less energetic sinners like Martin Luther.[24]

Perhaps even more important for understanding Luther's reluctance to specify the form of the Christian life too narrowly is his conviction that the essential form of the Christian life is freedom. The old Church had prescribed so many things so narrowly by canons, rules, regulations, and anathemas that it had succeeded in turning the freedom of the gospel into a law. Christ is not Moses, and the gospel is not a book of rules. There is no single pattern of true Christianity any more than there is a single pattern of human existence. Christians have been liberated through faith in Christ to live in love. Such freedom is not created by books of rules, and books of rules cannot nurture and sustain it. True Christians trust Christ for salvation rather than their fidelity in keeping fasts, going on pilgrimage, offering the corporal acts of mercy, or observing the days of holy obligation. Their good works are the spontaneous overflow of their lively confidence in God. Luther celebrated the diversity of the life of faith and resisted the efforts of canonists, old and new, to narrow and restrict what in his view God had created free and unbounded. Keeping a fast or breaking it may equally well be acts of Christian devotion. What matters is the faith from which the deed is done.

V

Things do not always work out exactly as planned. The reeducation of Latin Christendom in a Christian faith and practice shaped by the theology of Luther was more difficult to achieve than early Lutherans anticipated. To begin with, there were other voices raised in the Protestant camp that dissented from Luther, sometimes over minor matters like the celebration of a feast, sometimes over serious issues like the celebration of the eucharist. Even dedicated Lutherans found themselves caught in fierce struggles among themselves between Philippists and Gnesio-Lutherans over the meaning of Luther's theological heritage.

Moreover, Catholic theologians did not yield Scripture or the early Christian fathers to the Protestants without a fight. Thomas de Vio Cardinal Cajetan, who had made a name for himself as a philosopher and interpreter of Thomas Aquinas, dropped his philosophical studies in order to write a series of biblical commentaries that would demonstrate to Protestants and Catholics alike that the literal sense of the Bible supports Catholic theology. Domingo de Soto at Salamanca and Ambrosius Catherinus Politus at Rome similarly attempted to show that Protestants had misread Paul.[25]

Nevertheless, in spite of all obstacles to the re-formation of Catholic laity into evangelical, the Protestants, both Lutheran and Reformed, made some measurable progress toward their goals. By mid-century a permanent, self-perpetuating Protestant culture had developed. The older ex-Catholic leadership of former priests, nuns, friars, and monks was slowly replaced by a new leadership that had never attended mass, much less said one, and by a laity that had never confessed its sins to a priest, gone on pilgrimage, invoked patron saints, made a binding vow, or purchased an indulgence. Riddagshausen, Wienhausen, and Gandersheim were no longer cloisters to them but schools or evangelical communities for women. By the time the century was over, the Protestants had not only transformed formerly Catholic universities like Rostock and Leipzig into centers of Protestant intellectual life but had founded new universities like Helmstedt and Giessen that had no memory of a Catholic past.

While Protestants continued to write anti-Catholic polemics, their treatises lacked the passion and sense of betrayal of the polemics written by the first generation. Protestants were permanent outsiders with their own fixed institutions, parishes, confessions, catechisms, and settled sense of identity. They harbored no illusions about reunion and felt no twinges of nostalgia for a church that had never been their home. Unlike their grandparents they cherished no hope for an evangelical reformation of the Catholic church and settled into a mode of permanent opposition.[26]

In all these respects, the third generation of Protestants differed from the first. The Reformation began as an argument among Catholic insiders; it continued as an argument between Catholics and former Catholics until well past the middle of the century. The transformation of a movement led by former Catholics into a movement led by traditional Protestants took two generations to effect. Luther, Zwingli, Calvin, Hubmaier, Hooper, and Melanchthon were not Protestants in the way Voetius, Ames, Turrettini, Perkins, Wollebius, and Spener were. Indeed, the extent of the difference between them may prove in the end to be the best measurement of the success of their reform program.[27]

XII

LUTHER AND THE ASCENT OF JACOB'S LADDER

On the west front of Bath Abbey are carved two stone ladders stretching from heaven to earth on which twelve angels are climbing, six on each ladder. A tourist who sees the west front of the abbey for the first time is told that the carvings represent the dream of Oliver King, Bishop of Bath and Wells under Henry VII and his former chief secretary. The bishop had a nocturnal vision of angels climbing ladders to heaven. As he stood before the ladders in amazement, he heard voices saying that an olive should establish the crown and that the king should restore the church. He took the reference to olives and kings to be an allusion to his own name and concluded that he, Oliver King, should support the Tudor monarchy and rebuild the ruined abbey at Bath.[1]

There is, however, in the bishop's dream about politics and architecture more than a hint of something familiar, of a dream even more famous and ancient than the dream that inspired the restoration of Bath Abbey. The biblical setting and inspiration for Oliver King's dream of high intrigue and ecclesiastical ambition is Genesis 28, the story of Jacob's dream as Jacob camped by night at Bethel on his lonely journey from Beersheba to Haran. Like Bishop King, Jacob dreamed of a ladder stretching from earth to heaven, a ladder along which angels ascended and descended in a never-ending procession. While Jacob did not restore a ruined shrine (or support the political aspirations of that Labanesque monarch Henry VII), he did erect a stone monument at the place where he had slept as a memorial of his astonishing and wholly unanticipated vision.

If we leave the front of Bath Abbey and consult the biblical commentaries in the abbey library, we will discover that there are even more connections between Jacob's dream and the dream of Bishop King than we first thought. The commentaries on Genesis 28—the

Ordinary Gloss and the Postils of Hugh of St. Cher, Nicholas of Lyra, and Denis the Carthusian—all establish the relationship between Jacob's dream and sacred space. Jacob, so the medieval commentators thought, had slept by accident on the site of the future temple, a site that would therefore become famous both as the cultic center of ancient Israel and as the focal point for the activity of Jesus.

In other words, Jacob rested in the shadow of the altar and under the sign of the cross. Wherever the cross and altar are found, there is the place where Jacob slept, the place where heaven and earth are joined by an angelic ladder. Denis the Carthusian, Bishop King's older contemporary, put the matter this way:

> The place where Jacob rested is not only the universal Church but also any particular church, no, rather, even a material basilica dedicated to the Lord, which, because of the presence of the highest majesty, because of the presence of the sacraments of Christ, because of the celebration of the divine office, because of the devoted gathering and holy prayer of the faithful, is nothing other than the "house of God," "the gate of heaven." For in it sins are taken away through sacramental confession and the virtues infused through which the gates of the heavenly kingdom are opened.[2]

Bishop King's dream took him back to Bethel, took him to the sacred space where a stone monument to God should be erected, took him like Jacob to the "house of God" and the "gate of heaven," where the sacramental presence of Christ could be adored and celebrated. Bath Abbey is the place where Jacob rested. I mention this dream because of what seems to me a shining and obvious fact all too frequently overlooked or undervalued; namely, that the biblical stories, images, and themes that pervade the culture of late medieval and Reformation Europe have their own history in that culture.

The story of Jacob's dream has had a particularly rich history of interpretation in Western Christendom. Anders Nygren in his classic study, *Agape and Eros,* identified three principal strands in the dogmatic traditions of medieval Christianity that relied on the story of Jacob's dream for their inspiration and at least partial justification. According to Nygren, medieval theologians identified Jacob's ladder with (1) the ladder of grace and merit; (2) the analogical ladder of speculation; and (3) the anagogical ladder of mysticism.[3]

The first ladder—the ladder of grace and merit—was by far the most common. It was the ladder by which every Christian ascended from a state of sin to the beatific vision of God. The analogical ladder of speculation, on the other hand, was reserved for a smaller group of Christian intellectuals, who were able to use the material and sensible elements of this world as a ladder to enable them to rise to the contemplation of the immaterial and invisible realities of the spiritual world. The third ladder, the anagogical ladder of mysticism, was open in principle to every Christian, though in actual fact relatively few Christians attempted the ascent to the more rarefied heights of spiritual ecstasy.

Nygren argued that all three of these interpretations of Jacob's ladder were rejected by Martin Luther because they rested on a faulty conception of Christian love. In Nygren's view the difficulty for Luther lay in the fact that medieval conceptions of love merged the ancient Greek understanding of love as *eros,* which desires an object because that object has value in itself, with the biblical understanding of love as *agape,* which confers value on the otherwise valueless objects of its affections. Medieval theologians believed that the soul must have fellowship with God on God's level as that soul is purified and drawn upward by its attraction to God, even if the ascent to God is based on the *agape* or prior self-giving love of God. Luther believed that fellowship with God took place at the bottom of Jacob's ladder, with men and women who were still sinners, unpurified and incapable of ascent, and yet who were given value by the love with which they were loved. To use Nygren's sharp formulation, the medieval Church was concerned with "fellowship with God on God's own level, on the basis of holiness," while Luther was concerned with "fellowship with God on our level, on the basis of sin."[4]

It is undoubtedly the case that there are profound differences between medieval and Lutheran conceptions of justification and that the story of Jacob's ladder plays a role in this disagreement. But the medieval interpretation of Jacob's dream is considerably richer and Luther's relationship to that tradition considerably more complicated than Nygren suggests. In what follows I want to take a second look at the late medieval exegetical tradition surrounding Jacob's dream and at Luther's relationship to it in order to cast fresh light on the intellectual world of the early Reformation.

I

It may be useful to begin by summarizing the story of Jacob's dream as told in Genesis 28. With the help of his mother, Rebekah, Jacob defrauds his elder brother, Esau, of his inheritance and his father's blessing. Rebekah learns that Esau is plotting to kill Jacob and, fear-ing for the life of her younger son, persuades her husband, Isaac, to send Jacob to the distant home of his uncle Laban to find a bride among the family of his maternal cousins. Isaac agrees and sends Jacob on his way with a fresh blessing. Esau, observing what happens and hoping to regain favor with his father, takes a new bride from the family of his paternal cousins, daughters of his father's half-brother, Ishmael, though without giving up his Canaanite wives. Jacob meanwhile follows the road from Beersheba to Haran, avoiding the cities and sticking to the open country. At night he lies down in a field with stones for a pillow. In his dream he sees a ladder stretching from earth to heaven, with angels bustling up and down, engaged in heavenly business. The God of Abraham and Isaac stands above this ladder and addresses Jacob directly without any angelic intermediary. God renews the Abrahamic covenant with Jacob, promising him the land of Israel, innumerable descendents to fill it, and the continual presence of God himself throughout Jacob's earthly pilgrimage. Jacob awakens from his dream with a shudder of awe and amazement and with the knowledge that he has spent the night in an especially sacred place. He takes the stone he had used as a pillow and sets it up as a pillar. After anointing it with oil, he makes a vow that, if God would accompany him and protect him on his perilous journey, then he would regard the God of Abraham and Isaac as his God as well. He also vows to pay a tenth of what he earns as an offering to God. Jacob names the place where this dream occurred Bethel, or the "house of God," though it had formerly been known as Luz.

From the standpoint of the medieval commentators who analyzed this text, the story fairly bristles with problems. Is Jacob fleeing for his life, or is he simply obeying his parents? Esau, after all, for all his murderous intentions toward Jacob, has no plans to act against Jacob before their father's death. Why does Jacob sleep in the open field rather than in one of the villages along the way? Where is the field where Jacob sleeps, and why is it regarded as such holy space? Is it only because of Jacob's dream, or are there other reasons? How many stones did Jacob select for a pillow, since the story uses both the plural and singular forms for stone when it mentions Jacob's pillow? Does it matter how many stones Jacob selected? Who are the angels who ascend and descend Jacob's ladder, and what are they doing? What exactly is the status of Jacob's dream—or, indeed, of any dream—as a medium of divine self-revelation? Why does Jacob, who has received unconditional promises from God, talk about them conditionally, as though they were unreliable? Does Jacob, like Scrooge at the first appearance of Marley's ghost, not really believe what he has seen?

I want to examine these and other questions in the light of three standard medieval commentators whose works are widely read and quoted: Hugh of St. Cher, a thirteenth-century Dominican who taught at the University of Paris;[5] Nicholas of Lyra, a fourteenth-century Franciscan, often incorrectly thought to be a convert to Christianity from Judaism because of his knowledge of rabbinic literature;[6] and Denis the Carthusian, a fifteenth-century monastic reformer and ally of Nicholas of Cusa, whose commentaries were popular throughout the sixteenth century.[7] Rather than go through each commentary in turn, I want to reconstruct as briefly as possible a kind of composite interpretation of this passage, noting of course any important disagreements or points of controversy among these three commentators.

This is easier to do than one might think because of the nature of the biblical commentary as a genre of theological literature. A commentary tries to interpret a text written by someone else. The text that is being interpreted in its various logical and grammatical units sets the agenda for the interpreter and prescribes to a considerable extent the structure of the commentary itself. The commentary almost always concerns itself with philological, grammatical, and historical matters. While it contains dogmatic and polemical sections (sometimes quite lengthy dogmatic sections), it is not primarily a dogmatic or polemical treatise. Usually the commentator (at least in the period that concerns us here) tries to apply the text to the religious concerns of his readers. In any case the commentator invariably is conscious of, cites, and tries to correct other commentators. Indeed, it belongs to the art of commenting to read all the commentators who have gone before, or at least all the commentators one can find, and to incorporate their interpretations into one's own.

Hugh of St. Cher offers three levels of interpretation of Genesis 28, while Nicholas of Lyra and Denis the Carthusian offer only two. Hugh's three leves are: (1) the literal sense, which is the meaning of the text on its level as story or as straightforward exposition; (2) the allegorical or mystical sense, which is the deeper theological meaning not obvious in the text as letter; and (3) the tropological or moral sense, which is the significance of the text for Christian ethics and the moral life. Lyra offers only the literal and the moral senses and Denis only the literal and allegorical, though both include under the literal sense some of what Hugh labels as mystical interpretation.

It is important to bear in mind that Hugh, Lyra, and Denis do not mean by the literal sense of Scripture what a modern interpreter who approaches the text with the tools of historical criticism means. In modern historical-critical interpretations of the Bible, there is a split between the historical and the literal meaning of the text. Historical critics believe that the events described in the letter of Scripture cannot always be taken at face value but may refer to other events only hinted at in the biblical narrative.[8] The real story took place outside and back of the text and is sometimes very different from the story narrated in the text. For Hugh, Lyra, and Denis, the literal and historical sense of Genesis 28 is the story as it presents itself to the reader. Although they ask critical questions about the text, even historical-critical questions, their exegetical starting point is the canonical form of the text.

The literal sense of the text is the sense that most interests Lyra and Denis. While Hugh gives more attention to the allegorical or mystical sense, he too has pressing questions about the literal sense. The first cluster of issues that troubles them is geographical. Where did the dream occur? Jacob calls the place Bethel, though he later identifies it as Luz. On the basis of an argument that owes more to etymology than to a sound knowledge of geography, the commentators describe Luz as an open place where almond groves abound.[9] Following suggestions from Josephus, they conclude that Jacob did not dare to sleep in the villages on the way, both because the Canaanites were traditional enemies of his father, Isaac, and because Jacob was afraid that he might be corrupted by their wickedness.[10] The opinion that Bethel is Bethlehem, where Jesus was born, or Mount Moriah, where Isaac was offered as a sacrifice, are reported as possible interpretations but not taken very seriously.[11] Hugh, Lyra, and Denis are convinced that Bethel is the site of the future temple and lies therefore within the bounds of the Solomonic city of Jerusalem.[12] The medieval commentators regard Jacob as a prophet who announces that the place where he slept is sacred, not only because of his dream, but because he now knows that Bethel is the future cultic center of Israel, a place inextricably intertwined with the future passion and death of Jesus Christ.[13]

Denis provides the fullest psychological explanation of what occurs in Jacob's dream.[14] Jacob has an imaginary vision in his interior sense through sensible likenesses. This is the lowest level of prophetic ecstasy. When a prophet is cut off from the stimuli of his external senses as Jacob was cut off by sleep and when his imagination is illuminated by pictures and sensible images, then the prophet is given a vision of secrets that transcend human reason. Such a vision is not a hallucination because the prophet is also given an intellectual understanding of the sensible images implanted in his imagination.[15] In the case of Jacob these images, together with their meaning, were insinuated into his mind by an angel. Even though Jacob thought he saw

God in his dream, what he really saw was a sensible image of God, a much lower level of revelation than the intuitive vision of the divine essence granted to Paul or the intellectual knowledge of God through the intelligible species given to David. Still, even the lowest form of prophetic ecstasy is an unnerving experience and is rarely granted to someone who is wholly unprepared for it.

Jacob, of course, did not come to his dream wholly unprepared. Medieval theorists were aware that one of the most potent stimulants for the inducement of an ecstatic state of mind is the suffering brought on by persecution. While obedience to his parents was a virtue that also prepared Jacob for his vision, Genesis 28 is about both obedience and persecution.[16] Indeed, there are even manuscript variants that lead the reader to believe that Isaac, who was told nothing about Esau's vendetta by Rebekah, nevertheless knows about it.[17] Jacob comes to the open ground in Luz, persecuted, obedient, a man of prayer who chastises and disciplines his body. The proof of Jacob's ascetic practice is his selection of a stone for a pillow.[18]

Denis reports the citation by Lyra of unnamed Jewish commentators who believed that Jacob chose three stones for a pillow. During the night the three stones were fused into one as a sign that God wished Jacob to be united to him forever. Denis dismisses this interpretation with the wry comment that he finds it astonishing that such an extraordinary miracle is not mentioned in the text.[19] On the whole, Denis prefers the one stone theory.

Denis and Lyra identify the ladder in Jacob's dream as Christ.[20] The ladder stretches from earth to heaven because Christ assumed human nature in order to become mediator and savior. The ladder rests on earth to show Christ's solidarity with human beings; it stretches to heaven to show his consubstantiality with the Father. The rungs of the ladder are the generations of human ancestors from whom Christ descended. The angels ascend and descend this ladder to show that their ministry is subordinate to the ministry of Christ.

While Hugh agrees that one of the possible interpretations of Jacob's ladder is that it is Christ (particularly Christ in his kenosis or self-emptying), he prefers to regard this interpretation as mystical rather than literal.[21] Denis and Lyra retain it as literal, not only because they belong to a growing late medieval consensus that subsumes much of what had been regarded as allegorical or tropological under the literal sense, but also, and more importantly, because the identification of Jacob's ladder with Christ is the interpretation given to the text by Christ himself. When Jesus spoke of angels ascending and descending on the Son of Man (John 1:51), he removed the literal interpretation of Jacob's ladder from the realm of debate.

Although there may be, and are, other allegorical and moral senses of Genesis 28, the literal sense of the text for Denis and Lyra is determined by Christ himself.

It is the mystical and moral meanings of the text that set Hugh's imagination on fire. He identifies the ladder not only with Christ but also with the Bible, the cross, the sacrament of penance, and the cloistered life. The angels are not only the spirits who ascend to contemplate Christ and descend to serve him but also preachers, the four evangelists, the doctors, imitators of Christ, the penitent, and the monks.[22] Denis adds good priests, virtuous prelates, and contemplatives to the list of "angels."[23] All of this is offered in the spirit that one good interpretation need not exclude another. It is, furthermore, on this level of interpretation that what Nygren calls the ladder of grace and merit and the ladder of mysticism make their appearance. None of the commentators appear interested, however, in Nygren's analogical ladder of speculation.

The last cluster of problems has to do with Jacob's puzzling reaction to his dream. Although God has promised him an absolute renewal of the covenant with Abraham and Isaac, Jacob talks about the renewed covenant in conditional terms. If God will actually do what he promises, then Jacob in his turn will honor the God of his father and grandfather by paying tithes. Why, wonder the commentators, does Jacob greet his dream with such a pusillanimous response? Does he regard the covenant as uncertain? Does he think it will only take effect if he swears a vow and promises to pay tithes? Vows, after all, are works of supererogation.[24] They are not essential to salvation and therefore seem particularly inept and inappropriate in a context in which God renews his covenant of salvation.

Equally puzzling is the pillar of stone that Jacob erects. The later Mosaic law forbids the raising of stone monuments of this kind. Why does Jacob, who seems doubtful about the covenant to begin with and therefore swears an inept vow, compound his offense by raising an idolatrous shrine? Hugh suggests, following Augustine, that while it is true that the Mosaic law prohibits stone pillars, it does so in order to discourage idolatrous practices. Idolatry was the furthest thing from Jacob's mind. Jacob built his stone memorial for a figure and a sign of what had happened in this place, but not as an idol.[25]

Similarly, Jacob has no doubts about the reliability of the covenant offered to him in his dream any more than Christians have doubts about the reliability of the sacramental grace offered to them in the eucharist. But just as Christians examine their consciences before receiving the eucharist, so also Jacob wants to be certain that he interposes no obstacle to the working of grace. It is no contradiction in terms to say that eucharistic grace is present in the bread and wine apart from human faith or merit and to confess that that same grace may be ineffective because the recipients are still in a state of mortal sin. Jacob wants to be certain that he does not place any obstacles in the way of the promises of God. As a consequence, he vows that he will worship God through supererogatory acts of special devotion. Therefore the tithes he offers are tithes beyond the debt owed by natural or divine law.[26] In short, the medieval commentators are keen to make it clear that Jacob is a heroic figure. Any doubts Jacob entertains are doubts about himself and not about the covenant and promises of God.

II

It is not altogether certain what medieval commentaries Luther had before him as he interpreted Genesis 28. He mentions Lyra and the Ordinary Gloss by name, as well as Bernard and Bonaventure, but his allusions to a consensus on a disputed point among "nearly all commentators" suggests that he consulted other authors in addition to the commentators explicitly cited.[27] What is clear is that the medieval interpretations of this text advanced by Hugh, Lyra, and Denis are well known to him.

Luther rejects, for example, the medieval consensus that located Bethel on the site of the Solomonic temple.[28] Bethel was in Ephraim, three miles from Jerusalem. Therefore the notion that Bethel and Luz are earlier names of Jerusalem, as Lyra, Hugh and Denis argued, seems extremely doubtful to Luther. There is, of course, always the chance that place names have changed over time. However, it appears more likely to Luther that Jacob's Bethel is the place where Jeroboam later erected a shrine to the golden calf, a shrine that became in time a rival of the temple in Jerusalem as the cultic center of ancient Israel (1 Kings 12:28–29).

Luther appears to waver on the question of whether Jacob slept in a city or in the open field.[29] Early in his lecture he repeats the traditional suggestion that Jacob did not go into the city because he distrusted the people who lived there. Later he accepts the possibility that Jacob may have slept in the city or at least may have entered it in order to buy oil to anoint the stone he erected as a memorial of his dream.

What Luther wants to believe (although he admits he cannot prove it) is that Jacob slept on Calvary, where Christ was later crucified.[30] Luther identifies Calvary with Mount Moriah, where Seth preached and performed miracles and where Abraham offered Isaac as a sacrifice to God. It may even be the place where the tree of the knowledge of good and evil stood in Paradise. Thus Christ slept in a stone sepulcher at the place where Jacob slept on a stone pillow. If this interpretation is not true, Luther cheerfully concedes, it is at least harmless.

Unlike Denis, Luther is fascinated by the idea that Jacob took for a pillow three stones that were fused into one stone during the night. The three stones obviously represent the Trinity and the one stone, Jesus Christ. Although Lyra attributes the fundamental idea of the three stones fused into one to Jewish interpreters of the Bible, Luther suggests that the Jewish rabbis probably borrowed the idea from the Christian fathers and then proceeded to misinterpret it by rejecting its obviously trinitarian significance.[31]

Luther does not provide a psychological theory for dreams as a medium of divine revelation.[32] He accepts the notion that they can be instruments of divine self-revelation, but only insofar as they agree with the Word of God. As Luther sees it, Jacob had already been made a patriarch and an heir of the covenant of Abraham through Isaac's blessing.[33] The dream only repeats and confirms what Isaac has already conferred on Jacob through the word of his blessing.

While Luther does not provide a psychological theory for Jacob's dream, he does suggest the state of Jacob's mind on the eve of his vision.[34] This fascination with psychological motivation is characteristic of Luther's exposition of the Bible. Again and again in his commentary on Genesis, Luther fills in the text of the biblical narrative by providing insight into the state of mind and motivations of the characters in it.

Jacob, after all, had obeyed his parents and gone into voluntary exile. He had agreed to find a wife acceptable to his family. (At this point Luther introduces a long digression on marriage, attacking the celibate ethic of the medieval Church and the acceptance of clandestine betrothals and marriages in medieval theology and canon law.)[35] But Jacob's obedience to his parents had postponed the blessings promised to him in the word of his father, Isaac. Hope deferred makes the heart sick; worse, it makes God appear to be a liar.[36] To compound the uncertainties arising from the postponement of the promises of God, Jacob had a natural homesickness for his parents and a natural fear of the vengeance of his brother. Although Luther does not agree with the medieval tradition that holds that Jacob was prepared for his vision by his virtues (especially his filial piety and his asceticism), he does agree with the medieval tradition that believes that Jacob was prepared for his vision by his troubles.[37]

While Luther mentions Lyra's interpretation of Jacob's ladder as the genealogy of Christ and Gregory's interpretation of the "angels" as preachers and alludes benignly and vaguely to "many godly speculations" offered by other commentators, he himself offers three interpretations of the ladder: a literal interpretation, an allegorical interpretation, and a third interpretation that he leaves unlabeled.[38] The "historical, simple and literal" interpretation of Jacob's ladder is Christ incarnate in two natures.[39] Luther, like Denis and Lyra, cites John 1:51 as the warrant for this interpretation. The angels who ascend and descend are real angels, who marvel at the communication of attributes between the two natures of Christ and the condescension of a God who can be found in dust. While Luther goes on at greater length than Hugh, Lyra, or Denis about Christ as the ladder that links heaven and earth, he does not say anything very new.

The second, or allegorical, meaning of the ladder is the union of Christ and human beings in the community of the Church.[40] Luther is no supralapsarian in the manner of Duns Scotus or Andreas Osiander. The incarnation is for the purpose of redemption. Luther does not reject the ladder of grace and merit, as Nygren suggests. Rather he redefines it as a ladder of grace and good works.[41] The ascent to God is by grace alone. The Word justifies sinners absolutely by imputing to them the righteousness of Christ. Justified sinners, however, descend to their neighbors in good works performed in response to grace and out of gratitude for God's mercy. Works are not rejected, but they play no role in the ascent to God.

The third interpretation takes us back to the "spiritual interpretation" of Denis the Carthusian.[42] The ladder that links heaven and earth is not only the incarnate Word but also the preached Word. Wherever the gospel is preached and the sacraments rightly administered, there is the place where Jacob slept, there is Bethel, there is the "house of God" and the "gate of heaven." Luther is less inclined than Denis or Bishop Oliver King to link Jacob's ladder to a material building. Jacob's ladder is found where the gospel is preached and heard. That may take place in Bath Abbey as it may take place in any church. But the crucial thing is the preaching of the gospel and not the building that houses it. It is the exercise of the function that sanctifies the space.

Luther describes Jacob awaking from his dream with the language usually reserved for prophetic or mystical ecstasy. Jacob is so filled with joy that he is "altogether beside himself, thunderstruck, ecstatic."[43] This ecstatic rapture does not, however, prevent Jacob from having doubts about his dream and about the promises of God. Unlike the medieval commentators who are eager to preserve Jacob's status as a hero of the faith, Luther takes an almost perverse delight in uncovering Jacob's weakness. He does so because, as he confesses, the weaknesses of the saints console him more than their virtues.[44] Jacob can be an inspiration and consolation to the Church, not because he is free of defects, but because he has precisely the same defects all Christians have. The triumph of God is a triumph in the midst of human frailty.

Luther does not have the difficulty with Jacob's vow, however, that the medieval commentators have. Luther sees no connection between Jacob's vow and the guilt and remission of sins.[45] Jacob is not a monk. His vow and offering of tithes is a spontaneous response of thanksgiving to God for the grace first offered in Isaac's blessing and later confirmed in Jacob's dream. Indeed, Luther believes that Jacob intends out of gratitude to reopen a school of the prophets at Mount Moriah and to endow it with his tithes.[46] School endowments are an institution dear to Luther, and he launches a long excursus on their importance and on the importance of education generally.

III

When we place Luther's exegesis in the context of such standard medieval commentators as Hugh of St. Cher, Nicholas of Lyra, and Denis the Carthusian, we are led, I think, to draw several conclusions.

1. First of all, Luther does not appear to be repelled by what he calls the "godly speculations" of medieval commentators about Jacob's ladder. Nygren led us to expect that the very idea of ascent to God implicit in Jacob's dream was repugnant to Luther. Luther, however, not only tolerates the speculative exegesis of the standard commentators but even indulges in a number of godly speculations of his own. There is not a hint in his lecture that he disapproves of the idea that Christians ascend and descend Jacob's ladder. The problem is not with the metaphor of ascent and descent but with the notion that the ascent is helped along by the merit of good works. Good works belong to the descent and not to the ascent of the ladder. Christians ascend Jacob's ladder by the imputation of Christ's merits. Luther has taken what Nygren calls the ladder of grace and merit and the anagogical ladder of mysticism and reinterpreted them. To be sure, Luther has no place in his exegesis of Genesis 28 for Dionysius the Areopagite and his speculations. But, then, neither do Hugh, Lyra, or Denis.

2. What is more surprising is the extent to which medieval exegesis sets the agenda for Luther's interpretation of Jacob's dream. No one would be surprised to find remnants of traditional exegesis in Luther's early writings. In his first lectures on the Psalms, for exam-

ple, Luther talks about the allegorical, tropological, and anagogical meanings of Scripture and distinguishes the literal-historical sense from the literal-prophetic. What is astonishing, at least for historians who have been taught to identify Luther with a great sea change in biblical studies, is that Luther at the age of sixty is still talking about spiritual senses of Scripture and finding in the stories of Genesis the hidden prophetic meanings that the Enlightenment will later attempt to discredit.

Yet there is more to the medieval character of Luther's exegesis than the use of allegory or the appeal to a literal sense pregnant with deeper meanings. To a very great extent the questions Luther asks and answers are traditional questions. Why does Jacob flee? Where does Jacob sleep? Is Bethel inside the temple? Does Jacob enter any cities? How many stones does he choose for a pillow? Does he make a monastic vow?

Does he doubt his vision? Is Jacob a prophet? Why does he offer tithes? Luther not only repeats the traditional questions but demonstrates that he knows the traditional answers as well. Indeed, nowhere is Luther more traditional than when he identifies Jacob's ladder with Christ and insists that it is the saying of Jesus in John 1:51 that compels him to do so.

3. Luther's contribution to the interpretation of Jacob's dream lies more in what he adds to the reading of the text than in what he rejects from the antecedent tradition. What he adds, first of all, are his own characteristic theological insights. When he argues that the weaknesses of the saints provide more consolation for frail and tempted Christians than their alleged heroic virtues or when he insists that Jacob was created a patriarch and heir of Abraham's covenant by the word of Isaac's blessing rather than by his own dream, he is making original contributions to the debate over the meaning of Genesis 28 and pressing the understanding of the story in a new and untraditional direction. Even commentators who do not agree with Luther's doctrine of justification must take account of these new readings of the text, if only to quarrel with them.

Luther's second contribution is not so much theological as narrative. Luther attempts to get inside the minds of the characters in the biblical stories and to provide an imaginative reconstruction of their inner motives, anxieties, and hopes. He tries to make the stories understandable by providing access to the inner life of the characters in them. Jacob's troubled state of mind on the evening before his dream is a matter of considerable concern to Luther, who uses the rich resources of his narrative imagination to make the characters real by making them local.

Luther's exegesis, in other words, is not merely analytic in the manner of the exegesis of Hugh, Lyra, and Denis. He is not merely interested in the bird on the dissecting table; he wants to see and hear the bird on the wing. Analysis can clarify the text, but only synthesis can create the illusion of three-dimensionality that belongs to the text as a living narrative. The story of Jacob's dream is the story of a frail and sinful human being, frightened and homesick, exhausted by his hurried journey from Beersheba, overtaken by nightfall in the midst of an empty field, uncertain of the future toward which he is drawn by his own decisions and the providence of his father's God. Luther is not satisfied with his work as an interpreter until he has put us with Jacob in the middle of that lonely field, made Jacob's terror and homesickness our own, and laid our heads on Jacob's comfortless pillow. Therefore the final question Luther's exegesis poses is whether a two-dimensional representation of a three-dimensional reality (like a commentary on Jacob's dream at Bethel) ever properly interprets its subject unless it creates an illusion of three-dimensionality, unless it recreates by human art and imagination the contingent unfolding in time of the lives of its characters. That is a question for historians as well, though we are less certain how to answer it.

XIII

LUTHER AND CALVIN ON THE BANKS OF THE JABBOK

From 1536 to 1545 Martin Luther lectured on the book of Genesis, finishing his last lecture on November 17, 1545. His lectures were collected from student notes by some of his students and published in four volumes. The first volume appeared in 1544, while Luther was still lecturing on Genesis, and the last three after Luther's death in 1546. The final volume was published in 1552 and was devoted to the story of Joseph, the last of the patriarchs.[1]

Two years later, in 1554, Calvin published his own commentary on the book of Genesis and dedicated it in a foreword letter dated July 31 to the three sons of Johann Friedrich, the elector of Saxony, who had died in March.[2] Calvin had intended the dedication to be an ecumenical gesture toward the Lutherans and was therefore chagrined when the princes rejected the dedication on the recommendation of their theological advisors. The letter to Calvin from the Saxon Chancellor, Francis Burckhardt, indicated that the Lutheran theologians were convinced that Calvin taught an entirely unsatisfactory doctrine of the eucharist, a charge that Calvin tried to answer in his long controversy with Joachim Westphal and Tilemann Hesshusen (1554–1561).[3] Furthermore, they complained that Calvin had made insulting remarks about Luther in his commentary on Genesis, an accusation that Calvin flatly denied. Calvin admitted he was critical of some of Luther's exegesis but not in a spirit that denigrated Luther's contribution. Perhaps the Lutherans took offense at Calvin's dismissal of Luther's exegesis of Genesis 11:27 as "frivolous" or of 13:14 as "lacking solidity."

In his reply to Chancellor Burckhardt, Calvin regretted the rejection of his dedication by the Lutherans, though he noted wryly there was very little he could do about the unwanted dedication since the books in which it appeared had already been printed and placed in circulation.[4] While he confessed that he accepted as serenely as he could the

decision of the princes, he repudiated the grounds on which they had
made it. It seemed to Calvin that the Lutheran theologians in Saxony
brooked no deviation from Luther's exegesis, thereby demonstrating
what Calvin could only regard as a supine veneration for Luther's
words. If Luther were beyond criticism, there would be no need for
any future commentaries on Genesis. "This was the point to be examined," wrote Calvin, "whether I had eagerly sought after different
meanings, whether I had wantonly attacked, or spitefully carped at, or
insultingly inveighed against him. In truth, most accomplished sir, if
your leisure permitted you to read over the whole book, you would
find in it nothing of the kind."[5]

In a letter to Melanchthon written in early March, 1555, Calvin
complained bitterly that Melanchthon was not doing enough to
restrain the Lutheran theologians who were looking for a suitable pre-
text to crush him (and, by extension, Calvin as well).[6] It would not
be easy "to bridle such wild beasts," he admitted, but we must
"accomplish what God requires of us, even when we are in the greatest despair respecting the results." In a letter to a colleague at Erfurt,
Calvin contrasted the Gnesio-Lutherans in Saxony with Luther.
Although "they do not possess a single one of Luther's virtues, by
their lusty bawling they give themselves out for his genuine disciples."
Furthermore "they cannot assent to anything that comes from this
quarter" (Calvin may have had the rejection of his commentary on
Genesis in mind), "because we do not chime in with all the opinions
of the Saxons." They are violent, obstinate, incapacious, frenzied,
implacable, contumacious, ignorant, barbarous, and arrogant. They
go out of their way to "raise disturbances without a motive." While
they ape Luther, they do not imitate his virtues. In short, cried Calvin, "would that Luther were alive today!"[7]

What I want to do in this essay is accept Calvin's challenge to Chancellor Burckhardt to examine his exegesis of Genesis in the light of
Luther's interpretation of the same text. I am not interested, of course,
in demonstrating that Calvin was critical of Luther (he freely admitted
to the Saxon theologians that he was) or in measuring the degree of
Luther's influence on Calvin's interpretation of Genesis (though that
influence is measurable and can to a certain degree be tracked). What I
have in mind is a somewhat more modest goal; namely, to compare their
exegesis of Genesis in order to identify more accurately their similarities
and differences as biblical commentators. The point of this exercise is not
merely to clarify the nature of their relationship (though that is, in itself,
a worthy goal) but also to set in sharper relief than would otherwise be
possible the image of Calvin as an interpreter of Genesis.

In order to provide a larger context for this reassessment of Luther and Calvin, I want to sketch briefly a picture of the interpretation of Genesis on the eve of the Reformation. Although this could be done in a variety of ways, I have chosen to do it by examining the Genesis commentary of the great fifteenth-century biblical commentator, Denis the Carthusian (1402/3–1471). Denis's commentary on the literal and spiritual senses of the Pentateuch was available to Calvin's contemporaries in printed editions such as the attractive folio volume published by Peter Quentel in Cologne in 1534, the same year in which Calvin wrote his first theological treatise, *Psychopannychia*.[8]

Obviously it is not possible within the limits of one essay (or even a dozen) to examine the interpretations of the whole book of Genesis by Denis, Luther, and Calvin. What I propose to do is examine in detail the exegesis of what Luther called one "of the most obscure passages of the whole Old Testament"; namely, the story of the wrestling match beside the brook Jabbok, between Jacob, who was returning to the Promised Land to meet his alienated brother Esau, and a mysterious man who appeared to attack Jacob by night without provocation and who dislocated Jacob's hip shortly before dawn.[9] The story is found in Genesis 32:24–32.

> Jacob was left alone; and a man wrestled with him until daybreak. When the man saw that he did not prevail against Jacob, he struck him on the hip socket, and Jacob's hip was put out of joint as he wrestled with him. Then he said, "Let me go, for the day is breaking." But Jacob said, "I will not let you go, unless you bless me." So he said to him, "What is your name?" And he said, "Jacob." Then the man said, "You shall no longer be called Jacob, but Israel, for you have striven with God and with humans, and have prevailed." Then Jacob asked him, "Please tell me your name." But he said, "Why is it that you ask my name?" And there he blessed him. So Jacob called the place Peniel, saying, "For I have seen God face to face, and yet my life is preserved." The sun rose upon him as he passed Penuel, limping because of his hip. Therefore to this day the Israelites do not eat the thigh muscle that is on the hip socket, because he struck Jacob on the hip socket at the thigh muscle. (NRSV)

I

The first question that troubled Denis was whether the wrestling match was physical or spiritual.[10] Did Jacob actually wrestle with a mysterious stranger beside the Jabbok, or did he receive a private vision, unwitnessed by anyone else and in the nature of the case unverifiable? Supporters of the hypothesis that Jacob received a vision have to explain how Jacob could have been lamed by it. Supporters of the hypothesis that the match was wholly physical have to account for the fact that wrestling seems at times to be used metaphorically as a synonym for prayer. Although Denis did not take a strong position on the issue, physical or spiritual, he appears to agree with Hugh of St. Cher that Jacob's wrestling match was both, though in what proportion it was impossible for him to say.[11]

On the other hand, Denis was in no doubt whatever who the mysterious stranger was.[12] Jacob's opponent was a good angel appearing in the form of a man. Denis was eager to refute what he reported as a Jewish legend; namely that the angel with whom Jacob wrestled was Esau's guardian angel.[13] According to this reading of the text, Esau's guardian angel had met Jacob at the Jabbok to impede his progress into Palestine and to wrest from him, if possible, the primogeniture and blessing Esau had lost to Jacob. When the angel could not overcome Jacob, he wept and pled, both for himself and for Esau.

The difficulty with this story, of course, was that an angel would have known the mind of God in this matter and not have gone against it. God had judged Esau unworthy to receive the primogeniture and the blessing and had given them to Jacob. What had transpired had taken place by the will and direction of God. No angel would have attempted to undermine the plan of God. Besides, Denis added, angels do not cry; it is incompatible with their perfection.[14]

An alternative theory identified the stranger as Jacob's guardian angel rather than Esau's.[15] According to this account the angel had accompanied Jacob from Mesopotamia to Palestine and wanted to leave him at the Jabbok. But because Jacob feared his brother too much and did not trust God enough, he refused to let the angel go and kept him in place through prayer. The so-called wrestling match occurred because Jacob's mind had withdrawn from God through diffidence. When the angel lamed Jacob, he did so as a punishment for his lack of faith.

Other interpreters found no grounds in the story for assuming that Jacob was being punished by God for his faults. The story could be read in a far more hopeful vein. God wanted to give Jacob greater spiritual gifts, and greater gifts presuppose a greater struggle.[16] At any event, the point of the struggle was comfort. Through it "the angel saved [Jacob] from unadulterated human fear and comforted him in the Lord." Denis was even willing to claim that the angel "confirmed him in the hope of eternal salvation."[17]

The question not unnaturally arose in the minds of the readers of the Jacob story why the angel was unable to defeat Jacob. As a heavenly being the angel was surely more powerful than any mortal, even a patriarch who bore a divine blessing. Denis answered the question by appealing to the theological distinction between *potentia absoluta,* or absolute power, and *potentia ordinata,* or ordained power.[18] Considered absolutely, the angel could have crushed Jacob at any time. But it would have been unfitting for the angel to unleash overwhelming force against Jacob. It was never a question of "cannot" but only of "will not." What was at stake in the angel's defeat was not sheer energy (*potentia absoluta*) but divine purpose (*potentia ordinata*). In the end Jacob kept the angel in place by humility, devotion, love, and prayer, and not by his skill as a wrestler.[19]

Equally puzzling is why the angel asked to be released at daybreak.[20] Angels are creatures of light and ought not be alarmed at the rising of the sun. Devils may scatter at dawn but surely not angels. Denis offered several traditional exegetical suggestions to explain the baffling urgency of the angel's request.

Perhaps the angel was late for choir, because it was time to appear in the heavenly court and sing the praises of God.[21] Perhaps the angel thought it was time for Jacob to be on his way to the meeting with Esau he dreaded so much.[22] Or perhaps the angel thought no one should see him except Jacob, although, as Denis noted, this explanation was not very convincing.[23] Angels can only be seen by mortals when they want to be. An army of angels could be camped on the banks of the Jabbok without drawing attention to itself.

The angel then asked Jacob his name. Of course, the angel knew Jacob's name already; it would be unthinkable that he did not. The wrestling match was no random encounter. The angel asked Jacob his name (much as a priest asks the name of a child at baptism) so he could do more fittingly what he intended.[24] What he intended was to change Jacob's name to Israel. Denis engaged in some discussion of the philological history of the two Hebrew names and, like Jerome, accepted the interpretation of the names offered by Moses. Jacob was no longer the supplanter but like the angel a prince with God. The point of the change of name was to signify that if Jacob had not been conquered by the angel, he would not be conquered by Esau.[25]

Jacob in his turn asked the name of the angel, but the angel refused to tell him. Denis could find no fault in Jacob for asking, since Jacob only wanted to increase his knowledge of divine things and invoke and honor the angel by his own name.[26] Why the angel denied Jacob's request is less clear. Perhaps the knowledge Jacob sought from the angel was too high for a mortal to grasp without the gravest difficulty.

Or perhaps the question was unanswerable because most angels have no fixed names but derive their names from the tasks they are assigned (Michael and Gabriel are obvious exceptions).[27] Rather than disclose his name, the angel blessed Jacob. The form of the blessing was not recorded in the biblical text. Because of this silence concerning the words of the blessing, some interpreters have concluded that the blessing was in fact the change of name.[28]

After his encounter with the angel, Jacob made the astonishing claim that he had seen God face to face (*clare et facialiter*) and lived.[29] Denis was inclined to discount this claim. Jacob was no Moses. Unlike Moses, Jacob did not see God in the incomprehensible and invisible nature of his deity. Jacob's experience was not a theophany in that sense of the term. What Jacob saw clearly with his exterior eyes was an angel in human form who appeared and spoke to him in the person of God.[30] In that sense and that sense only was it appropriate for Jacob to claim that he had seen God and lived.

However, if one set aside the literal sense of the text, one could agree with Augustine and Isidore that the angel with whom Jacob wrestled was Christ.[31] After all, Denis believed that Scripture contained both a spiritual and a literal sense, even though he devoted his primary attention to the literal. On the spiritual level Denis compared Jacob to contemplatives who wrestle with God in prayer and will not let God go until God blesses them.[32] Such a wrestling match is never with a mere angel but always with Christ.

II

What Denis accepted as the spiritual sense of the text, Luther advocated as its literal-historical meaning. Jacob's antagonist was not an angel (certainly not Esau's guardian angel!), not a devil, and not flesh and blood. Jacob's antagonist was God (or as Luther would also say, Christ) appearing in hostile form.[33] Although God was not in reality hostile to Jacob—quite the contrary, he was and remained a loving Father—he nevertheless showed a dark and threatening face to Jacob in order to test his faith.[34]

To provide a New Testament frame of reference for Jacob's ordeal, Luther appealed to the story of the encounter between Jesus and the Syrophoenician woman. According to Matthew's account (15:21–28) an unnamed woman asked Jesus to heal her daughter. Jesus refused on the ground that she was not an Israelite and even compared her to a dog. "It is not fair," said Jesus, "to take the children's food and throw it to the dogs." "Yes, Lord," replied the woman, "yet even the dogs eat the crumbs that fall from their master's table" (NRSV). Jesus was so impressed with her answer and her faith that he granted her request and healed her daughter.

In his *Fastenpostille* published in 1525 Luther included a sermon on this pericope.[35] The Syrophoenician woman provided for Luther an outstanding example of the boldness faith must exercise in the presence of a seemingly hostile God. She accepted without a murmur the judgment of Jesus that compared her to a dog. Rather than defend herself from such a comparison, she demanded from Jesus a dog's rightful share. "Where could Jesus turn?" Luther asked triumphantly. He was trapped by his own words. What the woman discovered by boldly confronting Christ was that his "no" was not "no" at all but what Luther called "a deeply hidden yes." "Therefore," concluded Luther, "sweep your heart clean of such feelings and trust firmly in God's Word and grasp from above or from underneath the 'No' the deeply hidden 'Yes' and hold on to it as this woman did and keep a firm belief in God's justice. Then you have won and caught him with his own words."[36]

In his lectures on Genesis, Luther returned to this text and its themes.[37] Faith should not draw back when it feels the wrath of God or endures his inexplicable hostility. Like the Syrophoenician woman, Jacob did not falter or turn aside when faced with God's opposition in his lonely vigil beside the Jabbok. But against God's relentless opposition Jacob pressed forward and conquered God's wrath by God's promise. Although God appeared unfriendly, he was in reality a loving Father. Undeterred by the unexpected opposition of God, Jacob grasped the deeply hidden "yes" underneath God's "no." "I will not let you go," he cried, "unless you bless me!" (NRSV)

Luther's reconstruction of the wrestling match turned what Genesis described as a quiet struggle by night into a noisy and inelegant brawl.[38] Only three brief conversations are recorded in Genesis, all of which occurred at the end of the match. Luther found such silence unnatural. In his view the opponents "struggled" in the darkness "with arms and words alike as two wrestlers usually do." The stranger in a terrifying voice bombarded Jacob with a string of disquieting thoughts as they wrestled: "You must die, Jacob, for you are not the man to whom God gave the promise. God does not want to keep even the promise that has been given. You must perish Jacob; you are in for it!" To which Jacob responded "No, that is not God's will, I shall not perish! I may be pushed, assailed and thrown down, yet I shall not die."[39] In the deep darkness of that night, declared Luther, "Yes and no there assailed each other very sharply and violently."[40]

When the traditional questions were asked about Jacob's conflict with God, Luther gave a somewhat narrower range of answers than Denis had given. (1) Why was the stranger unable to defeat Jacob? Of course, the stranger could have defeated Jacob at any time, but he did not want to use more strength against Jacob than a man could use.[41] In addition, God helped Jacob in his struggle against the stranger through the power of the Holy Spirit.[42] (2) Why did the stranger demand to be released at daybreak? The stranger wanted Jacob to let him go because he needed to return to his own proper tasks.[43] (3) What was the name of the man who wrestled with Jacob? Luther believed that Jacob was completely in the dark about the stranger's identity until the very end of the conflict, when the stranger told him that he had triumphed over God and humans.[44] Only at that point did Jacob know he had wrestled with God in human form. That is why Jacob claimed to have seen God face to face; he saw him both hidden and disclosed in Christ. (4) What was the content of the blessing Christ gave to Jacob? Moses did not reveal the text of the blessing, but Luther suggested it must have been the same as the blessing given to Abraham and Isaac.[45]

The renaming of Jacob offered Luther an opportunity to underscore what he regarded as the main point of the story. Jacob's name was changed from Jacob to Israel, that is, from supplanter of Esau to conqueror of God.[46] Jacob had conquered God with God's own promises; he had grasped God's "deeply hidden yes." The notion that Jacob had conquered God as the Syrophoenician woman had trapped Jesus with his own words was and remains absurd to philosophy. Nevertheless, theology is willing to claim that God is conquered by faith, though it does not claim that God is thereby made submissive to human will.[47] God can be conquered; God cannot be tamed.

Against God's opposition but by God's will, Jacob triumphed over God by holding fast to the promises God seemed to have abandoned. He bravely and stubbornly opposed God's apparent hostility and refused to accept God's "no." For Luther bold opposition is what faith is all about; it is tested and triumphs in the dialectic of God's "yes" and "no." "Let us compose a proverb from this history," Luther concluded, "when you think our Lord God has rejected a person, you should think that our Lord God has him in his arms and is pressing him to his heart."[48]

Throughout his exposition Luther maintained a clear distinction between historical and allegorical interpretations of the Jacob narrative. Although he complained about the misuse of allegory by some theologians, he did not reject a limited use of allegorical approaches to the Bible. At the end of his exposition of the literal meaning of

Jacob's ordeal, he appended a fairly detailed allegorical interpretation. The principle that Luther invoked for his use of allegory was not new with him but a theological commonplace since the time of Augustine; namely, that only the literal sense can be used as a foundation for doctrine. Allegory has a lesser role and can be used for the illustration of meanings firmly grounded in the literal sense.[49]

Luther claimed that on the allegorical level Jacob could be viewed as the whole body of the faithful in every age. From this perspective Jacob provided the Church with a picture of all the saints who are tempted and tested by God.[50] In the history of Jacob, Christians can see their own history as well. Luther ended his allegorical exposition with an extended discussion of the meaning of eating or not eating the sinews of the thigh, over which we shall draw a merciful curtain.[51]

III

Whereas Denis was interested in overcoming Jacob's all-too-human fear of Esau and Luther in resolving Jacob's crisis of faith, Calvin was interested in Jacob as an exemplary model.

What Luther regarded as the allegorical sense of the text (namely, Jacob as an example of a tested believer) was collapsed by Calvin into the literal sense. Or to state that more precisely, the text as Calvin read it had two purposes: (1) to warn Jacob of the conflicts that still awaited him and to assure him that he would triumph over them; and (2) to represent all the servants of God as they are tested by God in this world and to remind them that what was once exhibited in visible form in Jacob is daily fulfilled in individual members of the Church.[52] As in Jacob, so also in us.

Unlike Denis and Luther, who thought the conflict was both physical and spiritual, Calvin insisted that Jacob's wrestling match was a vision.[53] Calvin did not deny that Jacob's struggle was a real event with real physical consequences, and commentators like Denis were, of course, correct to point out that Jacob's lameness was no figment of his imagination. But the wrestling match was not an external event that anyone else could have seen; it was a divine self-disclosure to Jacob alone. By the same token, Jacob's vision was not private; it was given to Jacob in order to benefit the Church.[54] That is why Jacob built a monument and named it Peniel; namely, to celebrate his vision and remind the Church of its continuing relevance for the life of the whole people of God in every age.

Calvin agreed with Luther that Jacob's enemy was not an angel, not a devil, and not flesh and blood. Jacob's adversary was God appear-

ing in the form of a man.[55] Like Luther, Calvin conceded that this
notion appeared absurd but assured his readers that reason and experience taught it to be true.[56] Jacob's enemy was God.

However, Calvin drew back from Luther's position when he refused
to identity the stranger who attacked Jacob with Christ. Instead he
drew an analogy between the stranger and the Holy Spirit. Just as the
Holy Spirit is sometimes called a dove, so Jacob's antagonist was
called a man, even though the dove is really the Holy Spirit and the
man was really God appearing in human form.[57] Obviously, such an
analogy (the dove is to the Holy Spirit as the man is to God) precludes
any notion of hypostatic union. For what seem to be reasons grounded
in his understanding of the unfolding history of salvation, Calvin was
reluctant to call Jacob's vision a revelation of Christ, although he did
concede in the *Institutes* that Jacob's vision was a disclosure of the
Logos in human form.[58]

Yet this disagreement between Luther and Calvin should not be
allowed to obscure the degree of agreement between them. God in
human form (if not yet Christ) was Jacob's enemy. Even though God's
intentions toward Jacob were loving and kind, he showed Jacob a harsh
and unfriendly face in order to test his faith. The harshness, however, is
more apparent than real. Indeed, God opposed Jacob with much less
force that he used to assist him in his resistance.[59] Jacob did not flee from
the hostile face of God but trusted in God's providential care and so triumphed over God's opposition. By so doing Jacob left an example, not
only for Christians who are tested by God's open hostility in the way
Jacob was but also for Christians subjected to any kind of conflict in
which God exercises the faithful.[60]

Calvin raised the interesting question of why Jacob had not been
tested earlier. His answer was that raw recruits are often spared from
conflicts in which veterans engage. Once Jacob had been seasoned by
suffering, he was led out to real war.[61] The timing was not accidental
but guided by God's providential hand.

Calvin also offered a new reason (or at least a reason not mentioned
by Denis or Luther) for God's withdrawal from the struggle. God
wanted to withdraw so that Jacob could rejoice in the grace afforded
him.[62] In this connection Calvin was particularly impressed by what
he called Jacob's "invincible perseverance."[63] Jacob provided for Calvin a model of how one ought to contend with God; namely, by never
growing weary until God leaves the conflict of his own accord.

Calvin did not explain how Jacob could be wounded by a vision, but
he did explain why. God wanted to leave an indelible mark on Jacob
so that he would not dismiss his vision as an idle dream.[64] Jacob rose
from his vision with a permanent, but apparently painless, limp.[65]

Furthermore, Jacob's wound continues to remind Christians that they emerge conquerors from their temptations only by being wounded in the conflict. The limp serves as a permanent sign that Jacob triumphed in God's strength and not in his own; and as in Jacob, so also in us.

Calvin agreed with Luther that Jacob did not know who his assailant was until daybreak. The key indicator that Jacob knew what had transpired was when he asked the stranger to bless him. Since in Calvin's view blessing is the act of a superior to an inferior, Jacob's request signaled his realization that the mysterious man was in fact God.[66] God then changed Jacob's name to Israel to indicate that his victory over God implied that he ought not to fear any lesser enemy.

Like Denis, Calvin tended to discount Jacob's claim to have seen God face to face. His vision of God appearing in human form was a lesser revelation than the self-disclosure of God to Moses or the apostles.[67] Jacob was not yet living in the time of the fuller self-revelation of God. Far better than Jacob's imperfect vision of God is the sight of Christ, the living image of God, in the mirror of the gospel.[68]

IV

When we place the three expositions of Genesis 32 by Denis, Luther, and Calvin side by side, we can see clearly several important similarities and differences. For example, Calvin is the only one of the three interpreters to opt for the story of Jacob's conflict with a mysterious stranger as a vision. Denis and Luther seem to accept it as both, an internal and external event, partly vision, partly physical trial. Similarly, Calvin is the only one not to refer to Jewish exegesis of the text. Both Denis and Luther mention especially the Jewish suggestion that the stranger was Esau's guardian angel, even though they emphatically reject it as a silly fable. Calvin does not allude to it at all.

More importantly, Calvin is the only one of the three not to use the distinction between the literal (or historical) and the spiritual (or allegorical) senses of the text. Luther praises the historical sense over the allegorical and may even at times create in some of his hearers the false expectation that he will reject the allegorical sense entirely. However, he has nothing of the sort in mind, preferring merely to restrict it. Allegory may properly be employed by theologians and preachers for the decoration and illustration of doctrine.

Because Denis accepts with a tranquil conscience the traditional notion that the Bible contains a spiritual sense as well as a literal, his literal exposition is remarkably free from spiritual applications. He focuses on the narrative and its meaning and postpones a discussion of its spiritual application until he has finished his discussion of its literal sense. His separation of letter and spirit and postponement of a discussion of the spirit gives his literal exposition a curiously modern feel, at least in comparison with Luther and Calvin.

Luther finds spiritual meanings on both levels of the text. On the level of letter, Luther uses the Jacob narrative to show how faith conquers God by opposing God with God's own promises. Jacob's opponent is not an angel but Christ, a view that Denis had reserved for the spiritual sense. On the other hand, Luther labels as allegorical the notion that Jacob provides an image of all the saints who are tempted and tested by God.

Calvin rejects, or, perhaps more accurately, makes no reference to or use of two levels in the biblical text. He does not believe it is appropriate to identify Jacob's opponent with Christ on either an allegorical or a literal level. Jacob's opponent is not Christ (contra Luther) and not an angel acting in the person of God (contra Denis) but God appearing in human form. Luther is also wrong to appeal to allegory in order to make the point that Jacob is the model of believers who are tested by God. Jacob as model clearly belongs to the literal sense.

While Calvin rejects two levels of the biblical story, he nevertheless affirms a twofold sense of the letter. The story as letter focuses both on Jacob, who provides an exemplary model of perseverance through severe testing by God, and on all believers, who are similarly tested in this life. The exposition moves back and forth between Jacob and the Church, between narrative and application, until it creates a layered effect in Calvin's exegesis. If we label the Jacob narrative *a* and the application to the Church as *b,* Calvin's exposition of the story scans as follows: *abababab.* What this scanning does not convey is the relative length of the two parts. Generally speaking, the application to the Church is longer than the interpretation of the narrative.

The most important similarity between Luther and Calvin may be the point at which both differ with expositors like Denis. It may also, perhaps, be their most important difference. Calvin agrees with Luther that Jacob's enemy is God, who shows a hostile face to Jacob (and by extension to all believers). Both agree that there is a difference between the appearance to us, which is hostile, and the reality that lies behind it. The underlying reality is that God is a loving Father who means such testing to be for our own good. Luther even speaks of a playful God who tests us.

Yet there is a very different development of this common theme by the two authors. For Luther the wrestling match is a boisterous and raucous brawl in which the opponents shout at each other and strain for an advantage. Luther even suggests what the two wrestlers might have bellowed at each other. Although the outcome is not in doubt *sub specie aeternitatis*, it is not altogether clear to Jacob in the heat of battle that the hostile God will not win and that his "no" will not be his final word. Jacob must counter God's sharp "no" (which is, after all, not the "no" of any creature, but the "no" of God the Creator) with an equally sharp "yes." He must exercise the boldness and cunning of faith in order to trap Christ with his own words. He must grasp the "deeply hidden yes" underneath the terrifying and implacable "no." When Jacob is finally proclaimed a conqueror of God and given a new name, he is lying exhausted on the banks of the Jabbok, weakly hanging on to the stranger who has wounded him.

For Calvin the atmosphere of the conflict is more serenely Augustinian. Gone are the noise and sweat of battle. The conflict is viewed from the perspective of God's providential care and not from the perspective of Jacob's terror. God is against us and for us; he fights against us with his left hand and for us with his right. While God opposes Jacob, he wills him to be conqueror and so opposes him less with his left hand than he supports him with his right. Unlike Luther, Calvin does not add dialogue not found in the biblical text or portray the conflict as the clash of a sharp and implacable "no" with an equally sharp and implacable "yes." Instead of a harsh dialectic of "yes" and "no," Calvin offers a gentler dialectic of "left" and "right," a left hand that never offers more resistance than the right hand can overcome. What Calvin commends in Jacob is his perseverance and not his boldness. Victory is certain for those who trust in the goodness of God's providence and persevere through their trials.

I do not want to overemphasize these differences or suggest that they are more important than they really are. In spite of differences of style and, to some degree, of substance, Luther and Calvin are allies in their interpretation of the Jacob narrative. They are never, as the Saxon court theologians unfairly alleged, irreconcilable rivals. For them the story is finally about a God who opposes Jacob and a faith that triumphs over God's opposition. It is about God's "yes" and God's "no," God's left hand and God's right. It is about terror and courage, about promises and perseverance, and about the conquest of God.

NOTES

Abbreviations

BhTh   Beiträge zur historischen Theologie (Berlin, 1929–)
BoA   [Bonner Ausgabe] *Luthers Werke in Auswahl*, 6 vols. (Bonn and Berlin, 1912–)
CR   *Corpus Reformatorum* (Halle and Berlin 1834– ; Leipzig, 1906–)
CSEL   Corpus Scriptorum Ecclesiasticorum Latinorum (Vienna, 1866–)
Kn.   J.K.F. Knaake, *Johannis Staupitii, opera quae reperiri poterunt omnia: Deutsche Schriften*, Vol. I (Potsdam, 1867)
LW   *Luther's Works*, 55 vols. (St. Louis: Concordia Publishing House and Philadelphia: Fortress Press, 1955–)
OC   *Ioannis Calvini opera quae supersunt omnia*, 59 vols. (Brunswick and Berlin, 1863–1900)
OS   *Ioannis Calvini opera selecta*, 5 vols. (Munich, 1926–36)
Sent.   Gabriel Biel, *Epithome et collectorium ex Occamo circa quatuor sententiarum libros* (Tübingen, 1501)
SMRT   Studies in Medieval and Reformation Thought (Leiden, 1966–)
SuR   Spätmittelalter und Reformation, Texte und Untersuchungen (Berlin, 1972–)
WA   *D. Martin Luthers Werke: Kritische Gesamtausgabe* (Weimar, 1883–)
WABr   *D. Martin Luthers Werke: Briefwechsel* (Weimar, 1930–)
WATR   *D. Martin Luthers Werke: Tischreden*, 6 vols. (Weimar, 1912–21)

All translations not specifically documented in the notes are mine.

I. Luther against Luther

1. *CR* 6.156–60. Translated by Ian D. Kingston Siggins in *Luther* (New York: Barnes and Noble, 1972), p. 34.

2. *WATR* 1.50.

3. *WATR* 1.50.

4. Erich Vogelsang, *Der angefochtene Christus bei Luther* (Berlin, 1932), p. 17.

5. *WA* 40.II.15.15. Translated by E. Gordon Rupp, in *The Righteousness of God: Luther Studies* (London: Hodder and Stoughton, 1953), p. 104.

6. On late medieval penitential traditions, see especially Gordon J. Spykman, *Attrition and Contrition at the Council of Trent* (Kampen, 1955), pp. 51–89, and Thomas N. Tentler, *Sin and Confession on the Eve of the Reformation* (Princeton: Princeton University Press, 1977).

7. For the critical edition of the text of Kolde, see Clemens Dress, ed., *Der Christenspiegel des Dietrich Kolde von Münster* (Werl, 1954) and the High German translation by Christoph Moufang, ed., *Katholische Katechismen des 16. Jahrhunderts in Deutscher Sprache* (Hildesheim, 1880). Citations in this chapter are from the English translation by Robert Dewell in *Three Reforma-*

tion Catechisms: Catholic, Anabaptist, Lutheran, edited by Denis Janz (New York and Toronto: The Edwin Mellen Press, 1982), pp. 31–130.
  8. For a brief assessment, see Steven E. Ozment, *The Reformation in the Cities* (New Haven and London: Yale University Press, 1975), pp. 28–32.
  9. Ian D.K. Siggins, *Luther and His Mother* (Philadelphia: Fortress Press, 1981), pp. 48–52.
  10. Janz, *Catechisms*, p. 59.
  11. Ibid.
  12. On this subject, see Tentler, *Sin and Confession*, pp. 162–232.
  13. Janz, *Catechisms*, p. 74.
  14. Ibid, p. 71.
  15. Ibid., p. 74.
  16. Ibid., p. 75.
  17. Ibid.
  18. Ibid.
  19. Ibid., pp. 75, 80. See Tentler, *Sin and Confession*, pp. 124–28.
  20. Janz, *Catechisms*, p. 80. See Tentler, *Sin and Confession*, pp. 304–18.
  21. Tentler, *Sin and Confession*, pp. 250–301.
  22. Janz, *Catechisms*, p. 75.
  23. Ibid., p. 81.
  24. Ibid., p. 82.
  25. Ibid.
  26. Johannes von Paltz, *Werke I: Coelifodina,* SuR 2, edited by Christoph Burger and Friedhelm Stasch (Berlin, 1983).
  27. Johannes von Paltz, *Werke II: Supplementum Coelifodinae,* SuR 3, edited by Berndt Hamm (Berlin, 1983).
  28. For an introduction to Paltz's theology, see especially Berndt Hamm, *Frömmigkeitstheologie am Anfang des 16. Jahrhunderts,* BhTh 65 (Tübingen, 1982).
  29. Ibid., pp. 250–53.
  30. On Biel, see H.A. Oberman, *The Harvest of Medieval Theology,* 3d ed. (Durham, NC: The Labyrinth Press, 1983), pp. 146–60.
  31. Paltz's views on the *via securior* are summarized by Hamm, *Frömmigkeitstheologie,* pp. 254–303.
  32. Ibid., p. 280.
  33. Ibid., pp. 291–99.
  34. *WA* 38.143.25; 40.II.574.8. Rupp, p. 103. For what is still an excellent brief treatment of Luther's *Anfechtungen,* see E. Gordon Rupp, *The Righteousness of God* (London, 1953), pp. 102–20.
  35. *WA* 40.II.15.15. Rupp, p. 104.
  36. *WA* 3.447.30. Rupp, p. 115.
  37. *WA* 40.II.15.15. Rupp, p. 104.
  38. *WA* 40.II.411.14.
  39. *WA* 49.629.1
  40. *WA* 1.557.33. Rupp, p. 110.
  41. *WATR* 1.50 (Nov.-Dec. 1531)
  42. For the theology of Staupitz in comparison with Luther, see my *Misericordia Dei: The Theology of Johannes von Staupitz in its Late Medieval Setting,* SMRT 4 (Leiden, 1968) and *Luther and Staupitz: An Essay in the Intellectual Origins of the Protestant Reformation* (Durham, NC: Duke University Press, 1980).

43. Otto Scheel, ed., *Dokumente zu Luthers Entwicklung*, 2d ed. (Tübingen, 1929), 512.
44. Ibid., 461.
45. Ibid., 138, 207, 209, 210.
46. Ibid., 225, 256, 262, 274, 456.
47. Ibid., 487.
48. *WA* 1.525. *LW* 48, pp. 65–66.
49. Staupitz, *Nachfolgung*, Kn. 86.
50. *WA* 1.184.22; 1.370.9.
51. *WATR* 1.496.

II. Luther and Augustine on Romans 9

1. Anders Nygren, *Agape and Eros* (Philadelphia: Westminster Press, 1953), pp. 681–741.
2. Uuras Saarnivaara, *Luther Discovers the Gospel* (St. Louis: Concordia Publishing House, 1951), pp. 3–18.
3. Adolf Hamel, *Der junge Luther und Augustin*, 2 vols. (Gütersloh, 1934–35).
4. Heiko A. Oberman, "Headwaters of the Reformation: *Initia Lutheri - Initia Reformationis*," in *Luther and the Dawn of the Modern Era*, edited by H.A. Oberman (Leiden, 1974), pp. 40–88.
5. David C. Steinmetz, *Luther and Staupitz: An Essay in the Intellectual Origins of the Protestant Reformation* (Durham, NC: Duke University Press, 1980), pp. 3–34.
6. Leif Grane, *Modus Loquendi Theologicus: Luthers Kampf um die Erneuerung der Theologie (1515–1518)* (Leiden, 1975), pp. 11–62.
7. The critical edition of *Expositio quarundum propositionum ex epistola ad Romanos* is found in *Sancti Aureli Augustini Opera*, Sec. 4, Pars 1 *CSEL* 54, edited by Joannes Divjak (Vienna, 1971), pp. 3–52.
8. *Expositio* 52 (60).
9. Ibid.
10. Ibid. 52 (60), 53 (61).
11. Ibid. 52 (60).
12. Ibid.
13. Ibid. 52 (60), 54 (62).
14. Ibid. 52 (60).
15. Ibid. 47 (55).
16. Ibid.
17. Retractationes I.23 (22) .2–4 in *Oeuvres de Saint Augustin* 12, edited by Gustave Bardy (Paris, 1950), pp. 412–418.
18. *De diversis quaestionibus ad Simplicianum*, Quaestio II, in *Oeuvres de Saint Augustin* 10, edited by G. Bardy et al. (Paris, 1952), pp. 442–509.
19. Ibid. II.3, 5.
20. Ibid. II.2.
21. Ibid. II.10.
22. Ibid. II.19.
23. Ibid. II.13.
24. Ibid. II.16.
25. Ibid. II.22.

26. For a brief discussion of these shorter works, see A.F.N. Lekkerkerker, *Römer 7 und Römer 9 bei Augustin* (Amsterdam, 1942), pp. 131–137.
27. Enchiridion sive de Fide, Spe et Charitate, XXV.98–99, in *Oeuvres de Saint Augustin* 9, edited by J. Rivière (Paris, 1947), pp. 274–283.
28. *WA* 56.396.6.
29. *WA* 56.405.8.
30. *WA* 56.405.11.
31. *WA* 56.394.28.
32. *WA* 56.395.4.
33. *WA* 56.396.14. Translated by Wilhelm Pauck, ed., *Luther: Lectures on Romans*, Library of Christian Classics 15 (Philadelphia: Westminster Press, 1961).
34. *WA* 56.397.1.
35. *WA* 56.397.2. Translated by Pauck.
36. *WA* 56.398.11. Translated by Pauck.
37. *WA* 56.399.8. Translated by Pauck.
38. *WA* 56.399.25.
39. *WA* 56.397.14. Translated by Pauck.
40. *WA* 56.397.17.
41. *WA* 56.400.5. Translated by Pauck.
42. *WA* 56.400.4.
43. *WA* 56.400.8. Translated by Pauck.
44. *WA* 56.401.7. Translated by Pauck.
45. *WA* 56.401.16. Translated by Pauck.
46. *WA* 56.402.25.
47. *WA* 56.404.1.
48. *WA* 56.404.9.
49. *WA* 56.404.21.
50. For an important recent treatment of Martin Luther and the Jews, see Heiko A. Oberman, *Wurzeln des Antisemitismus* (Berlin, 1981), pp. 125–183; now available in English translation (Philadelphia: Fortress Press, 1984).
51. *WA* 56.400.1. Translated by Pauck.

III. Luther and the Hidden God

1. *WATR* 4.198. The translations of Luther in this chapter are taken from *Day by Day We Magnify Thee*, translated and compiled by Margarethe Steiner and Percy Scott (Philadelphia: Fortress Press, 1951, 1982).
2. *WA* 37.42–43.
3. *WA* 18.685.5
4. *WA* 28.101–102.
5. *WA* 37.201–202.
6. *WA* 17.I.155–156.
7. *WA* 17.II.203.

IV. Abraham and the Reformation

1. This essay was originally written to mark the retirement of E. Gordon Rupp as Dixie Professor of Ecclesiastical History at the University of Cambridge and was given as a lecture to the Tenth Southeastern Institute of Medieval and Renaissance Studies at the University of North Carolina in 1979.

2. One can find a brief introduction to this dispute in my book, *Reformers in the Wings* (Grand Rapids: Baker Book House, 1981) pp. 135–39.

3. On the importance of Abraham for Paul, see especially the stimulating essay by Ernst Käsemann, "The Faith of Abraham in Romans 4," in *Perspectives on Paul* (Philadelphia: Fortress Press, 1971), pp. 70–101.

4. The phrase is quoted by Heinrich Bullinger in his commentary on Romans. See H. Bullinger, *In Omnes Apostolicas Epistolas, Divi videlicet Pauli xiii et vii Canonicas, Commentarii* (Zurich, 1537), p. 47.

5. There are some exceptions to this rule, as Maurice F. Wiles proves in his excellent book on the interpretation of Paul in the early Church, *The Divine Apostle* (Cambridge: Cambridge University Press, 1967).

6. John B. Payne complains of this neglect in his fine essay, "Erasmus and Lefèvre d'Étaples as Interpreters of Paul," *Archive for Reformation History* 65 (1974), 54–83. See also the essays by Feld, Payne, Roussel and Koch in *Histoire de l'exégèse au XVIe siècle*, Olivier Fatio and Pierre Fraenkel, eds., Études de philologie et d'histoire 34 (Geneva: Librairie Droz, 1978), pp. 300–350.

7. Thomas de Vio, Cardinal Cajetan, *Epistolae Pauli et aliorum Apostolorum* (Paris, 1540).

8. Jacopo Cardinal Sadoleto, *Opera quae exstant omnia*, Vol. IV (Verona, 1738).

9. Girolamo Cardinal Seripando, *In Pauli Epistolas Commentaria* (Naples, 1601). [Hereafter cited as Seripando.]

10. For an introduction to Wendelin Steinbach and his biblical exegesis, see Helmut Feld, *Martin Luthers und Wendelin Steinbachs Vorlesungen über den Hebräerbrief* (Wiesbaden, 1971). [Hereafter, *Hebräerbrief*.] H.A. Oberman dissents from some of Feld's conclusions about Steinbach in his book, *Werden und Wertung der Reformation* (Tübingen, 1977), pp. 118–40. As will become clear in what follows, I concur with Oberman in his dissent.

11. Helmut Feld, ed., *Wendelini Steinbach, Opera Exegetica Quae Supersunt Omnia*, Vol. I (Wiesbaden, 1976). [Hereafter cited as Steinbach.]

12. Zwingli's comments on Romans were published posthumously and may have undergone some revision by his editor. On Romans 4, see M. Schuler and J. Schulthess, eds., *Huldrici Zuinglii Opera*, Vol. VI.2 (Zurich, 1833), pp. 88–91.

13. Bullinger, *Commentarii*, pp. 37–48.

14. Johannes Brenz, *Liber Commentariorum in Epistolam Pauli ad Romanos Primus, qui est de Fide* (Tübingen, 1588), pp. 550–68. This is printed as Volume VII of the *Operum Reverendi et Clarissimi Theologi, D. Ioannis Brentii, Prepositi Stutgardiani.*

15. Philip Melanchthon, *Commentarii in Epistolam Pauli ad Romanos*, edited by Rolf Schäfer, *Melanchthons Werke in Auswahl*, Vol. V (Gütersloh, 1965), pp. 122–55.

16. A. Tholuck, ed., *Ioannis Calvini in Novi Testamenti Epistolas Commentarii*, Vol. I (Berlin, 1834), pp. 45–58.

17. The standard work on Seripando is by Hubert Jedin, *Girolamo Seripando*, Cassiciacum II-III (Würzburg, 1937).

18. Melanchthon, who was resident in Tübingen from 1512 to 1518 while pursuing his studies, called Steinbach an "adsiduus lector . . . sacrorum librorum, et Augustini." See Feld, *Hebräerbrief*, p. 9. Steinbach's marked copy of the Amerbach edition of Augustine has survived in the library of the University of Tübingen. See in this connection Oberman, *Werden*, p. 120.

19. On the theology of Biel, see H.A. Oberman, *The Harvest of Medieval Theology*, 3rd ed. (Durham, NC: The Labyrinth Press, 1983), pp. 131–184. For additional bibliography on this subject, see my article, "Late Medieval Nominalism and the *Clerk's Tale*," *The Chaucer Review* 12 (1977); 38–54.

20. Feld, *Hebräerbrief*, pp. 201–13; Oberman, *Werden*, pp. 118–40.

21. Oberman, *Werden*, p. 127.

22. Steinbach, III.17.136.1–7.

23. Ibid., III.17.135.1–11.

24. Ibid., V.30.262.24–28.

25. Feld, *Herbraerbrief*, pp. 208–9.

26. Steinbach, III.17.135.15–21.

27. Ibid., III.18.142.14–143.1.

28. Ibid., III.16.131.11–18.

29. Ibid., III.17.134.20–25.

30. Ibid., III.17.136.22–137.2

31. Ibid., V.30.264.5–8.

32. Ibid., III.16.131.11–18; 17.134.20–25; 17.136.22–137.2.

33. Ibid., III.17.134.12–17. See Oberman, *Werden*, p. 127: "Das 'sola fide' wird damit nicht, wie bei Biel und in der Tradition üblich, zurückgewiesen, sondern als *modus loquendi* des Apostels—und Augustins—durchaus akzeptiert, jedoch nur für den christlichen Anfänger, der noch nicht voll im Bilde ist, dass der Glaube allein Gott keinesfalls genügt."

34. Steinbach, II.12.97.1–4; III.15.118.16–20; 16.131.6–10; 17.136.5–9; 21.176.13–21. Cf. III.18.144.2–4; 19.152.7–9.

35. Ibid., III.16.129.26–130.6.

36. Ibid., III.19.152.7–9; 15.118.16–20; 15.119.1–15.

37. Ibid., III.17.132.19–133.1; III.17.136.1–7.

38 Oberman, *Werden*, p. 134.

39. *WA* 1.224.7–8.

40. *WA* 56.423.19–20; 446.11–16; 446.31–32; 447.19–27.

41. *WA* 56.334.14–18; 371.2–10.

42. *WA* 4.168.1. Cf. *WA* 3.649.17–20.

43. *WA* 3.419.36–420.1.

44. *WA* 3.419.25–31.

45. *WA* 3.420.2–5.

46. *WA* 3.410.16–19.

47. *WA* 3.410.16–19.

48. *WA* 4.355.29–32.

49. *WA* 55.I.20–13–15; 55.II.106.16–19; 3.127.19–24; 3.311.35–36; 4.81.25–27; 4.337.10–12.

50. *WA* 3.548.2–5; 4.95.1–4; 4.356.9–13; 3.651.19–22; 4.83.3–9.

51. *WA* 57.236.1–7. I have cited the translation of James Atkinson, ed., *Luther: Early Theological Works*, Library of Christian Classics 16 (Philadelphia: Westminster Press, 1962), p. 213.

52. *WA* 55.II.123.19–22; 3.128.18–21; 4.40.14–15.

53. *WA* 3.199.16–18; 4.2.20; 4.13.13–27; 4.245.34–37.

54. *WA* 4.272.16–26; 3.180.24–26.

55. *WA* 3.410.16–19; 3.419.25–420.5; 3.649.17–20; 4.168.1.

56. *WA* 3.288.4–5; 3.284.21ff.; 3.292.27–32.

57. *WA* 3.291.9–21.

58. *WA* 3.289.31–35.

59. *WA* 4.375.16–20.
60. *WA* 4.262.2–7.
61. *WA* 3.288.6–32; 3.291.26–28; 55.II.24.6–12; 55.II.33.1–4.
62. *WA* 56.267.9–12.
63. *WA* 42.563. I have cited the translation of George Schick in *Luther's Works*, Vol. III, J. Pelikan, ed. (St. Louis: Concordia Publishing House, 1961), pp. 20–21.
64. Seripando, p. 62.
65. Ibid., p. 65.
66. Ibid., p. 76.
67. Ibid., p. 65.
68. Ibid., pp. 448–49.
69. Ibid., pp. 72, 449–50.
70. Ibid., pp. 62–63.
71. Ibid., p. 62.
72. Ibid., p. 65.
73. Ibid., pp. 449–50.
74. Ibid., p. 450.
75. Ibid., pp. 64–65. Translation mine.

V. Luther among the Anti-Thomists

1. Joseph Lortz, *Die Reformation in Deutschland*, 2 vols., 4th ed. (Freiburg, 1962).
2. Denis R. Janz, *Luther and Late Medieval Thomism: A Study in Theological Anthropology* (Waterloo: Wilfrid Laurier University Press, 1983), p. 96.
3. Ibid., pp. 112–113.
4. Ibid., pp. 115–116.
5. Gerhard Hennig, *Cajetan und Luther: Ein historischer Beitrag zur Begegnung von Thomismus und Reformation*, Arbeiten zur Theologie, II Reihe, Band 7 (Stuttgart, 1966).
6. Leif Grane, *Modus Loquendi Theologicus: Luthers Kampf um die Erneuerung der Theologie (1515–1518)* (Leiden, 1975).
7. Hennig, *Cajetan*, p. 11.
8. Janz, *Luther*, p. 123.
9. For a brief review of scholarship on this question, see ibid., pp. 123–125.
10. Ibid., pp. 152–153.
11. The best study of Biel's understanding of Thomas Aquinas is the 1978 Duke University dissertation by John L. Farthing, "*Post Thomam:* Images of Thomas Aquinas in the Academic Theology of Gabriel Biel," which is currently being revised for publication by Duke University Press.
12. *WA* 10/II.329–330.
13. The most recent and reliable biographical material is found in R.R. Post, "Johann Pupper von Goch," *Nederlands Archief voor Kerkgeschiedenis*, N.S. 47 (1965/66): 71–97; and in *The Modern Devotion*, Studies in Medieval and Reformation Thought 3 (Leiden, 1968), pp. 469–92.
14. Goch's works include the following: *De quatuor erroribus circa legem evangelicam exortis et de votis et religionibus factitiis dialogus* [abbreviated: *Dial.*], edited by C.G.F. Walch, *Monimenta medii aevi*, Vol.I.4 (Göttingen,

1760), pp. 74–239; *De scholasticorum scriptis et religiosorum votis epistola apologetica* [Abbreviated: *Epist. Apol.*], edited by C.G.F. Walch, *Monimenta medii aevi*, Vol.II.1 (Göttingen, 1761), pp. 1–24; *De libertate christiana* [Abbreviated: *De lib. chr.*], edited by F. Pijper, *Bibliotheca Reformatoria Neerlandica*, Vol. VI (Hague, 1910), pp. 1–263; and *Fragmenta* [Abbreviated: *Frag.*] edited by F. Pijper, *Bibliotheca Reformatoria Neerlandica*, Vol. VI (Hague, 1910), pp. 267–347.

15. For discussions of Goch's theology, see Otto Clemen, *Johann Pupper von Goch*, Leipziger Studien aus dem Gebiet der Geschichte II.3 (Leipzig, 1896); Luise Abramowski, "Die Lehre von Gesetz und Evangelium bei Johann Pupper von Goch im Rahmen seines nominalistischen Augustinismus," *Zeitschrift für Theologie und Kirche* 64 (1967): 83–98; and David C. Steinmetz, "*Libertas Christiana*: Studies in the Theology of John Pupper of Goch (d.1475)," *The Harvard Theological Review* 65 (1972): 191–230.

16. *De lib. chr.* III.2.184–85.

17. Ibid. III.2.187.

18. Ibid. III.4.190–91.

19. Ibid. III.6.196.

20 *Epist. Apol.* 6, 8; *De lib. chr.* II.40.166.

21. Harry J. McSorley quite rightly complains in his essay, "Thomas Aquinas, John Pupper von Goch, and Martin Luther: An Essay in Ecumenical Theology" [in John Deschner et al., eds., *Our Common History as Christians: Essays in Honor of Albert C. Outler* (New York: Oxford University Press, 1975), pp. 97–129], that I do not discuss the problem of the two wills in my essay in the *Harvard Theological Review* 65 (1972): 191–230. Unfortunately, McSorley gives the impression that the natural will is the human will in a state of mortal sin, while the graced will is the human will after the infusion of sanctifying grace. For a clear discussion of the problem of the two wills, see Clemen, *Goch*, pp. 113–15. For Goch's text, see *De lib. chr.* II.29.140–31.147.

22. *De lib. chr.* II.29.142, II.31.146.

23. *Frag.* 302; *De lib. chr.* II.7.102; *Dial.* VIII.121; *Epist. Apol.* 19–20.

24. *De lib. chr.* II.29.141. The Pijper edition reads: "Et istae duae voluntates sunt realiter inter se distinctae, et a se invicem separabiles". Clemen cites it, however, as "realiter inter se distinctae et ad se invicem inseparables" [*Goch*, p. 113].

25. *Frag.* 306; *De lib. chr.* III.12.215.

26. *De lib. chr.* II.23.127; cf. I.22.80.

27. Thomas Aquinas, *Summa Theologiae cum textu ex recensione Leonina* (Turin and Rome), I-II, q.100 a.12 ad 3.

28. Ibid. q.114, a.1, a.4.

29. Ibid. q.114 a.1 ad 3.

30. *Frag.* 303, 304.

31. Ibid. 306.

32. *Summa Theologiae* II-II q.88 a.6.

33. *De lib. chr.* IV.1.226.

34. *De lib. chr.* I.6.53; *Epist. Apol.* 15.

35. *De lib. chr.* I.7.55.

36. *Dial.* XVII.181; *De lib. chr.* III.4.190–191, 5.193.

37. *De lib. chr.* IV.3.229, 4.231–32, 6.238; *Dial.* XVII.181.

38. *Epist. Apol.* 19; *Dial.* XVIII.183.

39. *Dial.* XVIII.184.

40. Ibid. XVII.178, XVIII.183.
41. Ibid. XII.159, XIV.164–65.
42. Ibid. XV.167.
43. Farthing, "*Post Thomam*," pp. 290–94.
44. Ibid., p. 347.
45. Book two of the *Collectorium* has not yet been issued as part of the new critical edition. It can be read, however, in a photo-offprint from Minerva Press of Frankfurt am Main, 1965: Gariel Biel, *Epithome et collectorium ex Occamo circa quatuor sententiarum libros* (Tübingen, 1501). Farthing discusses this passage in "*Post Thomam*," pp. 239–50.
46. Janz, *Luther*, pp. 46–47.
47. The critical edition of this text is Gabriel Biel, *Canonis Misse Expositio*, I-V, edited by Heiko A. Oberman and William J. Courtenay (Wiesbaden, 1963–76). See Farthing, "*Post Thomam*," pp. 251–66.
48. Farthing, "*Post Thomam*," p. 252.
49. *WA* 1.221–28.
50. Janz, *Luther*, p. 25.
51. *WA* 2.394.31–395.6. Translated by Denis R. Janz, *Luther and Late Medieval Thomism* (Waterloo: Wilfrid Laurier University Press, 1983), p. 32.
52. Janz, *Luther*, pp. 117–22.

VI. Luther and Hubmaier on the Freedom of the Human Will

1. Because this chapter was a lecture written for the University of North Carolina at Chapel Hill, the University of Bonn, and Cornell University and not a research paper in the strict sense of the term, I have kept the footnotes to a minimum. I have directed the reader to those books and essays where more extensive documentation can be found.
2. The critical edition of these texts is found in Balthasar Hubmaier, *Schriften*, edited by Gunnar Westin and Torsten Bergsten, Quellen und Forschungen zur Reformationsgeschichte 29 (Gütersloh, 1962), pp. 379–431. [Hereafter abbreviated as *HS*.]
3. The best biography of Hubmaier is Torsten Bergsten, *Balthasar Hubmaier: Anabaptist Theologian and Martyr*, edited and translated by W.R. Estep, Jr. (Valley Forge: Judson Press, 1978). This is an improved and abbreviated edition of the 1961 original, *Balthasar Hubmaier, Seine Stellung zu Reformation und Taufertum, 1521–1528*.
4. The best essay on the relationship of Hubmaier to Eck is Walter L. Moore, Jr., "Catholic Teacher and Anabaptist Pupil: the Relationship between John Eck and Balthasar Hubmaier," *Archive for Reformation History* 72 (1981): 68–97. The best general study of Hubmaier's theology is Christof Windhorst, *Täuferisches Taufverständnis: Balthasar Hubmaiers Lehre zwischen Traditioneller und Reformatorischer Theologie*, Studies in Medieval and Reformation Thought 16 (Leiden, 1976). On the relationship of Hubmaier to medieval theology generally, see my essays "Scholasticism and Radical Reform: Nominalist Motifs in the Theology of Balthasar Hubmaier," *The Mennonite Quarterly Review* 45 (1971), 123–44, and "The Baptism of John and the Baptism of Jesus in Huldrych Zwingli, Balthasar Hubmaier and Late Medieval Theology," in *Continuity and Discontinuity in Church History*, edited by F. Church and T. George, Studies in the History of Christian Thought 19 (Leiden, 1979), pp. 169–81.
5. *HS* 73, 291, 309.

6. For a discussion of this and related questions, see my *Luther and Staupitz: An Essay in the Intellectual Origins of the Protestant Reformation,* Duke Monographs in Medieval and Renaissance Studies 4 (Durham, NC: Duke University Press, 1980), pp. 3–34.

7. The most complete discussion of this question can be found in John L. Farthing, "*Post Thomam:* Images of St. Thomas Aquinas in the Academic Theology of Gabriel Biel" (Dissertation, Duke University, 1978).

8. While the following composite picture is based on many primary and secondary sources, the standard treatment of Biel's theology is still Heiko A. Oberman, *The Harvest of Medieval Theology,* 3d ed. (Durham, NC: The Labyrinth Press, 1983).

9. II *Sent.* d.39 q.1 art.2 concl.1.

10. II *Sent.* d.28 q.1 art.1 nota.2.

11. II *Sent.* d.27 q.1 art.3 dub.5Q.

12. II *Sent.* d.27 q.1 art.3 dub.30.

13. *Sent.* d.28 q.1 art.1 nota.2; d.27 q.1 art.2 concl.4.

14. I *Sent.* d.17 q.1 art.3H.

15. II *Sent.* d.28 q.1 art.2 concl.3.

16. The reconstruction of Luther's theology is based on research developed in my *Luther and Staupitz,* pp. 68–125.

17. *WA* 3.179.26ff.; 3.374.21–22; 4.422.21–22; 3.116.1–2; 3.116.25–26; 4.92.23–37; 4.81.20–22; 3.163.29ff.

18. *WA* 9.71.6, 23, 32; 9.72.36; 4.18.25–29; 4.43.8–12; 4.211.10–12; 3.212.4–7; 3.231.25–31; 4.207.22–27; 4.343.22–25.

19. *WA* 1.38.2–5.

20. *WA* 1.32.1–8, 14–26; 1.36.11–19; 1.37.3–18.

21. *WA* 1.184.22–26; 1.370.9–13.

22. *WA* 56.177.11–15; 275.19–22.

23. *BoA* 5.243.5–10. Translated by Wilhelm Pauck, ed., *Luther: Lectures on Romans,* Library of Christian Classics 15 (Philadelphia: Westminster Press, 1961).

24. *WA* 56.342.33–343.2; 356.4–6.

25. *WA* 56.351.23–352.7.

26. *WA* 56.343.16–23; 350.27–351.1.

27. *BoA* 5.320–326. Translated by James Atkinson, ed., *Luther: Early Theological Works,* Library of Christian Classics 16 (Philadelphia: Westminster Press, 1962).

28. *BoA* 5.378.22–22. Translated by Atkinson.

29. *BoA* 5.242.11–15. Translated by Pauck.

30. *HS* 382–397.

31. *HS* 386.

32. *HS* 418.

33. *HS* 416–17.

34. *HS* 313–15.

35. *HS* 315–16.

36. *HS* 434–457.

VII. Scripture and the Lord's Supper in Luther's Theology

1. Because this chapter was written originally for an audience of clergy rather than professional historians, references are to easily accessible English

translations of Luther's and Zwingli's works rather than to Latin and German critical editions.

2. *Luther's Works* 37, edited by Robert H. Fischer (Philadelphia: Fortress Press, 1961), p. 79. [Hereafter cited as *LW* 37.]

3. Ibid., p. 97.

4. Ibid., p. 231.

5. "Disputation against Scholastic Theology, Theses 35–53," in *Luther: Early Theological Works*, edited by James Atkinson, Library of Christian Classics 16 (Philadelphia: Westminster Press, 1962), pp. 269–70.

6. "Pagan Servitude of the Church," in *Martin Luther: Selections from his Writings*, edited by John Dillenberger (New York: Anchor Books, 1961), pp. 266–70.

7. Zwingli, "On the Lord's Supper," in *Zwingli and Bullinger*, edited by G.W. Bromiley, Library of Christian Classics 24 (Philadelphia: Westminster Press, 1963), p. 224, and Zwingli, *Commentary on True and False Religion*, edited by S.M. Jackson and C.N. Heller (Durham, NC: The Labyrinth Press, 1981), pp. 224–28.

8. *LW* 37, pp. 108–12.

9. For a brief sketch of Schwenckfeld's views, see David C. Steinmetz, *Reformers in the Wings* (Grand Rapids: Baker Book House, 1981), pp. 186–96.

10. Ibid., pp. 175–85.

11. *LW* 37, pp. 108–112.

12. Zwingli, *Commentary*, pp. 209–20. For an exposition of Zwingli's eucharistic views, see Jaques Courvoisier, *Zwingli: A Reformed Theologian* (Richmond: John Knox Press, 1963), pp. 67–78, and Gottfried W. Locher, *Zwingli's Thought: New Perspectives*, Studies in the History of Christian Thought 25 (Leiden, 1981), pp. 20–23, 220–28.

13. *LW* 37, pp. 95–98, 286–88.

14. Locher, *Zwingli's Thought*, p. 23.

15. Zwingli, *Commentary*, pp. 199–200; Courvoisier, *Zwingli*, pp. 74–77.

16. Dillenberger, ed., *Luther*, pp. 272–74.

17. *LW* 37, pp. 366–67.

18. Ibid., p. 188.

19. The heart of Zwingli's argument is found in "An Exposition of the Faith," in *Zwingli and Bullinger*, pp. 254–62.

20. Heinrich Heppe, *Reformed Dogmatics* (Grand Rapids: Baker Book House, 1978), pp. 441–45.

21. Zwingli, "Exposition," pp. 255–56.

22. Locher, *Zwingli's Thought*, p. 176.

23. *LW* 37, p. 215.

24. Ibid., pp. 215–16.

25. Ibid., p. 216.

26. Ibid.

27. Ibid. pp. 216–17.

28. Ibid., pp. 57, 218.

29. Ibid., p. 68.

30. Ibid., p. 69.

31. Courvoisier, *Zwingli*, pp. 70–72.

32. *LW* 37, p. 66.

VIII. Luther and Calvin on Church and Tradition

1. Calvin to Viret, May 19, 1540, *CO* 11:36 (no. 217).
2. *OC* 11:698 (no. 544); 12:99 (no. 657).
3. Cf. chapter 7, "Scripture and the Lord's Supper in Luther's Theology."
4. Brian A. Gerrish, "The Pathfinder: Calvin's Image of Martin Luther," in *The Old Protestantism and the New: Essay on the Reformation Heritage* (Chicago: University of Chicago Press, 1982), pp. 27–48.
5. *OC* 9:19, 91, 15:336; 16:263, 430; 17:139; 18:683–84, 733.
6. *OC* 11:774–5 (no. 586). Translated by Brian A. Gerrish, in *The Old Protestantism and the New* (Chicago: University of Chicago Press, 1982), p. 33.
7. *WABr* 8.569.29 (no. 3349).
8. *OC* 210.2:432 (no. 197). Gerrish, p. 32.
9. The Latin text is found in *OS* I:437–89. References to *Reply to Sadoleto* in this chapter are to the easily accessible English translation by John C. Olin in *John Calvin and Jacopo Sadoleto: A Reformation Debate* (New York: Harper Torchbooks, 1966), pp. 49–94.
10. *WA* 50. References 509–653 to *On the Councils and the Church* in this chapter are to the English translation by Theodore G. Tappert, ed., *Selected Writings of Martin Luther*, Vol. IV (Philadelphia: Fortress Press, 1967), pp. 197–370.
11. *Concilium Tridentinum: Diariorum, actorum, epistolarum, tractatuum, nova collectio*, edited by Görres-Gesellschaft (Freiburg, 1901–), Vol. IV, pp. 73–78.
12. For a discussion of this writing in the broader context of the polemics of the older Luther, see Mark U. Edwards, Jr., *Luther's Last Battles: Politics and Polemics 1531–46* (Ithaca and London: Cornell University Press, 1983), pp. 93–96.
13. "Councils," pp. 201–45.
14. Ibid., pp. 245–334.
15. Ibid., p. 325.
16. Ibid., pp. 335–70.
17. Ibid., p. 342.
18. "Reply," p. 50.
19. Ibid., p. 93.
20. Ibid., p. 62.
21. Ibid., p. 82.
22. Ibid.
23. Ibid., p. 92.
24. Ibid., pp. 77–78.
25. Ibid., p. 61.
26. Ibid., pp. 61–62.
27. Ibid., pp. 66–9.
28. Ibid., pp. 88–90.
29. Ibid., p. 90.

IX. Luther and the Drunkenness of Noah

1. *WA* 42.vii-x.
2. *LW* 2 (St. Louis: Concordia Publishing House, 1960), p. x.
3. The following comments are based on Gerhard von Rad, *Genesis: A Commentary* (Philadelphia: Westminster Press, 1972), pp. 134–39.

4. Robert Alter, *The Art of Biblical Narrative* (New York: Basic Books, 1981), p. 164.

5. For the literal interpretation of this passage, see Denis the Carthusian, *Doctoris Ecstatici D. Dionysii Cartusiani Opera Omnia*, Vol. I (Monstrolii, 1896), pp. 187–89.

6. Ibid., 191–92.

7. Ibid., 192–3.

8. *WA* 9.349.10–350.15; 9.421.4–36.

9. *WA* 14.204.15–208.32.

10. *WA* 42.377.25–393.36.

11. *LW* 2, p. 168. Translation of *WA* 42.379.35–42.

12. *WA* 42.388.8–9.

13. Luther gives an extended essay on the role of allegory in the midst of his exposition of the Noah story: *WA* 42.367.4–377.24.

14. In this connection, see the illuminating essay by Karlfried Froehlich, "Biblical Hermeneutics on the Move," *Word and World* 1:2 (1981): 140–52.

15. See my essay, "The Superiority of Pre-Critical Exegesis," *Theology Today* 27 (1980): 27–38.

X. Luther and the Two Kingdoms

1. Reinhold Niebuhr, *The Nature and Destiny of Man: II Human Destiny* (New York: Charles Scribner's Sons, 1941, 1943, 1949), p. 196, footnote 18.

2. Ibid., p. 196.

3. Ibid., p. 196–97.

4. Ibid., pp. 185–98.

5. Ibid., p. 191.

6. Ibid., p. 187.

7. Ibid., pp. 194–95.

8. Harry G. Haile, *Luther, An Experiment in Biography* (Princeton: Princeton University Press, 1980, 1983), pp. 180–84.

9. Ibid., pp. 78–80.

10. Ibid., pp. 19–20.

11. Ibid., pp. 133–147.

12. The literature on this subject is quite extensive. The best brief treatment is Heinrich Bornkamm, *Luther's Doctrine of the Two Kingdoms* (Philadelphia: Fortress Press, 1966). Also helpful for beginners are Heinrich Bornkamm, *Luther's World of Thought* (St. Louis: Concordia Publishing House, 1958), pp. 218–72; Gerhard Ebeling, *Luther: An Introduction to his Thought* (London: William Collins Sons and Co., 1970), pp. 159–225; and F. Edward Cranz, *An Essay on the Development of Luther's Thought on Justice, Law and Society*, Harvard Theological Studies 19 (Cambridge, MA: Harvard University Press, 1964).

13. Niebuhr, *Destiny*, p. 197.

14. On this point, see Bornkamm, *World*, pp. 240–41.

15. This chapter was written as a public lecture for a colloquium on Theological Anthropology sponsored by the Duke Divinity School and the Protestant Theological Faculty of the University of Bonn and held at Duke University in March, 1985. Students who attended were asked to read three well-known works of Luther: "The Freedom of a Christian," *WA* 7.49–73; "Secular Authority: To What Extent It Should Be Obeyed," *WA* 11.245–80; and "An Appeal to

the Ruling Class," *WA* 6.404–69. Since the students used the popular anthology edited by John Dillenberger, *Martin Luther: Selections from his Writings* (New York: Anchor Books, 1962), references in this chapter are to the anthology rather than to the Weimar edition.

16. Dillenberger, *Luther*, p. 54.
17. Ibid.
18. Ibid., p. 55.
19. Ibid.
20. Scholium on Romans 12:7 from Wilhelm Pauck, ed. and trans., *Luther: Lectures on Romans,* Library of Christian Classics 15 (Philadelphia: Westminster Press, 1961), pp. 335–36.
21. Dillenberger, *Luther*, p. 55.
22. Ibid., p. 57.
23. Ibid., p. 58.
24. *WA* 4.262.54–55.
25. Pauck, *Romans*, p. 151.
26. Ibid., p. 291.
27. Dillenberger, *Luther*, pp. 58–59.
28. Ibid., pp. 59–60.
29. Ibid., pp. 60–61.
30. Ibid., p. 68.
31. Ibid., pp. 68–69.
32. Ibid., p. 69.
33. Ibid., pp. 69–70.
34. Ibid., p. 72.
35. Ibid., p. 73.
36. Ibid., pp. 75–76.
37. Ibid., p. 79.
38. Ibid., p. 75.
39. Ibid., pp. 80–81.
40. Ibid., p. 81.
41. Ibid., p. 80.
42. Ibid., p. 369.
43. Ibid., p. 472.
44. Ibid., p. 369.
45. Ibid., pp. 370–71.
46. Ibid., pp. 374–75, 377–78.
47. Ibid., pp. 373–76.
48. Ibid., p. 373.
49. Ibid.
50. Bornkamm, *World*, pp. 240–42.
51. Ibid., pp. 246–47.
52. Ibid., p. 247.
53. Dillenberger, *Luther*, p. 393.
54. Bornkamm, *World*, p. 249.

XI. Luther and Formation in Faith

1. The first article of the Augsburg Confession begins with a reaffirmation of the decisions of the Council of Nicaea. Article XXII, dealing with communion in both kinds, appeals to Cyprian and ancient custom against the modern practice of deny-

ing the cup to the laity. For the appropriate texts, see *The Book of Concord,* translated and edited by Theodore Tappert (Philadelphia: Fortress Press, 1959).

2. See in this connection the valuable anthology by Gerald Strauss, ed., *Manifestations of Discontent in Germany on the Eve of the Reformation* (Bloomington, IN: Indiana University Press, 1972).

3. John Calvin, *OS* I: 437–89. Sadoleto's text is printed in his *Opera quae extant omnia,* Vol. 4 (Verona, 1737–1738). For further discussion of this question see "Luther and Calvin on Church and Tradition," chapter 8 in this book. See also John C. Olin, ed., *John Calvin and Jacopo Sadoleto: A Reformation Debate* (New York: Harper and Row, 1966).

4. Though there are small differences between Luther and Calvin on this question, the similarities are far more important. See again chapter 8.

5. On this question see John Calvin, *Institutes* IV.ii.11.

6. See in this connection Anthony N.S. Lane, "*Sola Scriptura*? Making Sense of a Post-Reformation Slogan, in *A Pathway into the Holy Scripture,* eds. P. E. Satterwhite and David F. Wright (Grand Rapids: Eerdmans, 1994), pp. 297–327.

7. Calvin's annotations have been particularly well studied. In this connection see Alexandre Ganoczy and Klaus Müller, *Calvins handschriftliche Annotationen zu Chrysostomus: Ein Beitrag zur Hermeneutik Calvins* (Wiesbaden: Steiner, 1981). Cf. David C. Steinmetz, "Calvin and the Patristic Exegesis of Paul," in *The Bible in the Sixteenth Century,* ed. D. C. Steinmetz, Duke Monographs in Medieval and Renaissance Studies 11 (Durham and London: Duke University Press, 1990), pp. 100–118.

8. David C. Steinmetz, "Calvin and his Lutheran Critics," *The Lutheran Quarterly,* 4.2 (summer 1990): 179–94.

9. Conrad Porta, *Jungfrawenspiegel,* Facsimile ed. of 1580, ed. Cornelia Niekus Moore (Bern: Peter Lang, 1990).

10. For a defense of celibacy against Protestant criticisms of the institution, see Johannes Eck, *Enchiridion,* pp. 222–30.

11. The Second Lateran Council of 1139 pronounced the marriage of clerics in major orders invalid.

12. Steven E. Ozment, *The Reformation in the Cities* (New Haven: Yale University Press, 1975), pp. 58–61. Following Oskar Vasella, Ozment notes: "Clerical marriage would have been a great financial loss to the bishop of Constance."

13. Zwingli explains his brief affair with the daughter of a barber in Einsiedeln in a letter to Heinrich Utinger in Zurich dated December 5, 1518. See *Huldreich Zwinglis Sämtliche Werke,* Band VII, eds. E. Egli, G. Finsler, and W. Köhler, CR 94 (Leipzig: M. Heinsius Nachfolger, 1911), pp. 110–13. The bishop himself was known to be intimate with the widow of the former burgomaster of Constance. See Euan Cameron, *European Reformation* (New York: Oxford University Press, 1991), p. 44.

14. G. R. Potter, *Zwingli* (Cambridge: Cambridge University Press, 1976), pp. 78–81. Frau Reinhart had been Zwingli's concubine before their marriage. Their secret marriage was publicly announced before the birth of their first child.

15. Even when the former priest's character was beyond reproach, many laity still regarded a married clergyman as something illegitimate and forbidden. The attitude lingered on even among people whose formal theological allegiance had shifted. Noto-

rious in this respect was the attitude of Elizabeth I of England toward the spouses of married clergy, including the wife of Matthew Parker, her carefully selected Archbishop of Canterbury.

16. Wilhelm Niesel, ed., *Bekenntnisschriften und Kirchenordnungen der nach Gottes Wort reformierten Kirche* (Zollikon-Zurich: Evangelischer Verlag, 1938), p. 223: "Praedicatio verbi Dei est verbum Dei."

17. On the education of the orator, see Jean-Claude Margolin, *Humanism in Europe at the Time of the Renaissance,* trans. John Farthing (Durham, NC: The Labyrinth Press, 1989), pp. 61–63.

18. For the career and thought of Geiler, see E. Jane Dempsey Douglass, *Justification in Late Medieval Preaching: A Study of John Geiler of Keisersberg,* SMRT 1 (Leiden: E.J. Brill, 1966).

19. Geiler attempted to argue for the primacy of preaching, but without great success. See ibid., pp. 82–91.

20. Luther's discussion of confession in the Large Catechism makes many of these points clear, Tappert, *Book of Concord,* pp. 457–61.

21. The Small Catechism can be found in ibid., pp. 337–56; the Large Catechism in ibid., pp. 357–461.

22. The English translation of "A Fruitful Mirror" is easily accessible in Denis Janz, *Three Reformation Catechisms: Catholic, Anabaptist, Lutheran* (New York and Toronto: Edwin Mellen Press, 1982), pp. 31–130.

23. See in this connection *WA* 38:351–73.

24. For an example of Luther's preference for the failings of the biblical characters over their virtues see my "Luther and Tamar," in *Luther, Faith, and Human Sexuality, Lutheran Theological Seminary Bulletin* 73.1 (winter 1993): 3–15.

25. Domingo de Soto, O.P., *In Epistolam divi Pauli ad Romanos Commentarii* (Antwerp: Jan Steelsius, 1550), p. 5: "Quocirca non sola fide (ut falso ipsi praedicant) sed fide per charitatem operante iustificamur: . . ." Ambrosius Catherinus Politus, O.P., *Commentarius in Omnes divi Pauli et alias septem Canonicas Epistolas* (Venice: Vincent Valgrisi, 1551), a2: "Nam si nostrae aetatis tractores spectemus (qui numerus hodie multus est) eorum longe maior pars haeretici sunt. . . ."

26. Richard A. Muller, in *Post-Reformation Reformed Dogmatics,* Vol. 1 (Grand Rapids: Baker, 1987), pp. 15–52, argues that the discursive, polemical theology of the early reformers, aimed at the reform of abuses in the life and thought of the medieval Catholic church, was replaced by a more sophisticated, dialectical theology, aimed at protecting and establishing the Protestant churches.

27. Readers who would like to pursue these questions further are encouraged to read Euan Cameron, *The European Reformation* (Oxford: Oxford University Press, 1991); Eamon Duffy, *The Stripping of the Altars: Traditional Religion in England 1400–1580* (New Haven: Yale University Press, 1992); Gerald Strauss, *Luther's House of Learning: Indoctrination of the Young in the German Reformation* (Baltimore and London: The Johns Hopkins University Press, 1978); and John Westerhoff and O. C. Edwards, eds., *A Faithful Church: Issues in the History of Catechesis* (Wilton, CT: Morehouse-Barlow Co., 1981).

XII. Luther and the Ascent of Jacob's Ladder

1. Spa Committee of Bath City Council, *Bath: Official Guide Book 1978* (Blackpool: United Printing Services, 1978), p. 10.

2. Denis the Carthusian, "Enarratio in Cap. XXVIII Genesis," in *Doctoris Ecstatici D. Dionysii Carthusiani Opera Omnia,* Vol I (Monstrolii: Typis Cartusiae S.M. de Pratis, 1896), p. 332. Further references will be abbreviated as Denis, "Enarratio."

3. Anders Nygren, *Agape and Eros* (Philadelphia: Westminster Press, 1953), pp. 621–37.

4. Ibid., p. 690.

5. Hugh of St. Cher, *Hugonis de Sancto Caro, Opera Omnia* Vol. I (Venice: Nicholas Pezzana, 1732), 53v–55v. Hereafter abbreviated as Hugh, "Expositio."

6. Nicholas of Lyra, *Prima Pars Biblie cum Glossa Ordinaria et Expositione Litterali et Morali,* Vol. I (Basel: Froben, 1498). Hereafter abbreviated as Lyra on the literal sense of Genesis 28.

7. Denis, "Enarratio."

8. The best treatment of this problem is by Hans W. Frei, *The Eclipse of Biblical Narrative: A Study in Eighteenth and Nineteenth Century Hermeneutics* (New Haven: Yale University Press, 1974)

9. For example, Hugh, "Expositio," 39r; Lyra on the literal sense of Genesis 28:19.

10. Hugh, "Expositio," 38r; Denis, "Enarratio," p. 329.

11. Denis, "Enarratio," p. 329. Hugh concedes that it may be called Bethel because it is near to Bethlehem, though he too identifies Bethel with Jerusalem.

12. Hugh, "Expositio," 39r; Denis, "Enarratio," p. 331; Lyra on the literal interpretation of Genesis 28:19.

13. Denis, "Enarratio," pp. 330–31.

14. Ibid.

15. See also my essay, "John Calvin on Isaiah 6: A Problem in the History of Exegesis," *Interpretation* 36 (April, 1982): 156–70, especially pp. 163–64, for the medieval treatment of the nature of Isaiah's vision. Cf. David C. Steinmetz, *Luther and Staupitz: An Essay in the Intellectual Origins of the Protestant Reformation* (Durham, NC: Duke University Press, 1980), pp. 129–31, 135–40.

16. Denis, "Enarratio," p. 329.

17. Hugh, "Expositio," 37v.

18. Denis, "Enarratio," p. 329.

19. Ibid.

20. Lyra on the literal sense of Genesis 28:12; Denis, "Enarratio," p. 329.

21. Hugh, "Expositio," 38r.

22. Ibid., 38r–38v

23. Denis, "Enarratio," pp. 331–32.

24. Lyra on the literal sense of Genesis 28:20–22; Denis, "Enarratio," p. 331.

25. Hugh, "Expositio," 39r.

26. Denis, "Enarratio," p. 331.

27. *WA* 43.595.36.

28. *WA* 43.594.38.

29. *WA* 43.602.12.

30. *WA* 43.596.25.
31. *WA* 43.575.4.
32. *WA* 43.591.20.
33. *WA* 43.592.28.
34. *WA* 43.573.9.
35. *WA* 43.561.21. On this subject see Steven E. Ozment, *When Fathers Ruled: Family Life In Reformation Europe* (Cambridge, MA: Harvard University Press, 1983), pp. 25–49.
36. *WA* 43.568.14.
37. *WA* 43.574.23.
38. *WA* 43.578.10.
39. *WA* 43.582.15.
40. *WA* 43.582.18
41. *WA* 43.576.6.
42. *WA* 43.597.31, 598.35.
43. *WA* 43.586.41.
44. *WA* 43.604.1.
45. *WA* 43.607.23.
46. *WA* 43.610.33.

XIII. Luther and Calvin on the Banks of the Jabbok

1. The four volumes correspond to the Weimar edition according to the following pattern: I (1544) = *WA* 42.1–428; II (1550) = *WA* 42.429–43.364; III (1552) = *WA* 43.365–44.231; IV (1554) = *WA* 44.232–825.
2. Wulfert de Greef, *The Writings of John Calvin: An Introductory Guide*, trans. by Lyle D. Bierma (Grand Rapids: Baker Book House, 1994), pp. 104–5. Cf. *OC* 15:196–201.
3. *OC* 15:260–61.
4. *OC* 15:453–55.
5. *OC* 15:454.
6. *OC* 15:488–89.
7. *OC* 15:501–2.
8. Denis the Carthusian, *Enarrationes piae ac eruditae in quinque Mosaicae legis libros* (Cologne: Peter Quentel, 1534). Citations are taken from the critical edition, *Doctoris Ecstatici D. Dionysii Cartusiani Opera Omnia*, Vol. I (Monstrolii: Typis Cartusiae S.M. de Pratis, 1896). Although there is no evidence that Calvin consulted Denis in his interpretation of Genesis 32, Denis was one of the few medieval authors collected by the library of the Academy in Geneva. See in this connection Alexandre Ganoczy, *La bibliotheque de l'Académie de Calvin* (Geneva: Droz, 1969).
9. *WA* 44.93.
10. Denis, *Enarrationes*, 357.
11. Hugh of St. Cher, "Liber Geneseos," *Opus Admirabile, Tomus Unus* (Venice: Nicolaus Pezzana, 1731), 45v.
12. Denis, *Enarrationes*, 356.
13. Ibid., 359.

14. Ibid., 359.
15. Ibid., 356–57.
16. Ibid., 357.
17. Ibid., 358–59.
18. Ibid., 357.
19. Ibid., 358.
20. Ibid., 357.
21. Ibid., 357.
22. Ibid., 357.
23. Ibid., 357.
24. Ibid., 358.
25. Ibid., 358.
26. Ibid., 358.
27. Ibid., 358.
28. Ibid., 358.
29. Ibid., 358.
30. Ibid., 358.
31. Ibid., 360.
32. Ibid., 360.
33. *WA* 44.99. Cf. 96–97 on Esau's guardian angel.
34. *WA* 44.105.
35. *WA* 17(2).200–204.
36. *WA* 17(2).203.
37. *WA* 44.103–4.
38. *WA* 44.100–101.
39. *WA* 44.100–101.
40. *WA* 44.100.
41. *WA* 44.101–2.
42. *WA* 44.100–101.
43. *WA* 44.103–4.
44. *WA* 44.106–8.
45. *WA* 44.107–8.
46. *WA* 44.105.
47. *WA* 44.105.
48. *WA* 44.111.
49. *WA* 44.93, 108–9, 114–15.
50. *WA* 44.114–15.
51. *WA* 44.115–16.
52. *OC* 23.442.
53. *OC* 23.442.
54. *OC* 23.446.
55. *OC* 23.442.
56. *OC* 23.442.
57. *OC* 23.443.
58. *OC* 23.445–46. Cf. *Inst.* I.xiii.10.
59. *OC* 23.442–43.
60. *OC* 23.443.
61. *OC* 23.443.

62. *OC* 23.444.
63. *OC* 23.444.
64. *OC* 23.444.
65. *OC* 23.447.
66. *OC* 23.444–45.
67. *OC* 23.445–46.
68. *OC* 23.447.

INDEX

Abraham, 14, 32–36, 42, 43; Luther on, 35, 39–40, 41; Steinbach on, 37–38, 41, 42

accidents, in theory of transubstantiation, 73

ad fontes, 128

alienation from God, 66, 166

allegorical interpretations: of Jacob story, 166–67; of Noah story, 103–4, 105–7, 109

Anabaptists, 32, 59, 70

anfechtungen, 1–2, 10

anti-Pelagianism, 17, 21

anti-Semitism, Luther on, 20

anxiety, 1–2, 19

appeal to antiquity, 127–30

Aristotelianism, 18, 39, 56, 73

Aristotle, 114, 116

ascension, 81, 83

attributes of Christ, 78, 80–81

attrition (imperfect contrition), 4, 6, 7, 10

Auerbach, Erich, 100

Augsburg Confession, 86

Augustine, St., 12–14, 36–37, 38, 49; on Romans, 9, 14–18, 20–21

Augustinianism, 12, 13, 64, 69,71; Seripando on, 35, 42, 43; and Thomas' theology, 47, 55

Augustinians, 5, 8, 13

authority, 2–3, 8; Calvin on, 91, 92–93, 94–96; Luther on, 88–90, 94–96

auxilium speciale, 53

baptism, 32, 33, 59, 60, 70; of heretics, 89, 95

belief *(credere),* 34

believers, 39, 105

Bible, 13–14, 43–46, 72, 102; as Holy Scripture, 109. *See also* New Testament; Old Testament; Scripture

Biel, Gabriel, 5–6, 21, 34–35, 36, 47; on human will, 60–63; Luther on, 56–57, 63–64, 65, 66–67; on Thomas Aquinas, 48, 52–56

bishops, 96, 104, 106, 109, 116, 118

body, 75–76

body of Christ: Luther on, 73–75, 79–80; Zwingli on, 76–77, 79–80

Bradford, Gamaliel, 110

bread and wine, 73–74, 76–77, 80, 81

Bucer, Martin, 85, 113

Bullinger, Heinrich, 131, 132–33

Cajetan, Thomas de Vio Cardinal, 48, 55

calling, divine *(vocatio),* 15, 16, 68

Call-Word *(Heissel-Wort),* 115, 135

Calvin, John, 24, 64, 85–88, 90–97, 128, 129, 156–58, 164–66

Canaan (son of Ham), 100, 102, 103, 105, 106, 107

Canaan, land of, 100–101

Canaanites (children of Ham), 100, 101, 103, 105, 106

Canon Law, Luther on, 121, 123

Capreolus, John, 48, 55

Carlstadt, Andreas Bodenstein of, 47, 57, 75

catechisms, 135–40

Catherinus, Ambrosius, 48

Catholic Church, 52, 90–94, 121–22. *See also* Church, the

causality, 37, 52, 53, 54
celibacy, 131–32
ceremonies, 120–21
Chalcedon, Council of, 88, 89, 130
charity, 37, 49, 63, 65, 104. *See also*
    love
Christ (Jesus Christ), 25–28, 29–30, 66,
    116, 119, 161–62; and the eucharist,
    73–76, 77, 79–80; as Jacob's ladder,
    148–49; Noah seen as type of,
    103–4, 105, 109; at right hand of
    God, 78–81
Church, the, 2–3, 6, 8, 44, 77; Anabap-
    tists on, 59; Calvin on, 87–88,
    90–97; covenant with God, 62, 65;
    Denis on, 104; Hubmaier on, 70;
    Luther on, 87, 90, 94–97, 114,
    115–16, 120–22, 123–24; and Paul,
    33–34; Zwingli on, 78–79
circumcision, rite of, and Abraham,
    32, 33, 34
circumscriptive presence, 79–80, 81
Coelifodina (Paltz), 5
coercion, 114, 115, 121–22
*Collectorium on the Sentences of Peter
    Lombard* (Biel), 48, 53
*Commentary on the Sentences of Peter
    Lombard* (Gorkum), 47
common sense, Luther on, 40–41
concupiscence, 50, 61, 65–66
Concursus dei generalis, 53, 54, 57, 61
condign merit, 54, 55
confession, 2, 3–5, 6, 10–11, 65, 135,
    137–38; and tradition, 92, 95
congregation, and the eucharist,
    76–77, 79
congruity, merit of, 36, 37, 42, 55–56,
    57
conscience, 1, 2, 8, 112, 121; Biel on,
    61, 62; Hubmaier on, 67–68
consecration, and transubstantiation,
    73
Constantinople, Council of, 88, 89
contrary appearance, 27–29
contrition, 4, 5–8, 10–11, 61
Corinthians, I, 73, 76–78
councils, 87–90, 94–95, 96

covenant, 6, 14, 20, 33, 34, 55, 149–50;
    between God and the Church, 62,
    65, 69; Lord's Supper as, 77
credere (belief), 34
credulitas, 33
creed, the, 78, 81
crucifixion, 19, 104
curse on Canaan, 100, 102–3, 105, 106,
    107
Cyprian, 89, 95, 103

d'Ailly, Pierre, 47, 48, 52, 56–57
De congruo merit. See congruity, merit
    of
*De diversis quaestionibus ad Simpli-
    cianum* (Augustine), 16–17
Deed-Word *(Thettel-Wort),* 115–16,
    135
defeatism, 113
definitive presence, 79–80
De libero arbitrio (Augustine), 14
Denck, Hans, 68
Denis the Carthusian, 99, 102–5, 109,
    143, 146–48, 152, 158–61, 166–67
depression, suffered by Luther, 1, 9
De Servo Arbitrio (Luther), 59, 63
destiny, Augustine on, 14
Deus absconditus. See hidden God
Deus revelatus, 26
devil, 9, 10, 31
Dictata super Psalterium (Luther), 63,
    98
dietary laws, and the Council of Jeru-
    salem, 89, 95, 96
Dietrich, Veit, 98–99
dignity, 50
disposing grace, 54
disposition, 2–5, 7, 11, 40–41, 64–65
*Disputation against Scholastic Theol-
    ogy* (Luther), 56–57, 66
divine acceptation, 50, 51, 56
divine calling *(vocation),* 15, 16, 68
divine nature of Christ, 79
divine ordination, 55
divine providence, 38
divine will. *See* will of God
doctrine, Calvin on, 91–92, 93

Dominicans, 49, 52, 105
doubts, Luther on, 19
drunkenness of Noah, 99–111
dualism, 14, 75–86, 113

Eck, John, 59–60
effectual calling, 16, 21
elect, the, 14, 16, 20
election, 8–9, 15–17; Luther on, 10,
    17–22, 63–64, 66
empirical evidence, 29, 39
Enchiridion (Augustine), 17, 20
Enchiridion (Eck), 59
Ephesus, Council of, 88, 89
equity, 123
Erasmus, 17, 21, 59
Esau, 15–17, 20, 26, 144, 159
ethics. *See* morality
eucharist (Lord's Supper), 72, 76–78;
    Luther on, 73–75, 77–78, 82–84;
    Zwingli on, 76–77, 78–79, 82
evangelical Christianity, in contempo-
    rary America, 124
evil, 14, 18, 65, 112, 119
exegesis, 96–97, 98–99, 109–11
Exposition of the Canon of the Mass
    (Biel), 54
*Expositio quarundam propositionum
    ex epistola ad Romanos* (Augus-
    tine), 14–15
extra-Calvinisticum, 79
extreme unction, 6–7
Ezekiel, 102

Faber Stapulensis, 17, 21
faith *(fides),* 26, 33, 124–25; Augustine
    on, 15–17; Calvin on, 92–94; and
    the eucharist, 74, 77–78; formed by
    love, 37, 41, 42; and good works,
    119–20; and the hidden God, 27,
    28–29, 31; Luther on, 10, 11, 39–40,
    71, 83–84, 162–63; and the Word of
    God, 116–18. *See also* justification
    by faith
fall, the, 61, 66, 67, 69
Farel, Guillaume, 90–91
Fathers, 87, 89, 94–95, 128
fides. See faith

fiducia, 33
figura, 74, 75
flesh, 66, 67–68, 75–76
foreknowledge, 15, 16, 20, 64
Fourth Lateran Council, 73
Franciscans, 3, 105
Free Church, and Hubmaier, 70
freedom, Luther on, 115–16, 117,
    120–22, 124, 140
free will, 6, 37, 47, 48, 49–50, 51;
    Augustine on, 14, 15, 16, 18; Biel
    on, 6, 60–62, 65; Hubmaier on,
    67–68, 69, 70; Luther on, 17, 18, 21,
    57, 65, 66, 71

Galatians, Luther on, 35
Genesis, 98–99, 109, 110; Gen. 9:
    18–29, 99–102; interpretations of,
    103–11, 142–43, 146–53, 156–68
Geneva, 90–91
Gentiles: as children of Abraham, 14,
    33; as Christians, 20, 32, 89; in
    Noah story interpretations,
    100–101, 103–4, 105, 108–9
Gerrish, Brian, 86
gift of God, 50, 61, 116–17; faith as, 16,
    42, 83
Goch, John Pupper of, 48–52, 56,
    57–58
God, 8–9, 14–15, 40, 79, 161; and the
    eucharist, 75, 82; and government
    of the state, 122–23; hiddenness of,
    23–31, 39; Hubmaier on, 68–69;
    Luther on, 31, 63–64, 82–84, 114,
    115–18, 120, 124; proofs for the
    existence of, 25. *See also* gift of
    God; promises of God; will of God
good (goodness), 17–18, 61–62, 64
good works, 37, 49–51, 53–54, 55, 56,
    93; Augustine on, 15, 16; Biel on,
    53–54, 55, 63; Luther on, 10, 57, 64,
    117, 118–20. *See also* works
Gorkum, Henry of, 47
gospel (good news), 25, 62, 68–69; and
    the Law, 29–30, 71; Luther on, 115,
    116–17, 121–22. *See also* Word of
    God
government of the state, 122–24

governments, two *(Zwei-Regimente-Lehre)*, 115, 121–24
grace, 6, 7, 26, 43, 113, 120; Augustine on, 12, 15; Biel on, 36, 37, 53–55, 61, 62, 65, 67; and free will, 47, 48; Goch on, 49–50, 51; Hubmaier on, 68–69, 70; Luther on, 10, 11, 12, 17, 40–41, 57–58, 63–67, 71, 76, 80–82; in Noah story interpretations, 103–4, 106; Staupitz on, 8–9, 10; Steinbach on, 37–38; Zwingli on, 76, 77
graced will, 50, 56
Grane, Leif, 13
Gregory of Rimini, 13, 53, 55, 57
guilt, 64, 100, 102

Haile, Harry, 113
Ham (son of Noah), 10, 101, 102, 103–4, 105–8, 109–10
Ham, children of (Canaanites), 100, 101, 103, 105, 106
Hebrews (book of), on faith, 39
Heidelberg Disputation (Luther), 66, 85
Heissel-Wort (Call-Word), 115, 135
Hennig, Gerhard, 48
heresy, 47, 89
hermeneutics, 36, 38–39, 98–99, 109
hidden God, 23–31, 39
history, 94–95; and interpretations of the Bible, 43–46, 102, 108–9; theology conditioned by, 36–37, 38–39
Hoen, Cornelius, 74
Holy Spirit, 15, 54, 76, 93, 96, 107; Hubmaier on, 67, 68; Zwingli on, 76–77, 79
Holy Scripture. *See* Scripture
Hubmaier, Balthasar, 59–60, 67–70
Hugh of St. Cher, 143, 146–49
human nature, 42, 54, 70, 75–76, 107; of Christ, 78–79, 80–81; Luther on, 28, 66
hypostatic union, 78–79

Ignatius Loyola, 127
immanence, 24, 83
imperfect contrition. *See* attrition

incarnation, 24, 75, 78, 81, 82, 104
ineffectual calling, 16, 21
infant baptism, 32, 70
innovation, theological, 92, 95
ironic evil, 112
Isaac, 15, 39, 145
Israel (people), 14, 20–21, 33, 100–102. *See also* Jews

Jacob, 15–17, 20, 143–45, 147–55, 158–68
James, St., 33, 37, 42
Janz, Denis P., 48, 56–57
Japheth, 100–101, 102, 103–4
Japheth, children of, 100–101, 103–4
Jerusalem, Council of, 88–89, 95, 96
Jesus Christ. *See* Christ
Jews, 14, 23, 103; as Christians, 32; in Noah story, 100, 103–4, 105. *See also* Israel
John 6, 75–76
J (Yahwistic) primal history, 100–101
Judaism, and the Church, 32, 33
Judaization of Christianity, 66, 71
judgment, 26, 40–41, 114, 123–24
judicial system, of Catholic Church, 121
justice, 112–13, 114, 122; of God, 16–17, 18, 19, 21, 49, 50–51, 56
justification, 17, 40–41, 49, 56, 69; Augustine on, 15, 16–17; Biel on, 36, 55–56, 62; Luther on, 10–11, 65–66, 117–18
justification by faith, 12, 31, 42; and Abraham, 32–34, 37, 39–40, 41, 42; Calvin on, 92–94; and Christian ethics, 114, 118, 119; Luther on, 11, 40–41, 42, 90, 105, 112

Kingdom of God, 112, 114, 122
kingdoms, two *(Zwei-Reiche-Lehre)*, 113, 115–22
Kolde, Dietrich, 3–6, 7, 136–39

laity, role of, 127
larvae (masks) of God, 24
Last Judgment, 78

law, the, 33, 41, 61, 63, 115, 119; and
  the Gospel, 29–30, 71; Luther on,
  66–67, 89, 116–17, 120, 121
laws of the state, 121–23
Lewis, C. S., 42
literal interpretations: of Jacob story,
  147, 152; of Noah story, 102–3,
  109–10
Lord's Supper. *See* eucharist
Lortz, Joseph, 47
love, 12, 37, 42, 43; for neighbor,
  118–21, 122–23. *See also* charity
love of God (God's love), 9, 19
love of God (love for God), 37, 53,
  61–62, 120
Luke 22:19, 73
Luther, Martin, 1–3, 7–10, 12–14,
  98–99; on Abraham and Paul, 35,
  38–41, 43, 44; and Calvin, 85–88,
  156–59; on church and councils,
  87–90, 94–97; on drunkenness of
  Noah, 105–11; on the eucharist,
  73–75, 77–78, 82–84, 134–35; on
  Fathers, 129–30; on the hidden
  God, 23–31; and Hubmaier, 59–60,
  70–71; on Jacob, 144, 150–55,
  162–64; on Occamism, 56–58,
  63–67, 70–71; political and ethical
  theories, 112–25; reforms of church
  practice, 126–41; on Romans 9,
  17–22; and Thomas Aquinas,
  47–49; on Thomism, 56–58; on
  Zwingli, 79–81
Lyra, Nicholas of, 99, 105, 108, 143,
  146–48

magisterium 95–96
magistrates, 122, 123, 124
manducatio infidelium, 77
Manicheans, 14
Marcion, 23
marriage, 131–32
Mary, role of, 130–31
masks *(larvae)* of God, 24
massa peccati, 16, 21
massa perditionis (mass of perdition),
  17, 21
Matthew 26:26, 73, 75

Maurois, André, 110
Melanchthon, Philip, 1, 85, 86–87, 131
  n. 18, 157
Mellerstadt, Martin Pollich of, 47
mendicants, 49, 52
mercy, 9, 18–19, 30, 31, 41, 71
merit, 30, 42, 49–52, 56; Augustine on,
  12, 15–17; Biel on, 36, 53–56, 63;
  Luther on, 17, 57–58, 63, 64, 117;
  Steinbach on, 37–38, 42
metaphor, as explanation of eucharist,
  74, 75
ministry, Luther on, 116
miracles, and the eucharist, 73–74
Mirror for Christians (Kolde), 3–5,
  135–39
monarchy, 123
monasticism, 7, 49, 51–52
morality (ethics), 24, 33, 37, 50, 59, 62;
  Luther on, 112–13, 114, 115–21
moral interpretations. *See* tropological
  interpretations
mortal sin, 9, 54, 55, 66, 103; and
  penance, 4–5, 6
Moses, 23, 66, 100–101

natural law, 24, 63, 114, 123, 124
natural theology, 23, 24–25
natural will, 49–50, 51, 56
neighbors, 118–21, 124–25
New Testament, 32, 39, 43–44, 51,
  73–75. *See also* books by name
Nicaea, Council of, 88, 89, 130
Niebuhr, Reinhold, 112–13, 114,
  124–25
Noah, 99–111
nominalism, 34–35, 38, 42, 57, 70

Oberman, H. A., 13
Occamism, 49, 50, 55, 57, 70, 79; and
  Luther, 48, 56–58, 60, 63–67, 70–71;
  and Steinbach, 36, 37, 42. *See also*
  Biel, Gabriel
Ockham, William, 46, 47, 56
Oecolampadius, 59–60, 72, 74, 80
offices (in the Church), 118; Calvin on,
  91, 95–96; Luther on, 89–90, 91,
  95–96

Old Testament, 32, 101. *See also*
    Genesis
On the Councils and the Church
    (Luther), 87–90
On the Freedom of the Will (Hub-
    maier), 59

Paltz, John of, 5–7
parable of workers in the vineyard, 51
pastor, office of, 91
patriarchs, Luther on, 105, 106
Paul, St., 23, 35–36, 64, 69, 118; on
    faith of Abraham, 32–33; Luther
    on, 35, 38–39, 65; Romans 9, 14–22;
    Seripando on, 42–43; Steinbach on,
    36, 37–38
Paul III (pope), 35, 88
Peasants' War, Luther's stance on, 113
Pelagianism, 36, 38, 42, 47, 55–56, 70;
    Luther on, 57–58
penance, 7–8
penance, sacrament of, 6, 10–11. *See
    also* confession
perfect contrition, 6
Pharaoh, 15, 16, 19–20, 26, 106
Philippians 2, 120
piety, 43
political theory, of Luther, 112–25
polity, for the Church, 121–22
Pope, 96, 122
prayer, 5, 40
preachers, role in state, 114, 124
preaching, 67, 68–69, 81, 82–83, 133–34
predestination, 12, 15, 26, 67; Luther
    on, 17, 19–20, 64, 66
predetermination, 62, 64
preordination, 55
priests, 96, 116
princes, 113, 114, 123–24, 125
promises of God, 43, 51, 54–55, 69,
    108–9; and Abraham, 14, 32–33, 38,
    39–40; Luther on, 40–41, 66, 83,
    116–18, 120
proofs for the existence of God, 25
public office, 114, 121, 122–23, 124

*Questions on the Sentences of Peter
    Lombard* (d'Ailly), 48, 52
quietism, 113

real presence, 73–75, 80, 82
reason, 24, 61, 62, 67–69; Luther on,
    25–26, 40–41, 64; and revelation of
    God, 23, 29; and rule of state, 114,
    122, 123, 124
redemption, 12, 14, 23, 78, 109
regeneration 69, 70
Regimente-Lehre, Zwei (two govern-
    ments), 115, 121–24
Reiche-Lehre, Zwei (two kingdoms),
    113, 115–22
religious (monastic) vows, 49, 51–52, 56
repletive presence, 79
Reply to Sadoleto (Calvin), 87–88,
    91–94, 128
reprobation, 18, 19, 20, 21
resurrection, 78
Retractiones (Augustine), 15–16
revelation, 39, 68–69; and the hidden
    God, 23–24, 25–28, 29–30, 31
righteousness, 10, 42, 115, 117–18, 120;
    and Abraham, 32–33, 38, 41
Romans, Luther on, 35; Rom. 9, 14–22

sacraments, 2–3, 6–7, 10–11, 72, 96,
    122, 133–34; Luther on, 77, 81, 83,
    133. *See also* baptism; eucharist
Sadoleto, Jacopo Cardinal, 87, 90–94, 128
saints, Luther on, 105
salvation, 7, 20–21, 62, 68–70; Augus-
    tine on, 12, 16; Luther on, 18, 20,
    21, 65; and Noah story, 100–101, 103
Sarah (wife of Abraham), 33, 41
Schmalkalden, League of, 88
scholasticism, 18, 47, 48, 89; Luther
    on, 39, 56–58, 65, 73
Schwenckfeld, on the eucharist, 74–75
Scotism, 50, 56, 57
Scripture (Holy Scripture), 89–90, 116;
    Bible as, 45–46, 109; as source of
    authority, 87, 92–95, 97, 129. *See
    also* Bible
*Second Booklet on Human Free will,
    The* (Hubmaier), 59
Seripando, Girolamo Cardinal, 34, 35,
    41–43, 44
Sermon on the Mount, 114, 122–23
sexual sins, 3, 101

Shem, 100, 101, 102, 103–4, 105, 106, 107–8
Shem, children of, 103, 106
sin, 3–5, 9, 50, 67, 102–3, 122; Biel on, 54, 61–63; and coming of Christ, 27–28; and crucifixion of Christ, 19; Luther on, 65, 65, 112, 118; and natural theology, 24–25
sinners, 29–30, 50, 67–69, 112; Biel on, 6, 36, 53, 54, 55, 61–63; Luther on, 76, 115, 117
Spina Bartholomew, 48
spirit, 66, 67–68, 75–76
state, the, 114, 121–24
Staupitz, John, 8–10, 11, 13, 19, 21, 64
Steinbach, Wendelin, 34–35, 36–38, 39, 41, 42–43, 44; Melanchthon on, 131 n. 18
substance, 39, 40, 73
Summa Theologiae (Thomas Aquinas), 53–54
Supplementum Coelifodinae (Paltz), 5
Symbolism, as explanation of the eucharist, 74–75
synagogue, 104
synderesis, 61, 62, 64, 65, 67–68

Tabletalk (Luther), 24–25
temptation, 2, 9
theocracy, 123, 124
theological innovation, 92, 95
Thettel-Wort (Deed-Word), 115–16, 135
Thomas Aquinas, St., 47–56, 60
Thomism, 47–49, 56–58
Tillich, Paul, 65
tradition, 89, 95, 97
transcendence, 23, 24, 83
transubstantiation, 73–74, 92, 95; of the congregation, 77
tropological (moral) interpretations, 19–20; of Noah story, 104, 106, 109
trust, 28–29, 33, 41, 116
two governments *(Zwei-Regimente-Lehre),* 115, 121–24

two kingdoms *(Zwei-Reiche-Lehre),* 113, 115–22

ubiquity, as attribute of Christ, 80–81, 82
unbelief, Luther on, 28–29

Vincent of Lerins, 93
vineyards, role in drunken Noah story, 99–100, 101
virtue, 37, 42, 53, 112; Luther on, 18, 41, 64, 65
vocatio (divine calling), 15, 16, 21, 68
Von Rad, Gerhard, 100, 108–9
vows, 7, 49, 51–52, 56

will, human, 60–62, 64, 65–66; Hubmaier on, 59, 67–68, 69. *See also* free will
will of God (divine will), 14, 24, 69–70, 81, 159; Luther on, 18, 64
wisdom, as instrument of state, 114, 122, 123
Word of God, 26, 29–30, 40, 83, 115–17; and the eucharist, 74, 81; proclamation of, 67, 68–69, 120, 122, 133–35; as source of authority, 90, 91, 92–93; 96–97
works, 15, 16, 77, 105, 116; relationship to faith, 33, 42, 43. *See also* good works
wounds of Christ, 9, 19, 22

Yahweh, 100–101
Yahwistic (J) primal history, 100–101

Zechariah, 27–28
Zwei-Regimente-Lehre (two governments), 115, 121–24
Zwei-Reiche-Lehre (two kingdoms), 113, 115–22
Zwingli, Ulrich, 59–60, 75–76, 78–80, 86, 131, 133; on the eucharist, 74, 76–77, 78–79, 82; Luther on, 72, 73, 79–81

David C. Steinmetz (Th.D., Harvard University) is Amos Ragan Kearns Professor of the history of Christianity at Duke Divinity School and a former president of the American Society of Church History. He is the author of *Luther and Staupitz* and *Calvin in Context,* and serves as the general editor of the Oxford Studies in Historical Theology series.